大学英语教学及语言评价研究

刘志朋／著

国家一级出版社
中国纺织出版社
全国百佳图书出版单位

内 容 提 要

《大学英语教学及语言评价研究》一书分为两部分，第一部分为大学英语实践教学研究，第二部分为英语语言评价研究。在第一部分中，主要探讨了英语词汇学习策略教学和英语写作与听力教学等。第二部分内容主要探究英语新闻语篇中的中评价资源分析、中西文化对比研究以及泰山茶文化的翻译研究。

图书在版编目（CIP）数据

大学英语教学及语言评价研究 / 刘志朋著 . —北京：中国纺织出版社，2018.7

ISBN 978-7-5180-5135-9

Ⅰ. ①大… Ⅱ. ①刘… Ⅲ. ①英语—教学研究—高等学校 Ⅳ. ① H319.3

中国版本图书馆 CIP 数据核字（2018）第 130375 号

策划编辑：陈希尔　　　　责任印制：储志伟

中国纺织出版社出版发行
地址：北京市朝阳区百子湾东里A407号楼　邮政编码：100124销售电话：010—67004422　传真：010—87155801
http：// www.c-textilep.com
E-mail：faxing@c-textilep.com
中国纺织出版社天猫旗舰店
官方微博http：// weibo.com / 2119887771
北京虎彩文化传播有限公司印刷　各地新华书店经销
2018年 8 月第 1 版第 1 次印刷
开本：710×1000　1 / 16　印张：19
字数：260千字　定价：83.00 元

阶段性成果

《大学英语教学及语言评价研究》一书为山东省高等学校科研发展计划项目（人文社科类）“学术英语写作中因果关系的篇章建构功能研究”（J17RA062），山东省社会科学规划研究项目“大学英语课程设计与大学生自我效能感之相关性研究”(12CWJJ01)，山东省艺术科学重点课题——“一带一路”战略下齐鲁茶文化的外宣翻译策略研究（1607457）的阶段性成果。

第一部分　大学英语教学研究

Chapter 1
The Effect of Vocabulary Learning Strategy Training on Non-English Majors' English Vocabulary Learning

Chapter 2
阅读法在大学英语写作教学中的应用

Chapter 3
任务教学法与英语写作教学

Chapter 4
文化差异对英语听力的影响及其对策

Chapter 5
大学生英语写作中“Chinglish”的现象分析

Chapter 6
背诵在大学艺术、体育类学生英语学习过程中的作用

Chapter 7
英语专业学生学术论文写作中因果连词运用研究

Chapter 8
The Motivation Approach in College English Learning and Teaching

Chapter 9
Research of Listening Strategies in Non-English Majors' College English Learning

Chapter 10
The Lexical Approach in College English Learning and Teaching

第二部分 英语语言评价研究

Chapter 1
Invoking Implicit Evaluation: the Play of Graduation in News Text

Chapter 2
Realization of Implicit Evaluation in News Text

Chapter 3
隐性评价在新闻语篇中的体现

Chapter4
隐性评价在英语新闻语篇宏观层面上的体现

Chapter 5
隐性评价与大学“英文报刊选读”教学

Chapter 6
Comparison between Oriental Philosophy and Western Philosophy

Chapter 7
Textual Contrastive Studies

Chapter 8
政治语篇中的评价意义研究

Chapter 9
新闻语篇中概念意义的隐性评价

Chapter 10
泰山茶文化内涵翻译研究

第一部分
大学英语教学研究

Chapter 1
The Effect of Vocabulary Learning Strategy Training on Non-English Majors' English Vocabulary Learning

1.1 Introduction

1.1.1 Importance of Vocabulary Learning in Second Language Acquisition (SLA)

It is well known to us that vocabulary, the building material, is essential to a language, in which vocabulary is the basic component, and the other two are phonology and grammar. In other words, vocabulary is of utmost significance to people's communication and language learning. The linguist David Wilkins (1972) once summed up the importance of vocabulary in his book Linguistics and Language Teaching: Without grammar and vocabulary, the language learners will obtain nothing. Without enough words one cannot communicate with others, no matter how wonderful his grammar and pronunciation are, because vocabulary is the carrier for people to communicate with each other (McCarthy, 1990).

To achieve the aim of better interaction, it is the first task for people to learn vocabulary. Without vocabulary, people are unable to speak, read and write with clarity. With rich vocabulary, people are confident in their communication. Moreover, to learn a new language is to some extent to form a new network, which is made up of words. Without doubt, it is a fact that vocabulary is the backbone and essence of any language. Accordingly, it is of critical significance for language learners to acquire adequate vocabulary and communicate well with others. In general, the vocabulary that a learner owns reflects his or her English level. Since vocabulary is very important in language learning, it is of critical significance for language learners to memorize plenty of words in order to master a language. To some degree, vocabulary is the crucial part of English learning and teaching.

Vocabulary is the important part of language and significant to language learners. English is rich in vocabulary; there are about 1,000,000 words. It is clear that a small number of words (around 2,000 to 3,000) can be used effectively to express an enormous number of ideas. In case of speaking, it is important to get learners to be able to make the best of a small productive vocabulary. With writing, however, learners need to extend their productive vocabulary to include the specialized vocabulary of their areas of study and interest. In academic settings, writing is most often used as the form of assessment, and learners need to be able to show their knowledge of the field through the use of the specialized vocabulary. The research on native speakers indicates that second language learners in the same school system as native speakers of English may have to increase their vocabulary by around 1,000 words a year, besides making up a 2,000 to 3,000-word gap, in order to match native speakers' vocabulary growth. Learners with special goals, such as study at a university, need to acquire a further 1,000 high-frequency words. According to the College English Curriculum Requirements (CECR) (2007), the college students' general vocabulary size is 4,794 words. A high-level student vocabulary size should reach 6,395, among which 2,364 words belong to the active vocabulary.

Vocabulary is the important part of language and significant to the language learners. Nevertheless, the teaching and learning of vocabulary have not been given more attentions in English teaching throughout its varying stages and up to the present day. As is shown to us, the vocabulary is of critical importance to learn English. So how vocabulary is learned and how vocabulary is taught is the focus of the research. The methods of learning vocabulary well are taken for consideration by the researchers and language learners.

As Krashen and Terrell (1983) write in their book "The Natural Approach" that "of the two tools for communication, vocabulary and grammar, the former is clearly the most essential one." However, nowadays in the field of vocabulary learning, what interest researchers and language teacher in the west is how they can do to teach English vocabulary to non-native English learners well. In the world, English has become the commonly used language. And in our country, with the development of economy and politics, English has become one part of our daily life, especially in the field of economics. In students' eyes, learning English is not only a course in the school, but also the tool for them to interact with outside world. Furthermore, it is becoming increasingly popular that some students go abroad to further their studies. However, we cannot ignore the fact that after many years of English study, our students cannot express themselves clearly and read in English. It is universally recognized that vocabulary plays a fundamental role in successful SLA. Therefore, it is of great importance to master vocabulary in SLA. So as to be competent in second language learning, we must acquire adequate vocabulary.

1.1.2 The Present Situation of Vocabulary Learning

In recent years, the English learning in our country has been given more attention, in which the focus of English learning is shifted from how to teach to how to learn. Therefore, more and more language researchers begin to pay more attention to the mastery of basic learning skills. The interests of linguists and researchers shift from the learning product to the learning process in the field of language acquisition. In English language acquisition, some research results show that the English acquisition has been shifted from how the teachers teach to how the students learn well. At the same time, a number of researches are carried out from special perspectives. Therefore, in the field of language acquisition and research, a clear phenomenon appears that research on learners and learning methods outweighs that on teachers and teaching methodology.

Students should be encouraged to become more autonomous and to "Learn how to learn" (Cohen, 2000). Researches (O' Malley & Chamot, Oxford, Cohen and Wen Qiufang) show that the learning strategies are the key to learner's success. Furthermore, the study of learning strategy and the effects of language learning have been administered since students' autonomy of language learning is improved. In western countries, language researchers become more interested in language learning strategies. With an aim to improve the learners' autonomy of language acquisition, the researchers are involved in language learning training of the students.

With the focus shifting from teachers' teaching to students' learning, language learning strategy instruction research is given more attention. In western countries, a large body of research supports the positive effects of training on strategies in language learning performance (Carrell, 1998; Oxford 1990, 1996), although not all the researches about VLST reach the satisfactory results. In our country also appear some studies on the effect of these training, which began in the 1980s.

When it comes to the learning strategy instruction, most of researchers in the west concentrate on reading strategies (Carrell, 1998), and on cognitive strategies as one of the main categories of learning strategies. Besides, the studies on vocabulary learning strategies also concentrate on cognitive strategies. Recently, a study on the effects of listening strategy training was made by Zhou Weijing. After the training in her experiment, she found that the performance of the experimental group students were better than that of the control group students in 2002. Nevertheless, it is a clear fact that there are few researches on the effects of language learning strategy training now in language acquisition. This research is the one in which the vocabulary learning training is administered among the students in Taishan College. In this research, the teacher (the researcher) intended to explore the result of vocabulary learning strategy training (VLST). Then some implications and suggestions are drawn from this training. The purpose of this research is to help the teachers to overcome the barriers of vocabulary learning and facilitate the non-English majors in this college to learn vocabulary more effectively.

1.1.3 The Necessity of Study on Training

It is universally recognized that vocabulary is of importance in language acquisition in the eyes of English learners and educators. Without doubt, vocabulary is the foundation of L2 proficiency development. Obviously, in recent years, vocabulary has received the recognition it deserves in the field of language acquisition. Vocabulary is the important part of language and significant to the language learners.

Vocabulary learning is an indispensable part of the students' language acquisition. Vocabulary size was shown to be the best predictor of reading comprehension in L1 and L2 (Coady, 1997). In addition, vocabulary size has been shown to correlate highly with global assessment of writing quality and with general language proficiency scores (Bachman & Palmer, 1996). Vocabulary is thought of as the significant element in language learning; the number of words that the learners are familiar with are related to language application. In terms of the importance of vocabulary acquisition, it is critical for the learners to acquire as many words as possible. And a considerable vocabulary serves a solid basis for further English learning (Zang Xueyun, 2006). Without the basis, it is impossible to obtain detailed language information, let alone the fluent use of language. More teachers and students are realizing the fact that for English learners, enlarging the vocabulary is the biggest barrier to language learning.

It is critical to give to students the instruction on how to learn vocabulary with the use of proper strategies. But in China, there are few researches on vocabulary learning strategies. Most researchers put more emphasis on cognitive strategies for vocabulary learning, not the meta-cognitive strategies. Yet the importance of meta-cognitive strategies has been emphasized by O'Malley (1987), who states students who don't know how to use the meta-cognitive strategies are considered as the learners without clear purposes in their language acquisition. According to Anderson (2002), developing meta-cognitive awareness in learners may also lead to the development of stronger cognitive skills and much deeper processing.

The result of the studies on VLST shows that the training is very effective for language learning. McDonough (1995) reviews strategy training research and concludes that improvement caused by strategy training may be better for beginning students. We draw a conclusion from the past researches that vocabulary strategy training is very effective to improve the learners' English achievements. After the training, the performance of high-level learners is better than that of low-level learners. The present study indicates that VLST is very helpful for learners' present and future learning. In practice, the research can improve students' autonomy of English learning. After learning strategy training, the students become more active and proficient in English learning. Furthermore, they are more willing to use these strategies in the classroom learning activities. This research explores the effects of strategy training. The purpose of the present study will shed light on the issue of strategy training.

1.1.4 The Layout of the Thesis

The paper is made up of four chapters and it is organized in the following ways:

In introduction the researcher briefly presents some main issues, including the importance of vocabulary learning, the current situation of vocabulary acquisition, and the necessity of the study on vocabulary learning strategy training. The first chapter is the literature review, in which the researcher firstly introduces the general situation about the vocabulary learning strategies, and then the classification of vocabulary learning strategies. Furthermore, in this chapter the researcher also introduces the survey of research on VLS abroad and at home. Chapter two is the clear presentation of the research design. Then in the next chapter the researcher gives the analysis of the research results in detail. Lastly, the researcher summarizes conclusions, findings and implications.

In the field of English teaching and learning, vocabulary learning has always been the most discussed issue. Since vocabulary learning is the foundation of second language acquisition, the mastery of vocabulary is of significance to students' listening, speaking, reading, writing and translating as well as their communicative ability. A survey of the relevant literature shows that the last decade has witnessed the great development in researches into vocabulary learning strategies both in China and abroad. And many language teachers have come to realize that the essence of teaching is to help learners to learn how to learn. The close link between the learning strategies and learners' autonomy is also emphasized by researchers and educators. Most researchers believe that vocabulary learning strategy training is an effective way to facilitate students' vocabulary knowledge and their English study. In China, the previous related study is limited to key university students, but less research has been conducted in local colleges. Based on previous study, the thesis tries to make a further research in the local college students.

In this paper, the researcher conducted the vocabulary learning strategies training with the students in the experimental class. In class, the researcher gives explicit guidance in the strategies to the students. In addition, the researcher encourages the students to plan, to monitor and to evaluate their learning by themselves.

O'Malley and Chamot's (1990) classification of learning strategies was used in the study due to the importance of meta-cognitive and cognitive learning strategies. O'Malley and Chamot distinguished three major types of strategy: meta-cognitive strategies, cognitive strategies and social/affective strategies. The present study mainly selected some meta-cognitive strategies, cognitive strategies and social/affective strategies, and focused on the effect on non-English students' vocabulary learning. In this study, eighty students of Taishan College took part in the survey of vocabulary learning strategy training. They are from two classes. One class is randomly chosen as the experimental class, and the other as the control class. The participants in the experimental class received the regular four-month strategies-based instructional treatment, while the comparison students did not receive the training. Both classes took a pre-test before the training and a post-test after the training, and the experimental class filled out two questionnaires on the vocabulary learning strategy before and after the training. Two questionnaires and two vocabulary tests were delivered to the students. One questionnaire (the vocabulary learning awareness questionnaire), which is based on the framework of O'Malley and Chamot (1990), is adapted from that of Gu and Johnson (1996).

The other questionnaire is the vocabulary learning strategies questionnaire, which is based on Rebecca L. Oxford's Strategy Inventory for Language Learning (SILL). The two vocabulary tests are randomly selected from reference list of College English Vocabulary in College English Curriculum Requirements (2007) designed by College English Teaching Group.

With the help of the statistical software SPSS 13.0, the researcher analysed the data. The result shows that the vocabulary learning strategies training exerts positive influence on the participants. This research and the strategies-based vocabulary teaching in class give some implications and suggestions to the actual teaching for both teachers and learners. As to the problems occuring in the training process and in the research, the researcher also puts forward his own ideas and careful reflection. In teaching and learning English, the teacher should give students more instruction on strategy knowledge. Furthermore, more researches concerning vocabulary learning strategies training is needed to facilitate the students' learning in the future.

1.2 Literature Review

1.2.1 Language Learning Strategy

What is a learning strategy? Since 1975, various theorists have contributed to the definition of language learning strategy. Different models have been proposed to categorize and create a hierarchy of strategies on the basis of how they relate to the learner and the task and how they are employed in the learning process.

1.2.1.1 Definition of Language Learning Strategies

In Oxford Advanced Learner's English-Chinese Dictionary, the term strategy is defined as “a plan that is intended to achieve a particular purpose.” It is also defined as “A particular plan for gaining success in a particular activity, e.g., in a war, a game, or a competition, or for personal advantage” in Longman Dictionary of Contemporary English (1998). Some people think that language learning strategy is defined as the competence that people try to communicate with others. It is well known that since the 1970’s, studies on learning strategies have begun. In the past decades, the researches on language learning strategy have been on the rise. The following are the definitions given by some famous researchers.

Table 1 Definitions of learning strategies (Ellis, 1994)

Source	Definition
Stern 1983	‘In our view strategy is best reserved for general tendencies or overall characteristics of the approach employed by the language learner, leaving techniques as the term to refer to particular forms of observable learning behavior.’
Weinstein and Mayer 1986	‘Learning strategies are the behaviors and thoughts that a learner engages in during learning that are intended to influence the learner’s encoding process.’
Chamot 1987	‘Learning strategies are techniques, approaches or deliberate actions that students take in order to facilitate the learning, recall of both linguistic and content area information.’
Rubin 1987	‘Learning strategies are strategies which contribute to the development of the language system which the learner constructs and affect learning directly.’
Oxford 1989	‘Language learning strategies are behaviors or actions which learners use to make language learning more successful, self-directed and enjoyable.’

The definitions of learning strategies are very clear and different from each other. However, these definitions also reveal several problems (Ellis,

1994). Oxford (1989) considers the strategies as learners' behaviors. However, Weinstein and Mayer (1986) refer to them as learners' physical and mental behaviors and then the exact characteristics of the behaviors are given more concerns. Stern (1983) makes a distinction between 'strategies' and 'techniques'. The former are defined as universal methods to learn language. The latter consist of forms of language acquisition performances which are clear in language learning. The third problem is whether these learning strategies are thought of as conscious and subconscious.

1.2.1.2 Classification of Language Learning Strategies

A variety of researches focused on the language learning strategies. In these researches, the language learners were given instruction on how to use strategies. However, few researches were conducted to make the detailed classification of strategies.

When it comes to the classification of language learning strategies, Skehan (1989) concentrates on three fields. The first field is the students' ability to incorporate themselves into the learning environment. Naimen et al. (1978) refer to 'an active task approach', which is evident in such behaviors as seeking out and responding positively to learning opportunities and engaging in practice activities. 'Classification/verification', which Rubin (1981) puts at the top of her list of strategies, also belongs to this area. This strategy includes checking the examples of word usage, arranging words in a sentence to check understanding, looking up words in a dictionary, and paraphrasing a sentence to check understanding. Wong-Fillmore lists two strategies that fall into this area: 'get some expressions' and 'make the most of what you have got.' The second field is about the learner's 'technical predispositions'. The third general area involves the learner's capacity to evaluate. For example, Naiman et al. and Rubin both refer to the importance of monitoring.

However, the early taxonomies differ in a number of ways, reflecting the particular subjects that researchers worked with (Ellis, 1994). Thus Rubin and Naimen et al., who elicited information from adults, emphasized the importance of learners reflecting on their own learning and of conscious analysis, while Wong-Fillmore, who studied 5~7-year-old Spanish-speaking children in play situations, emphasized the social aspects of learning. For example, Rubin lists "memorization" and "deductive reasoning" among her strategies, while Wong-Fillmore indentifies "join a group" and "count on your friends" as important. These differences also seem to reflect whether the setting is a formal or informal one, raising the possibility that the learning strategies involved in classroom and naturalistic acquisition may not be the same.

The following studies have been endeavoured to identify broad classes of learning strategies.

Rubin's (1987) classification of language learning strategies is listed as follows.

Table 2 Rubin's classification (1987)

- Language learning strategies
  - Learning strategies
    - Cognitive strategies
    - Meta-cognitive strategies
  - Communication strategies
  - Social strategies

Rubin (1987) classifies language learning strategies into three groups. The first group is the learning strategies, which "contribute to the development of the language… and affect learning directly". The learning strategies are categorized as cognitive and meta-cognitive strategies. Cognitive strategies refer to clarification/verification, guessing, deductive reasoning, practice, memorization, and monitoring. Communication strategies are the second group, which are used by a learner when he has difficulty communicating with others. The last group is social strategies, which include question to fellow students/teachers/native speakers, initiating conversations, listening to L2 media, etc.

Table 3 O'Malley and Chamot's typology of learning strategies (Chamot, 1987)

Learning strategies	Definition
Meta-cognitive	
Advance organizers	Making a general but comprehensive preview of the concept or principle in an anticipated learning activity.
Directed attention	Deciding in advance to attend in general to a learning task and to ignore irrelevant distractors.
Selective attention	Deciding in advance to attend to specific aspects of language input or situational details that will cue the retention of language input.
Self-management	Understanding the conditions that help one learn and arranging for the presence of those conditions.
Advance preparation	Planning for and rehearsing linguistic components necessary to carry out an upcoming language task.
Self-monitoring	Correcting one's speech for accuracy in pronunciation, grammar, vocabulary, or for appropriateness related to the setting or to the people who are present.
Delayed production	Consciously deciding to postpone speaking to learn initially through listening comprehension.
Self-evaluation	Checking the outcomes of one's own language learning against an internal measure of completeness and accuracy.
Cognitive	
Repetition	Imitating a language model, including overt practice and silent rehearsal.

Learning strategies	Definition
Resourcing	Defining or expanding a definition of a word or concept through use of target language reference materials.
Directed physical	Relating new information to physical actions, as with response directives.
Translation	Using the first language as a base for understanding and/or producing the second language.
Grouping	Recording or reclassifying and perhaps labeling the material to be learned based on common attributes.
Note–taking	Writing down the main idea, important points, outline, or summary of information presented orally or in writing.
Deduction	Consciously applying rules to produce or understand the second language.
Recombination	Constructing a meaningful sentence or larger language sequence by combining known elements in a new way.
Imagery	Relating new information to visual concepts in memory via familiar easily retrievable visualizations, phrases, or locations.
Auditory representation	Retention of the sound or similar sound for a word, phrase, or longer language sequence.
Key word	Remembering a new word in the second language by (1) identifying a familiar word in the first language that sounds like or otherwise resembles the new word, and (2) generating easily recalled images of some relationship with the new word.
Contextualization	Placing a word or phrase in a meaningful language sequence.
Elaboration	Relating new information to other concepts in memory.
Transfer	Using previously acquired linguistic and/or conceptual knowledge to facilitate a new language learning task.
Inferencing	Using available information to guess meanings of new items, predict outcomes, or fill in missing information.
Social/affective	
Cooperation	Working with one or more peers to obtain feedback, pool information, or model a language activity.
Questions for classification	Asking a teacher or other native speaker for repetition, paraphrasing, explanation and/or examples.

In the above table, we can see that O'Malley and Chamot classify the learning strategies into three main kinds. Cognitive strategies are about learners' behaviors that tend to solve the problems in language learning. By using cognitive strategies, learners can analyze and transform the language learning materials. Learners tend to learn language with meta-cognitive strategies in cognitive process and also try to make an regulation on language learning. Social/affective strategies are about the approaches with which language learners choose to communicate with other people.

In Oxford (1990) a new taxonomy is presented, the general framework of which is shown in Table 4.

Table 4 Oxford's classification of learning strategies (1990)

Learning Strategies	Direct strategies	Memory strategies
		Cognitive strategies
		Compensation strategies
	Indirect strategies	Meta–cognitive strategies
		Affective strategies
		Social strategies

In the above table, we can see that the subcategories of direct and indirect categories shown in the table have familiar labels. Direct strategies include memory strategies, cognitive strategies and compensation strategies. Memory strategies help learners store and retrieve information. Cognitive strategies facilitate the understanding and production of a new language. Compensation strategies are used by learners to bridge large knowledge gap and use the language.

Cohen's Framework

Table 5 Cohen's classification of learning strategies (1998)

Theorist	Main Categories	Definitions or Subcategories	Examples
Cohen	learning strategies	identifying the material to be learned distinguishing the material from other material.	
		grouping	
		making repeated contact with learning material	
		committing the material to memory	
	use strategies	retrieval strategies	mental imaging
		rehearsal strategies	practicing
		cover strategies	producing simple language
		communication strategies	negative transfer

In Cohen's (1998) model, language learning strategies include those used for identifying the material that needs to be learned, distinguishing it from other material if needed, grouping it for easier learning, having repeated contact with the material, and formally committing the material to memory when it does not seem to be acquired naturally. For example, the strategies for learning the subjunctive in Spanish as a foreign language could include grouping together the list of verbs that take a subjunctive and memorizing them. The specific strategies for memorizing this group might involve the use of a keyword mnemonic.

Language use strategies include four subsets: (a) retrieval strategies, (b) rehearsal strategies, (c) cover strategies, and (d) communication strategies. Retrieval strategies are used to activate language material from storage through memory searching strategies such as mental linkages or sound association. Rehearsal strategies are used for practicing the target language structures and include both language learning and language use strategies. Cover strategies involve creating the impression that learners have control over the material when they do not. Examples of them are simplification, i.e., producing simplified utterances and complexification, i.e., saying something by means of an elaborate and complex circumlocution, both of which are used to bridge knowledge gaps in the target language. Communication strategies focus on approaches to conveying meaningful and informative messages to the listener or reader. Intralingual strategies are such examples. These include overgeneralizing a grammar rule or vocabulary meaning from one context to another where it does not apply, and negative transfer, i.e., applying the patterns of a native or another language in the target language where those patterns do not apply.

1.2.2 Definitions and Classifications of Vocabulary Learning Strategies

In the field of second language acquisition, we have seen the good development in vocabulary study and vocabulary learning strategy training. In the process of identifying and categorizing learning strategies, many studies dealt indirectly with strategies specifically applicable to vocabulary learning (Schmitt, 1997). In this part, a taxonomy of vocabulary learning strategies is listed as follows.

1.2.2.1 What is Vocabulary Learning Strategy

Vocabulary knowledge can be defined as the knowledge of lexical meanings of words and the concepts connected to those meanings. In some people's opinions, vocabulary learning strategies can be explained as the techniques that are helpful to memorize the words. However, according to Gu & Johnson (1996) and Hatch and Brown (1995), memory strategies are only one of the many aspects of vocabulary learning strategies, while vocabulary learning strategies refer to a broad range of strategies for vocabulary learning.

Vocabulary learning strategies are defined as: vocabulary learning strategies refer to both general approaches and specific actions or techniques (either mental or behavioral) used by a learner to make the vocabulary learning become easier, faster and better (cited in Fan Ling, 2002).

Ahmed (1989) suggests that vocabulary learning strategies refer to any kind of approaches or techniques that learners adopt to cope with vocabulary learning both consciously and subconsciously. Schmitt and McCarthy (1997) defined vocabulary learning strategies as the process by which information is obtained, stored, retrieved, and used, here 'use' means vocabulary practice rather than interactional communication.

1.2.2.2 Classifying Vocabulary Learning Strategies

Now there are various definitions of vocabulary learning strategies, among which Nation's (1990), Oxford's (1990), Schmitt's (1997) and Stoffer's (1995) are introduced.

1.2.2.2.1 Nation's (1990) Classification

Nation (1990) classifies vocabulary learning strategies into three categories: (1) Guessing the meaning of words in context, (2) Using mnemonic techniques to memorize word meanings, (3) Using prefixes, roots and suffixes to learn words. He pays special attention to the skill of guessing word meaning in context and suggests five steps involved in this strategy: (1) Look at the unknown word and decide its part of speech, (2) Look at the clause or sentence containing the unknown word, (3) Look at the relationship between the clause or sentence containing the unknown word and other sentences or paragraphs, (4) Use the knowledge you have gained from step 1, 2 and 3 to guess the meaning of the word; (5) Check whether your guess is correct.

In the skill of using mnemonic techniques, the learners can create an unusual association between the word form and its meaning. For example, if English-speaking learners want to master the Thai words khaaw saan, meaning "uncooked rice" , they would think of an English word (the key word) which sounds like khaaw saan, for example, council.

1.2.2.2.2 Oxford's (1990) Classification

Oxford (1990) classifies vocabulary learning strategies into three categories: social strategies, memory strategies, cognitive strategies and meta-cognitive strategies. Social strategies are related to the communication with other people. Memory strategies are defined as the approaches to memorize the words with the previous knowledge. Cognitive strategies mean to use some mechanical methods, together with some aids, to learn vocabulary. Meta-cognitive strategies are related with reference to a conscious overview of the language learning.

Oxford's classification system was unsatisfactory in categorizing vocabulary-specific strategies in several aspects (Schmitt, 1997). Oxford's classification is also inadequate in some aspects.

1.2.2.2.3 Schmitt's (1997) Classification

Schmitt (1997) categorized two kinds of vocabulary strategies: Discovery strategies and Consolidation strategies. Discovery strategies refer to the strategies that are for gaining initial information about a new word. Consolidation strategies are used to for learners to make some effect to remember words that have been exposed to them. Discovery strategies consist of determination strategies (when confronting a word for the first time, learners use their knowledge of the language, contextual clues, or reference material to discover the meaning of the new word) and Social strategies (ask someone else who knows); consolidation strategies include social strategies of cooperation, memory, cognitive, and meta-cognitive strategies groups. However, inquiry and cooperation are both social strategies, the former belongs to discovery strategies and the later is consolidation strategies, so there are no clear boundary between the two types of Schmitt's classification.

1.2.2.2.4 Stoffer's (1995) Classification

Stoffer (1995) developed a vocabulary learning strategy inventory, which contained fewer items. With the use of factor analysis, Stoffer found that the vocabulary learning strategy inventory items cluster into the following nine categories: (1) strategies about authentic language acquisition, (2) strategies used for self-motivation, (3) strategies used to organize words, (4) strategies used to create mental linkages, (5) memory strategies, (6) strategies about innovative language learning activities, (7) strategies related to physical activities, (8) strategies applied to solve anxiety and (9) auditory strategies.

1.2.3 Studies on Vocabulary Learning Strategies in the West

Several studies have explored the acquisition through context hypothesis. Krashen (1989), for example, argues that we get a better language acquisition in the process of reading and spelling. He advocates the Input Hypothesis (IH), which applies to reading as well as to oral language acquisition. It postulates that successful language learning results from comprehensible input as the essential external ingredient coupled with a powerful internal language acquisition device. In short, he believes that IH is more efficient than the other hypotheses. Ellis (1994), for example, has pointed out that attention is present in the case of both incidental and intentional learning and that this "distinction rests, somewhat uncomfortably, on a secondary distinction between focal and peripheral attention" . Nagy and Herman (1984) and Nagy and Anderson (1984) argue that the number of L1 words that are learned by a child in elementary school is too enormous to rely on word-by-word instruction. Nagy, Herman, and Anderson (1985) then conclude from their experimental study that children indeed to learn large numbers of words by means of incidental learning from written context.

Oxford and Scarcella (1994), for example, argue that it is crucial to teach students explicit strategies for learning vocabulary. They think that it is even appropriate at times to use some partially decontextualized activities.

Cohen (1990) puts considerable emphasis on learning words through association, and particularly mnemonic techniques, because his research results have found that learners do not use such aids systematically and therefore need instruction. Ellis and Beaton (1993) investigated forty-seven students learning German and using repetition, keyword, or "own" strategy conditions. They found that phonological and orthographic similarity of L2 to L1 was facilitative. Oxford and Scarcella (1994) stress that it is very necessary and helpful to give to adult learners direct advice on how to memorize words. Students are unable to obtain plenty of vocabulary they need only by reading and writing. In Oxford and Scarcella's eyes, language learners must be given instruction on how to memorize new words themselves by using satisfactory vocabulary learning strategies. It is not effective to learn vocabulary without clear strategies.

Sanaoui (1995) identified two distinctive approaches to L2 vocabulary learning. Some adult students are clearly capable of independently and actively managing their own learning. Others are much more in need of assistance in order to develop adequate learning strategies and increase their self-awareness.

A study by Brown and Perry (1991) made a research on vocabulary learning strategies. They investigated three kinds of strategies, which were keyword strategies, semantic strategies and keyword-semantic strategies. Keyword strategies mean to relate the words with some visual words that have been learned by learners. Semantic strategies mean that the language learners memorize the new words in the semantic situation. Keyword-semantic strategies are the combination of keyword strategies and semantic strategies. They carried out a research of three groups of students in university. The research results indicated that the students who were trained to use keyword-semantic strategies performed better than those who were trained to use keyword strategies and semantic strategies.

Bialystok (1983 b) carried out two experiments to investigate a number of ways in which the ability of Grade 10 students of L2 French to infer the meanings of words in a continuous text could be improved. In one of the experiments, a fifteen-minute lesson on how to infer resulted in more effective overall comprehension of a written text than providing the learners with picture cues or letting the learners use a dictionary. However, dictionary use resulted in better scores on a vocabulary test than the strategy training. In the second experiment the strategy training proved less effective in promoting either comprehension or vocabulary acquisition than the other two conditions.

Cohen and Aphek (1980) gave adult learners of L2 Hebrew a short training session in how to learn vocabulary through associations. The results indicated that forming associations helped in vocabulary recall tasks and that failure to employ an association often led to incorrect recall. Cohen and Aphek also reported that those students who were more proficient at the outset were also the most successful in using association in recall tasks, suggesting that training in forming associations might be most helpful for advanced rather than beginner learners.

1.2.4 Studies on Vocabulary Learning Strategies in China

Since the 1990's, many Chinese researchers and educators have made contributions to the exploration of English vocabulary learning. Gu and Johnson (1996) made a research, in which 850 non-English majors at a university were involved. They analyzed the relationship between strategies, vocabulary size, and language proficiency. A language proficiency test and a vocabulary test, together with a questionnaire, were used in their research. Their study arrived at the conclusion that the participants generally did not dwell on memorization, which was a popular belief about Asian students. Gu also made a case research about two students in CET-4. He found that in terms of vocabulary learning beliefs, the two students held different opinions in their vocabulary acquisition. The student who got higher marks performed better than the student who got lower marks in the vocabulary acquisition.

Wang Wenyu (1998) conducted a research among 50 college students, half of whom majored in English and the half not. The results of this research included: (1) Some strategies used by them are conducive to long-term retention of vocabulary. Management strategy, word list strategy, repetition strategy, encoding strategy and application strategy are given more emphasis; (2) English learners in China think that vocabulary is memorized with clear instruction rather than being learned naturally; (3) The students' vocabulary proficiency is closely related to the strategy they use.

Wu Xia and Wang Qiang (1998) investigated 202 sophomore non-English majors in a survey of vocabulary learning strategies. The quantity and vocabulary, coupled with the depth of vocabulary was investigated. Their findings are nearly similar to Wang Wenyu's on the correlation between application of strategies and test results. All the meta-cognitive strategies relate closely to both quantity and depth of vocabulary. Cai Xin (1998) conducted a research about vocabulary learning strategies among 100 Chinese senior school students. He argued that students were willing to use learning strategies in their acquisition of new words. The students tended to use meta-cognitive strategies and cognitive strategies. The frequency of strategies use is closely related to vocabulary size. Besides, Zhang Qingzong and Wu Xiyan (2002) made a research on the effect on vocabulary learning. They conducted an experiment on 139 non-English major students in Hubei University. The results indicated that the semantic processing was useful for learners' language learning. The learners who were involved in semantic processing performed better than those who were in formal group.

From the above analysis of the relevant literature about the vocabulary learning, we can see that English learners both in the west and in China all use the strategies to acquire the vocabulary. The aim of this thesis is to find out the effectiveness of some vocabulary learning strategies use by non-English majors in Taishan College.

1.3 Research Methodology

1.3.1 Objectives

The purpose of the research is to tell language learners the effects of vocabulary learning strategy training and facilitate them to learn and use a foreign language effectively. At the same time, it also encourages them to regulate their vocabulary learning. The research is also intended to make an exploration in feasibility of helping learners improve their vocabulary acquisition by empowering them with vocabulary learning through the training process.

The training, at the same time, is beneficial for the students to be autonomous language learners and also to regulate their learning in the future. Moreover, by means of training the students, the students can be encouraged to improve their consciousness in language learning. In order to effectively carry out the research, the vocabulary learning strategy training is carried out in the classroom teaching. The teacher (the researcher), takes charge of the class teaching and inspires the students' awareness of learning strategy in the class. Some strategy-based activities are integrated into the daily class teaching.

The following questions are answered in this training:

a. What effects does VLST have on VLS use?

b. What effects does VLST have on vocabulary proficiency?

c. What is the relationship between VLS use and vocabulary proficiency after the training?

1.3.2 Subjects

The subjects in this study are 80 first-year students majoring in accounting in Taishan College, half of whom are chosen randomly as the experimental class and another half as the control class. All the subjects have the experience of learning English in junior and senior high school. The students in these two classes are taught by the same teacher. They all attend the intensive reading class twice a week.

1.3.3 Instruments

Two questionnaires were used in this research. The first (Appendix Ⅰ) was the questionnaire about vocabulary beliefs and the second (Appendix Ⅱ) about vocabulary learning strategy. The second instrument (Appendix Ⅱ) made a research about the subjects' belief on their vocabulary acquisition. There were 32 statements about vocabulary learning behaviors in this questionnaire. These learning behaviors covered meta-cognitive strategies, cognitive strategies and social/affective strategies. In addition, two vocabulary tests were used before and after the training respectively.

1.3.3.1 Teaching Material

In the process of research, Reading and Writing Course Ⅰ and Ⅱ of New Horizon College English published by Foreign Language Teaching and Research Press were used as the textbooks of intensive reading class for both the experimental and control classes.

1.3.3.2 Vocabulary Tests

To check the benefits of training, two similar vocabulary tests were adopted to examine the result before and after VLST respectively. Thus, in the process of training, the researcher made adoption of vocabulary tests which were used as pre-test and post-test respectively. The tests were reliable and valid. Furthermore, the results were also satisfactory. The two tests were randomly selected from reference list of College English Vocabulary in College English Curriculum Requirements (2007) designed by College English Teaching Group. In each test, there were 40 items of words provided with four choices in Chinese. These words were sorted out randomly and the students were required to choose a correct answer from the four choices. The students in CC and EC all attended the first vocabulary test (pre-test) before VLST. And the second one (post-test), was given in CC and EC after VLST. After the test, all the students' papers were collected and marked. Then, the analysis would be given finally. After collecting the students' papers, the researcher inputted the results into the computer. To check the reliability, the researcher adopted SPSS 13.0 statistical analysis.

1.3.3.3 Questionnaire on Vocabulary Learning Awareness

Vocabulary Learning Awareness Questionnaire, developed by Gu Yongqi & Johnson (1996), can be used to analyze the learners' beliefs on vocabulary acquisition. In this questionnaire, the personal information of the participants is included. In the previous studies, this questionaire was proved to be a high, valid and reliable questionnaire. The beliefs include six statements, which are listed as follows.

a. Skills of memorizing are needed in vocabulary learning

b. I'm interested in learning vocabulary.

c. Clear plan and specific goal is the basis of efficient vocabulary learning.

d. Vocabulary learning is a mechanical task.

e. Vocabulary learning demands no creativity.

f. Students play a decisive role in vocabulary learning.

The participants were required to judge these statements on a 5-point Likert scale questionnaire from Absolutely Agree (5) to Disagree (1).

1.3.3.4 Questionnaire on Vocabulary Learning Strategies

The questionnaire, designed by the researcher, is based on Rebecca L. Oxford's Strategy Inventory for Language Learning (SILL). To evaluate the use of learning strategies by the subjects, the questionnaire was seen as a standardized measurement in the process of research. The participants were required to judge these statements on a five-point scale. The five-point scale respectively indicates "always or almost always true", "usually true", "somewhat true", "usually not true" and "never or almost never true". In addition, the value of 5, 4, 3, 2, 1 respectively is assigned to these categories in the learning strategies. Therefore, if higher marks are achieved by the subjects, we can infer that greater usage of strategy happens to them. The items describing the details of strategies are divided into meta-cognitive strategies, cognitive strategies and social/affective strategies, each of which contained many categories. Each subcategory of vocabulary learning strategies consisted of various behaviors of learners.

1.3.4 Research Procedures

In the regular class teaching, only the EC students were given the strategy-based instruction (SBI), which lasted four months. They were required to fill out the VLS questionnaire before and after the training. Before filling out the questionnaire, all the participants were informed by teacher of the fact that they should take the questionnaire seriously and spare no efforts to finish the task. As to the control class, the teacher just gave them the normal teaching. While in EC, the teacher spared 20 minutes each week to give the participants instruction on vocabulary learning strategies. The researcher found that the students longed for the introduction of VLS.

1.3.4.1 Psychological Preparation for the Training

The training process lasted four months. So, it was vital for the teacher to make the participants psychologically ready for the training. Group discussion was utilized to make the learners keep the belief in their minds that they must reflect on language learning and take themselves as new language learners.

1.3.4.2 Pre-test and Questionnaire

To check the homogeneity of the EC students and CC, an English vocabulary test (pre-test) was used in the training. To begin with, eighty students in two classes all took part in the pre-test. The test was reliable and valid. And the test results were also satisfactory. The marks in the vocabulary test achieved show that there is no tremendous difference between CC and EC. Two questionnaires (vocabulary learning awareness questionnaire and vocabulary learning strategy questionnaire) were answered only by the EC students to examine their vocabulary learning situations before the training.

1.3.4.3 Strategy-Based Instruction (SBI)

1.3.4.3.1 Selection of Strategies

Clearly, there are many issues that need sorting out before strategy training can be implemented effectively. First, more work is needed to discover what strategies and, in particular, what combinations of strategies should be taught. Second, ways have to be found of taking into account learners' own preferred learning strategies. Third, some learners may need convincing that strategy training is worthwhile. Fourth, it is not clear whether learner training will work best when it exists as a separate strand in a language programme. (Nation, 1990)

The language learners' motivation has a strong influence on the quantity of strategies in their language learning. Oxford and Nyikos (1989) argued that the degree of motivation which was expressed by the learners imposed the powerful effects on the use of learning strategies. The language learners who are highly motivated employ more strategies than those who are poorly motivated.

1.3.4.3.2 Preparation of Materials and Activities

It is necessary to decide what vocabulary will be selected for teaching, how it will be sequenced, and how it will be presented. In the research, the researcher must incorporate vocabulary development into communicative activities, and improve learners' access to vocabulary that has already been partly learned. There may be vocabulary exercises, which may include word-building exercises, matching words with various types of definitions, studying vocabulary in context, semantic mapping, and split information activities focusing on vocabulary.

1.3.4.4 Vocabulary Strategies Training Process

The textbooks used for this course were Reading and Writing Course Ⅰ and Ⅱ of New Horizon College English published by Foreign Language Teaching and Research Press. The author was in charge of students in both CC and EC. The students in both classes used the same textbooks (Reading and Writing Course Ⅰ and Ⅱ) in the process of regular teaching. However, only the experimental class were given the clear instruction on vocabulary learning strategies in this study. The vocabulary learning strategies, developed by O'Malley and Chamot, were explained in details to the EC students. The teacher made an instruction of these learning strategies to the EC students in the process of the training.

The training adopted the model of integrated teaching, in which the teacher incorporated the training of vocabulary learning strategies into the regular teaching in language curriculum. With this model, the training of learning strategies was administered together with the learning of language knowledge and skills in the class. At first, the teacher directly introduced some learning strategies and made the students attempt to understand these strategies and use them. Meanwhile, the teacher gave them the instruction on the memorization of some certain words in the textbook on the basis of the classification of the words, as well as the similar characteristics in the phonetic symbol, form and meaning. Words are not reserved in our minds separately, but classified according to some certain criteria. If the learners are efficient to memorize the new words after the training of vocabulary learning strategy, they will benefit a lot.

The detailed training process can be listed as follows.

(1) Group discussion was employed in learning new words of each unit each time. Before learning a group of new words, the teacher told the students to discuss how to memorize them effectively and whether the words shared the characteristics in common. If they were able to memorize the new words by using the same characteristics between new words, they would be encouraged to further the memorization of new words. If not, the teacher would explain to them the tips on how to find the similarity between new words and memorize them effectively.

(2) The teacher made a detailed explanation of vocabulary learning strategies to the students and then rehearsed the use of vocabulary learning strategies in the process of learning new words in the textbook. In the regular classroom teaching, the teacher would practice the previously learned strategies before introducing the new learning strategies.

(3) The students were required to apply the strategies to learning new words in the successive exercises in the textbook. Based on the textbook contents, the

students were left assignments after class to master the use of learning strategies. After the training of each vocabulary learning strategies, the teacher should check the students' ability of application of VLS.

1.3.4.5 Post-test and Questionnaire

The post-test was carried out to see the effectiveness of strategies training at the end of the strategy training. Both the EC and CC students all took part in the vocabulary capacity test (post-test) and were told to take the test seriously. After the regular four-month strategies-based training, the EC students were required to fill out the vocabulary learning strategy questionnaire with an aim to make an analysis on the effect of the research. At the last stage, the researcher gathered the questionnaire and the test results. The descriptive statistics (mainly mean) was used to analyze the data.

1.3.5 Data Collection

The pre-test was carried out before the research, and both the EC and CC students all took part in the test. However, only the EC students filled out the two questionnaires before the research. Four months later, all the students in the CC and EC took part in the post-test. Meanwhile, the questionnaire about the VLS was filled out only by the EC students. It was required that the questionnaire be finished within 30 minutes and collected in time. The teacher made an instruction to the students on how to fill out the questionnaire. All the data collected was analyzed by the computer.

1.4 Analysis of the Research Results

1.4.1 Results

The result of the survey and vocabulary tests indicates that the training of vocabulary learning strategies is effective to advance the students' vocabulary learning and improve their awareness of strategy use.

To sum up, the results of the training in EC show that the students tend to use vocabulary learning strategies and firmly believe that VLS is beneficial to their vocabulary learning. Although the result cannot arrive at the conclusion that the students are more automatic to learn vocabulary after the short duration of vocabulary learning strategy training, it still indicates that they make great progress thanks to their application of the strategies.

1.4.2 Data Analysis

1.4.2.1 Analysis of the Tests' Results

Table 6 Statistics of the pre-test in EC and CC (a=0.01)

	Pre-test in EC (N=40)	Pre-test in CC (N=40)	Difference	Z
Mean	34.09	34.16	0.07	0.11
Std. Deviation	2.95	2.77		

From the Table 6, we can see that the mean score in EC is 34.09, and that of CC is 34.16. The standard deviation of the EC is 2.95 and that of CC is 2.77. The researcher uses the statistical analysis of Z-test to examine the difference between the performances of both the EC and CC students on the vocabulary test before the research. The data [Z=0.11<2.58=Z(0.01/2)] indicates that little difference appears between the mean scores achieved by the EC students and CC. In other words, the students in both classes perform at the same level before the research.

The mean score of EC is slightly lower than that of CC. The standard deviation of EC is 2.95 and that of CC is 2.77. The standard deviation can tell us the average deviation of all the scores from the mean. The larger the standard deviation, the more deviant the scores away from the central point in the distribution; the smaller the standard deviation, the closer the scores to the central point (Seliger & Shohamy,1999). Through the Table 6, we can infer that the scores in EC are widely spread than those in CC. Moreover, we also draw a conclusion that the EC students are slightly poor at English compared with those in CC.

To examine the efficiency of VLST on the vocabulary learning of EC, and to see the difference of the performance between two groups (EC and CC), both groups all took part in a post-test after the training. Z-test statistical procedure was used to analyze the data of the two classes. We can see from the mean scores that there is a significance difference between two classes. The EC students performed much better than the counterparts in CC in terms of lexical learning. The result can be analyzed as follows.

Table 7 Statistics of the post-test in EC and CC (a=0.01)

	Post–test in EC (N=40)	Post–test in CC (N=40)	Difference	Z
Mean	37.15	33.75	3.4	5.01
SD	2.82	3.13		

From the Table 7, we can see that there was a great difference between the results of the two classes. The mean score of EC is 37.15, and that of CC is 33.75. The Standard Deviation of EC is 2.82, but that of CC is 3.14. The result indicates that the participants in two classes made improvement in lexical knowledge and that participants in EC achieved better performance than the CC students after training.

In the table, we can see that the mean score of EC is 37.15, which is higher than that (33.75) of CC. The mean difference between two classes is 3.4. Z-value is 5.01>2.58= =Z (0.01/2). It means that there is a vital difference between two classes in the post-test at the 0.01 level. According to the analysis of the post-test results, we can draw a conclusion that the EC students have made greater progress than those in CC. It also shows that the training of vocabulary learning strategies is effective in the vocabulary learning.

1.4.2.2 Analysis of the Vocabulary Learning Awareness Questionnaire

In this research, only the EC students filled out the vocabulary learning strategy questionnaire, whereas the CC students did not answer this questionnaire. In this part, the researcher used the beliefs on vocabulary learning to check the students' (in EC) awareness of strategy. Meanwhile, the researcher made a comparison between the students' beliefs on VLS before and after training. Due to the use of the 5-point Likert scale in the study, if a mean score is larger than 3.00 it will show that the students agree to such a belief while a mean score smaller than 3.00 shows that the students do not agree to such a belief.

Table 8 Statistics analysis of the subjects' belief on VLS in EC before the training (N=40)

EC	Skills of memorizing are needed in vocabulary learning.		I'm interested in learning vocabulary.		Clear plan and specific goal is the basis of efficient vocabulary learning.		Vocabulary learning is a mechanical task.		Vocabulary learning demands no creativity.		Students play a decisive role in vocabulary learning.	
1	1	2.5%	2	5%	7	17.5%	2	5%	3	7.5%	6	15%
2	3	7.5%	2	5%	12	30%	10	25%	9	22.5%	10	25%
3	6	15%	7	17.5%	9	22.5%	9	22.5%	10	25%	11	27.5%
4	18	45%	16	40%	10	25%	17	42.5%	15	37.5%	11	27.5%

EC	Skills of memorizing are needed in vocabulary learning.		I'm interested in learning vocabulary.		Clear plan and specific goal is the basis of efficient vocabulary learning.		Vocabulary learning is a mechanical task.		Vocabulary learning demands no creativity.		Students play a decisive role in vocabulary learning.	
5	12	30%	13	32.5%	2	5%	2	5%	3	7.5%	2	5%
average		4.02		3.95		2.80		3.18		3.20		2.90

As Table 8 shows, most EC students know the importance of memorizing techniques in learning vocabulary. The average score of item 1 is 4.02. However, the average score of item 3 is 2.80, which indicates that the students do not know the clear plan and specific goal is efficient to learn vocabulary. The mean score of item 6 is 2.90 and shows that the students do not realize that they are the decisive roles in vocabulary acquisition.

Table 9 Statistics analysis of the subjects' belief on VLS in EC after the training (N=40)

EC	Skills of memorizing are needed in vocabulary learning.		I'm interested in learning vocabulary.		Clear plan and specific goal is the basis of efficient vocabulary learning.		Vocabulary learning is a mechanical task.		Vocabulary learning demands no creativity.		Students play a decisive role in vocabulary learning.	
1	1	2.5%	1	2.5%	1	2.5%	6	15%	5	12.5%	2	5%
2	2	5%	2	5%	2	5%	9	22.5%	10	25%	3	7.5%
3	3	7.5%	6	15%	6	15%	10	25%	12	30%	5	12.5%
4	1	2.5%	12	30%	16	40%	13	32.5%	11	27.5%	14	35%
5	33	82.5%	19	47.5%	15	37.5%	2	5%	2	5%	16	37.5%
average		4.65		4.15		4.05		2.95		2.90		4.01

1.4.2.3 Analysis of VLS Questionnaire

The VLS questionnaire is used to prove whether the autonomy of students' vocabulary learning is raised after training. Table 10 gives the data analysis of the students' use of VLS.

Table 10 The average percentage of pre-training strategy survey (N=40)

Never	Seldom	Sometimes	Often	Always	Mean
8.5	18.5	28.4	24.8	19.8	3.30

Table 11 shows the percentage of frequently used strategies by the EC students before the training. From the table, we can see that the students' vocabulary learning is considered to be a mechanical task. Item 32 gets the highest mean score (4.24) among all the items. Meanwhile, 84% of the participants in EC often or always memorize new words by consulting teachers and classmates. The mean scores of Items 31 and 6 are also very high, respectively 4.16 and 4.01.

Table 11 Statistics description of frequently applied strategies

<table>
<tr><td colspan="2" rowspan="2"></td><td colspan="4">Item</td></tr>
<tr><td>32</td><td>31</td><td>6</td><td>15</td></tr>
<tr><td colspan="2">Strategy Description</td><td>I consult teachers and classmates on how to learn vocabulary.</td><td>I guess the word meaning in terms of analyzing word formation.</td><td>I associate it with the thing it refers to when memorizing the word.</td><td>When trying to memorize a word, I read and write it repeatedly.</td></tr>
<tr><td rowspan="3">Before survey (%)</td><td>O/A</td><td>84</td><td>76</td><td>69</td><td>71</td></tr>
<tr><td>S</td><td>12</td><td>18</td><td>23</td><td>16</td></tr>
<tr><td>N/S</td><td>4</td><td>6</td><td>8</td><td>13</td></tr>
<tr><td colspan="2">Mean</td><td>4.24</td><td>4.16</td><td>4.01</td><td>3.91</td></tr>
</table>

The percentage of strategy category differs before the training. The following Table 12 shows the detailed difference between meta-cognitive, cognitive, and social/affective strategies.

Table 12 The percentage of strategy category for pre-training

Strategy Category		Meta-cognitive Strategies	Cognitive Strategies	Social/ Affective Strategies	Average Score
Strategy Items		1,2,3,11,14	4,5,6,7,8,9,10,12,13,15,16,17,20, 21,22,23,24,25,26,27,28,29,30,31	18,19,32	
Before Survey (%)	O/A	39	45.4	50.33	44.6
	S	24.2	29.7	23	28.4
	N/S	36.8	24.9	26.67	27
Mean Score		3.05	3.34	3.37	3.3

From the mean scores of three categories, we can see that there is a low usage of vocabulary learning strategies before the training, especially the meta-cognitive strategies. Therefore, it is very necessary to train the students. Then the Table 13 analyzes the comparison before and after the training in strategy use.

Table 13 Comparison of strategy application before and after the training

			Meta-cognitive Strategies	Cognitive Strategies	Social/ Affective Strategies	Average Score
Strategy Application Percentage (%)	A/O	Before	39	45.4	50.33	44.6
		After	66.2	72.5	73	71.5
	S	Before	24.2	29.7	23	28.4
		After	22.8	17.6	19.33	18.6
	N/S	Before	36.8	24.9	26.67	27
		After	11	9.9	7.67	9.9
Mean Score		Before	3.05	3.34	3.37	3.301
		After	3.89	4.03	4.07	4.015
		Change	0.84	0.69	0.70	0.714

From the table, we can see that the percentage of strategy use has been greatly improved than before. The mean score of strategy application in EC is more than 4. But in terms of the comparison between these three categories of strategy, there is also an obvious difference in strategy application frequency. The percentage of strategy application in columns ‘Always or Often’ and ‘Sometimes’ changed greatly after the training. The percentage of strategy application in ‘Always or Often’ is 44.6% before the teacher starts the training. In contrast, the percentage of in ‘Always or Often’ is 71.5% after the training. The average percentage in ‘Seldom or Never’ is 27% before the training, while it is 9.9% after the training. The great changes also happen in application of each strategy category. The mean scores changes greatly after the training, especially that of meta-cognitive strategy usage. The change of mean score in meta-cognitive strategy is obvious (0.84), and that of cognitive is 0.69, while social and affective is 0.70. All these differences show that there is a great change in vocabulary strategy use and each category strategy use. The following Table 14 shows the most changed strategies usage in the training.Table 14 Statistics description of the most changed strategies

	Strategy Description	Average Score		
		Before	After	Change
Item 15	I read and write it repeatedly when trying to memorize a word.	3.91	3.61	–0.30
Item 32	I consult teachers and classmates on how to memorize a word.	4.24	4.06	–0.18
Item 22	I consult a dictionary to memorize a word.	3.15	3.02	–0.13
Item 12	I take down the unknown words and the words that are difficult to spell and write and then review them when time is available.	2.80	4.11	1.31
Item 14	I often reflect on my vocabulary learning.	2.23	3.58	1.35
Item 21	I make use of context to guess the word meaning.	2.65	4.03	1.38

	Strategy Description	Average Score		
		Before	After	Change
Item 1	I make a plan for vocabulary learning and learn certain amount of new words at regular time.	2.76	4.17	1.41
Item 4	When memorizing a word, I associate it with other English words that sound or spell similarly to it.	2.82	4.23	1.41
Item 9	When memorizing a word, I associate it with a known word.	2.98	4.41	1.43

According to the data in the table, we can see that there is great change of mean score after the training in 6 items, the highest of which is item9 (1.43) and the lowest of which is item 12 (1.31). This indicates that students' autonomy of vocabulary learning is higher than before. The change of mean score after the training in 3 items (items 22, 32 and 15) is -0.13, -0.18 and -0.30 respectively, which indicates that after the training the students have realized that the vocabulary learning is not a mechanical task but one that needs strategy application. At the same time, they understand that they are the decisive roles to learn vocabulary.

Table 15 Statistics of the strategy application in EC (a=0.01)

	Pre-survey in EC (N=40)	Post-survey in EC (N=40)	Difference	Z
Mean	3.301	4.015	0.714	7.95
SD	0.479	0.309		

Table 15 shows the difference before and after the training. From the data in this table, we can see that the mean score of the EC students is 4.015 after the training, while it is 3.301 before the training. Before the survey, the SD of the EC students is 0.479, while it is 0.309 after the survey. These statistics indicate that the students make more progress than before. Z-value is 7.95>2.58==Z(0.01/2) and the mean score difference is 0.714. It indicates that noticeable improvement appears after the training. Therefore, the training of vocabulary learning strategy is necessary. The change of SD also happens in the table. The statistics shows that the EC students become more aware of applying strategies to learn vocabulary than before. From the standard deviation in table above, we can understand that the data is more widely spread before the vocabulary learning strategy training. So we also arrive at a conclusion that the EC students make a better performance in vocabulary learning after the training.

1.4.3 Discussion after the Training

According to this research result, the VLST is beneficial to improve the students' efficiency to learn vocabulary. The participants in EC tend to adjust the vocabulary learning strategies and apply these strategies to vocabulary learning to some extent. In addition, the students are encouraged to memorize new words by way of spaced recall, grouping, story and so forth. Therefore, in practice, this training is very helpful for the students to learn vocabulary. In addition, the students are more willing to use these learning strategies in a context. After the training, the students realize that vocabulary learning strategies are important and necessary to their vocabulary learning. Meanwhile, their awareness of applying strategies has been improved. The training results also accord with the previous research results that the learning instruction is very necessary to help the students to be the autonomous learners (O'Malley and Chamot, 1990). To conclude, the statistics analysis of the research greatly support to the necessity of VLST.

1.5 Findings and Implications

The research results prove that the vocabulary learning strategy training is effective and the EC students perform better than those in CC. The questionnaire survey results accord closely with the research result, which makes the study reliable.

1.5.1 Findings of the Research

The vocabulary learning strategy training is carried out in this thesis. The aim of this research is to help the participants find the ways of regulating their vocabulary learning. Meanwhile, the study also tests the effectiveness of the strategy training among the participants in the college. The following is the conclusion of the four-month training.

(1) The study result proves that the students' efficiency is improved in learning vocabulary. In terms of the analysis of the marks in pre-test and post-test, we can see that students performed better after the training. Therefore, the VLST is helpful in improving the students' efficiency of vocabulary learning. The training also makes the students realize that VLS is significant and necessary for their vocabulary learning. The students' awareness of applying different strategies is greatly improved. Besides, the students are inspired to memorize new words by several effective means, thus improving their efficiency of vocabulary learning.

(2) Within the four-month training, with the researcher's help the students became familiar with several strategies. The study indicated that the training was effective to improve the students' efficiency to learn vocabulary and students' awareness of applying these strategies was also improved. The students tended to use the strategies to memorize the words. After the training, the students' beliefs about strategy application changed greatly. The study also proved that the vocabulary learning instruction was beneficial to help the students become better vocabulary learners.

1.5.2 Implications

(1) In the process of training, the teacher found that students liked to learn the knowledge about the use of learning strategies. When they were required to guess the meaning of unknown words, they longed for expressing their ideas and being successful. Therefore, it was very significant for the researcher to inspire them to be active in learning vocabulary. Because the teacher was the learner's trainer to some degree, he or she must be trained on how to give instruction on vocabulary learning. The students should also be trained on how to put the strategy instruction into practice in the training. As a learner trainer, the teacher should try every means to provide students with more chances to put the strategies into practice.

(2) We can also obtain other implications from the results of the study. When the teacher gave instruction to students on how to apply vocabulary learning strategies to their vocabulary learning, most of them shew great interest and longed for the training. They participated actively in the training and cooperated well with the teacher. This indicated that the students shew great interest in the training and desired to get useful instructions on vocabulary learning. On the other hand, teachers can facilitate the English learners to apply the different strategies.

(3) Vocabulary learning strategies are beneficial to make students become autonomous learners. In general, the students like to learn the words independently, thus it is necessary to make them use their own learning plans with an aim to memorize new words. On the other hand, as the trainer, the teacher should give more instructions to poor learners. Good learners know how and when to use these strategies to memorize the word; however, the poor learners cannot. Thus, the teacher must give special attention to poor learners in the training.

1.6 Conclusion

The subjects in this study are 80 first-year students majoring in accounting in Taishan College, half of whom were chosen randomly as the experimental class and the other half as the control class. The study explores the effectiveness of the VLST on the non-English majors of college students. The research concentrates on the students' improvement of their vocabulary learning in EC and lasts four months. The data, which is analyzed with the help of SPSS 13.0, is collected by using the questionnaires and tests. In this study, vocabulary learning strategies (including meta-cognitive, cognitive, and social/affective strategies) are designed in this training. The objective of the research is to find the ways of facilitating the college students to regulate their vocabulary learning. Furthermore, the research aims to check whether the strategy training is effective to improve the students' efficiency of vocabulary learning. Through the four-month training, the research reaches the following conclusions.

Firstly, the participants in the training become more aware of using the learning strategies. According to the research result, positive changes occur to the students' beliefs about vocabulary learning. The participants' efficiency to learn vocabulary is improved after the training. The students' performance in the post-test is better than that in the pre-test. Therefore, there is no doubt that the explicit vocabulary learning strategy training contributes to the improvement of students' learning.

Secondly, the data indicates that the vocabulary learning strategy training exerts positive influence on the students. After the training, the EC students are more willing to use strategies to learn vocabulary. Thus, the findings of the research indicate that explicit VLST exerts positive influence on the improvement of students' awareness of strategy employment. The strategies that language learners tend to employ show their L2 learning performances. The good learners are more willing to use learning strategies than the poor language learners.

It seems urgent and necessary for the teacher to give the students guidance and instructions on how to use vocabulary learning strategies more efficiently and appropriately. The researcher should give an detailed explanation on the effectiveness of certain strategy in theory first, and then instruct them to use it efficiently in practice.

1.6.1 Limitations of the Study

There are some limitations in this study, though the study brings some useful findings. And some weak points still appear in this research paper owing to the limitation of the researcher's academic knowledge.

Firstly, owing to the time limitation, the researcher does not cover all the strategies. In future study, more learning strategies will be analyzed and applied in the research. When it comes to instruments of the tests, they cannot ultimately reflect the participants' vocabulary proficiency. Furthermore, the test materials in this study are also limited in content and quality.

Secondly, the study is small-scale and the sample is not large. Owing to the time limitation and other practical restrictions, the sample of the subjects consists of only 80 students in the college and is not sufficient to represent the actual teaching situation.

Thirdly, the findings tend to be partial or fragmented in that they have focused on isolated aspects of classroom life. And it has to be pointed out that this study is only the initial step in the VLS research. Some findings concerning the efficiency of students' vocabulary learning should be further explored. The method of filling out the questionnaire is applied in this research, but it is not informative. Thus, other methods, such as oral interviews, should be applied in this research.

Fourthly, the study is methodologically flawed. The research is performed only from perspective of vocabulary learning strategies to examine the effects of students' vocabulary learning. Other factors, such as intelligence, motivation, language aptitude, personality and learning style, should be taken into consideration in the future study.

To conclude, the VLST is only an initial study of the students' English learning. In the future research, a more reliable and appropriate training should be implemented.

1.6.2 Promoting Students' Roles of Autonomous Learning

A question of a possible mismatch between teachers and learners in their perceptions of their aims and outcomes of classroom activities has been one focus of recent research. A perspective on learner-centeredness is that of learners' contributing to the design of language learning activities, an idea which would certainly ensure that the purpose of classroom activities was well understood. Another perspective on learner-centeredness is that of encouraging learners to shoulder the responsibility for their own successful learning.

1.6.3 Emphasizing the Teachers' Roles in Learning Strategy Training

According to Fu Daochun (2001), teachers' roles are not static. In China, teachers' contribution and dedication to education and society has been widely acknowledged, but their professional development and creativity have been very much ignored. With the implementation of the new English curriculum, students and teachers are expected to take on new roles in autonomous learning.

In some previous researches, we find that teachers need considerable exposure to the concept of learning strategies as opposed to teaching strategies, and repeated practice in designing and providing learning strategy instruction before they feel comfortable with incorporating strategy training in their classrooms.

Good teachers are very sensitive to learners' needs and keen on improving their teaching and their students' learning on the basis of researching the in the classroom. During the process of research they try to make sense of what they do and how they affect learners. Learner's autonomy does not mean that teachers should stand in front of the classroom doing nothing in an activity that has started. Besides, monitoring the class, the teacher can also join one or two groups as an ordinary participant. However, the teachers should change his role once he joins the students. He should not dominate or appear to be authoritative.

That means that teachers are not only controller, organizer, promoter and resource provider, but also facilitator, guide, researcher, and assessor.

Bibliography

[1]Ahmed, M. O. Vocabulary learning strategies. In P. Meara (Ed.), Beyond Words (pp. 3-14). London: CILT, 1989.

[2]Anderson, N. J. The role of metacognition in second language teaching and learning. ERIC Digest. Education Resources Information Center, 2002.

[3]Bachman, L. F., & A. S. Palmer. Language testing in practice. Oxford: Oxford University Press, 1996.

[4]Bialystok, E. 'Inferencing: testing the "hypothesis-testing" hypothesis' in Seliger and Long (eds.), 1983(b).

[5]Brown and Perry. A comparison of three learning strategies for ESL

vocabulary acquisition. TESOL Quarterly, 1991 (25): 655-70.

[6]Carrell, P. L. Can reading strategies be successfully taught? http://langue.hyper.chubu.ac.jp./jult/pub/tlt/98/mar/carrell.html, 1998.

[7]Chamot, A.U. Learning Strategies in Language Learning. New York: Present Hall, 1987.

[8]Coady, J. L2 vocabulary acquisition through extensive reading. In J. Coady & T. Huckin (Eds.), Second language vocabulary acquisition. Cambridge: Cambridge University Press, 1997.

[9]Cohen, A. D. Strategies in Learning and Using a Second Language. London: Addison Wesley Longman Limited, 1998.

[10]Cohen, A. D. Language Learning: Insights for Learners, Teachers, and Researchers. New York:Newbury House, 1990.

[11]Cohen, A. D. Strategies in Learning and Using a Second Language. Foreign language Teaching and Research Press, 2000.

[12]Cohen, A. D. and Aphek, E. Retention of second language vocabulary over time: investigating the role of mnemonic associations. System, 1980,8 (3): 221-235

[13]David Wilkins. Linguistics and Language Teaching. Cambridge: Cambridge University Press, 1972.

[14]Ehrman, M. The role of personality type in adult language learning: An ongoing investigation. In J. Parry and C. Stansfield (eds.) Language Aptitude Reconsidered (pp. 23-47). Englewood Cliffs, NJ: Prentice Hall, 1990.

[15]Ellis, N. C., & Beaton, A. Psycholinguistic determinants of foreign language vocabulary learning. Language learning, 1993, 43(4): 559-617.

[16]Ellis, R. The Study of Second Language Acquisition Oxford: Oxford University Press, 1994.

[17]Fan Ling. A Study on English Vocabulary Learning Strategies.

Unpublished Master's Thesis. CNU, 2002.

[18]Gu Yongqi & R. K. Johnson. Vocabulary learning strategies and language learning outcomes, Language Learning 46, 1996.

[19]Hatch， E. & C. Brown (Eds.). Vocabulary, Semantics and Language Education. Cambridge: Cambridge University Press, 1995.

[20]Krashen, S. D. & T. D. Terrel. The Natural Approach: Language Acquisition in the Classroom. San Francisco: Alemany Press, 1983.

[21]Krashen, S. D. "We acquire vocabulary and spelling by reading: additional evidence for the input hypothesis." Modern Language Journal,1989, 73: 440-464.

[22]McCarthy, M. Vocabulary Oxford England: Oxford University Press, 1990.

[23]McDonough, S. H. Strategy and skill in learning a foreign language. London: Arnold, 1995.

[24]McDonough, S. H. Learner Strategies. Language Teacher ,1999,32:1-18.

[25]Nagy, W. E., & Anderson, R.C. How many words are there in printed school English? Reading Research quarterly, 1984,19(3): 304-330.

[26]Nagy, W. E., & Herman, P. A. Limitations of vocabulary instruction. (Tech. Rep. no. 326). Champaign: University of Illinois Center for the Study of Reading, 1984.

[27]Nagy, W. E., Herman, P. A., & Anderson, R.C. Learning words from context. Reading Research quarterly, 1985, 20(2): 233-253.

[28]Naiman, N., M. Frohlich, H. Stern, and A. Todesco. The Good Language Learner. Research in Education Series No7. Toronto: The Ontario Institute for Studies in Education, 1978.

[29]Nation, I. S. P. Teaching and Learning Vocabulary. New York: Newbury

House, 1990.

[30]O'Malley, J. M. The Effects of Training in the Use of Learning Strategies on Learning English as a Second Language. In Wenden, A. & Rubin, J (Eds.), Learner Strategies in Language Learning. (P133-144). Hemel Hempstead: Prentice Hall, 1987.

[31]O'Malley, J. M., & Chamot, A. U. Learning Strategies in Second Language. Acquisition. Cambridge: Cambridge University Press, 1990.

[32]Oxford, R. L. Use of language learning strategies: A synthesis of studies with implications for strategy training. System, 1989,17: 235-247.

[33]Oxford, R. L. Language Learning Strategies: What Every Teacher Should Know. New York: Newbury House, 1990.

[34]Oxford, R. L. 1996. Employing a questionnaire to assess the use of language learning strategies. Applied Language Learning, 7:1& 2, 25-45.

[35]Oxford & Nyikos. Language learning strategies in a nutshell: Update and ESL suggestions. TESOL Journal , 1989 (2): 18-22.

[36]Oxford, R. L. & R. Scarecella. Second Language Learning among Adults State of Art in Vocabulary Instruction. System, vol.22, No. 2,1994.

[37]Rubin, J. 'Study of cognitive processes in second language learning'. Applied Linguistics , 1981,11: 117-31

[38]Rubin, J. Learning strategies: theoretical assumptions, research history and typology, In Wenden and Rubin (Eds.), 1987.

[39]Sanaoui, R. Adult learners' approaches to learning vocabulary in second Languages. The Modern Language Journal, 1995 (79): 15-28.

[40]Schmitt, N. Vocabulary learning strategies. In Vocabulary: Description, Acquisition and Pedagogy. Cambridge: Cambridge University Press, 1997.

[41]Schmitt & M. McCarthy, Vocabulary learning strategies: Vocabulary: Description, Acquisition, and Pedagogy. Cambridge: Cambridge University

Press, 1997.

[42]Seliger, H. W. & E. Shohamy. Second Language Research Methods. Oxford: Oxford University Press, 1999.

[43]Skehan, P. Individual Differences in Second-language Learning. London: Edward Arnold, 1989.

[44]Stern, H. H. Fundamental Concepts of Language Teaching. Oxford: Oxford University Press, 1983.

[45]Stoffer, I. University Foreign Language Students' Choice of Vocabulary Learning Strategies as Related to Individual Difference Variables. Unpublished Doctoral Dissertation. Alabama: University of Alabama, 1995.

[46]Weinstein, C. & Mayer. R. "The teaching of learning strategies" In M. C. Wittrock (Ed.) Handbook of research on teaching. New York: Macmillan, 1986.

参考文献

[1] 蔡新 . 高中学生词汇学习策略调查报告 . 外语教学与研究 ,1998（7）: 37-40.

[2] 范琳，王庆华 . 英语词汇学习中的分类组织策略实验研究 . 外语教学与研究 ,2002（3）: 50-53.

[3] 傅道春（主编）. 教师的成长与发展 . 北京：教育科学出版社，2001.

[4] 黄小萍 . 英语词汇学习方法实验研究 . 国外外语教学 .2003（1）:37-41.

[5] 胡春洞 . 英语教学法 . 北京：高等教育出版社，1990.

[6] 刘润清 . 外语教学中的科研方法 . 北京：外语教学与研究出版社，1999.

[7] 刘津开 . 外语学习策略研究——猜词能力与外语水平 . 外语教学，

1999（3）：31-35.

[8] 吕文澎 . 英语难词记忆法的实验研究 . 外语教学与研究，2000（9）：33-36.

[9] 马光惠 . 理工科大学生英语词汇水平研究 . 外语教学，2001（2）：49-53.

[10] 束定芳，庄智象 . 现代外语教学 - 理论、实践与方法 . 上海：上海外语教育出版社，1996.

[11] 王立非 . 第二语言学习策略研究、问题与对策 . 国外外语教学，2001（4）：7-15.

[12] 王文宇 . 观念、策略与英语词汇记忆 . 外语教学与研究，1998（1）：49-54.

[13] 王海啸，文秋芳 . 大学生英语学习观念与策略的分析 . 解放军外国语学院学报，1996（4）：61-66.

[14] 文秋芳 . 英语学习成功者与不成功者在方法上的差异 . 外语教学与研究，1995（3）：63-68.

[15] 文秋芳 . 英语学习策略论 . 上海：上海外语教育出版社，1996.

[16] 文秋芳 . 大学生英语学习策略变化的趋势与特点 . 外语与外语教学，1996（4）：42-46.

[17] 文秋芳 . 学习和运用第二语言的策略 (导读). 北京：外语教学与研究出版社，2000.

[18] 吴霞，王蔷 . 非英语专业本科学生词汇学习策略 . 外语教学与研究，1998（1）：55-59.

[19] 吴增生 . 值得重视的“学习者策略”的研究 . 现代外语，1994（3）：24-29.

[20] 减学运，石磊，黄迎 (主编). 英语词汇学习策略与实践 . 济南：齐鲁书社，2006.

[21] 章兼中，俞红珍 . 中小学英语学习策略的研究 . 中小学英语教学

与研究，1997（5）：40-44.

[22] 张庆宗，吴喜燕 . 认知加工层次与外语词汇学习—词汇认知直接学习法 . 现代外语，2002（2）：70-79.

[23] 张萍 . 硕士研究生基础英语和专业英语词汇学习策略的研究 . 外语教学与研究，2001（6）：43-50.

[24] 张文鹏 . 中学生英语学习策略运用研究 . 中小学英语教学与研究，1999（4）：30-33.

[25] 张烨，邢敏，周大军 . 非英语专业本科生英语词汇学习策略的调查 . 解放军外国语学院学报，2003（4）：47-51.

Appendix I

Vocabulary Learning Awareness Questionnaire

你填写的内容不会对你的英语成绩有任何影响，请根据你的实际情况填写：

姓名 __________ 年龄 __________ 性别 __________ 班级 __________

为了调查研究非英语专业大学生的英语词汇学习状况，请仔细阅读题目的要求，问卷所有的问题都不存在正确或错误的答案，这是因为每个人都有自己的学习方法，对问题的回答自然不同。本问卷中每一策略的使用情况都采用 5 分制：

以下问卷旨在了解您在平时词汇学习中的一些看法。每项内容后设有一组数字 5, 4, 3, 2, 1，请根据每个数字代表的含义选择其中一个。希望每个同学针对自己的英语词汇学习情况来选择与自己实际使用相符合或接近的选项，并用 2B 铅笔涂在答题卡上 ,(1= 坚决不同意 2= 不同意 3= 不好确定 4= 同意 5= 坚决同意) 十分感谢您的合作！

1. 词汇学习需要记忆技巧　5 4 3 2 1
2. 我对词汇学习很感兴趣　5 4 3 2 1
3. 有效的词汇学习应有计划性和明确的目标　5 4 3 2 1
4. 学习词汇是很机械的活动　5 4 3 2 1
5. 词汇学习是一种缺乏创造性的活动　5 4 3 2 1
6. 学生在词汇学习中起着决定性的作用　5 4 3 2 1

Appendix II
Vocabulary Learning Strategies Questionnaire

以下是问卷的第二部分，旨在了解您在平时词汇学习中的一些策略使用情况。每项内容后设有一组数字 5, 4, 3, 2, 1，请根据每个数字代表的含义选择其中一个。希望每个同学针对自己的英语词汇学习情况来选择与自己实际使用相符合或接近的选项，并用 2B 铅笔涂在答题卡上。十分感谢您的合作！

1= 完全或几乎完全不适合我的情况

2= 通常不适合我的情况

3= 适有时适合我的情况

4= 大多数情况下适合我的情况。

5= 完全或几乎完全适合我的情况

1 制定词汇学习计划，规定每天或每周每月学习多少单词　5 4 3 2 1

2 定期检测单词的记忆情况　5 4 3 2 1

3 当发现自己的词汇学习方式不太有效时就进行调整　5 4 3 2 1

4 把发音相同的词或拼写相似的词放在一起记　5 4 3 2 1

5 通过记住某一单词出现的文章内容来记单词　5 4 3 2 1

6 记单词时把单词和其所指的事物相联系，如记单词“sea”时，脑海里就想到大海　5 4 3 2 1

7 通过记住一个包含有某一单词的句子来记住该单词　5 4 3 2 1

8 将所学单词组合在一个故事情节内来记忆　5 4 3 2 1

9 把生词和已学的词联系起来一起记忆　5 4 3 2 1

10 借助同义词或反义词来帮助记单词 5 4 3 2 1

11 安排记单词的时间，如每天的早晨几点记单词 5 4 3 2 1

12 把自己认为不懂的词，容易错的词和难记的词记录下来，定期翻阅 5 4 3 2 1

13 定期有计划地复习前面所学单词 5 4 3 2 1

14 对自己的词汇学习方式进行反思，找出不足和进步 5 4 3 2 1

15 记单词时，反复地读或写单词，或边写边读帮助记忆 5 4 3 2 1

16 把单词按不同的词根，词缀进行记忆 5 4 3 2 1

17 利用单词表来记单词 5 4 3 2 1

18 在自己单词取得进步时，采取自我奖励等方式 5 4 3 2 1

19 和同学利用相互提问，回答等方式复习单词 5 4 3 2 1

20 根据单词意思划分类别记忆，如分成交通工具，服饰，水果，植物或家电等不同类别后加以记忆 5 4 3 2 1

21 我利用上下文中所提供的例子来猜测词义 5 4 3 2 1

22 通过查字典来学习和记忆单词 5 4 3 2 1

23 我根据句子的语法结构来猜测词义 5 4 3 2 1

24 我经常记忆短语 5 4 3 2 1

25 我根据单词的词性来猜测词义 5 4 3 2 1

26 我尽量通过大量阅读来扩大词汇量 5 4 3 2 1

27 我通过做练习来巩固记忆 5 4 3 2 1

28 我利用汉语的帮助来记忆英语单词 5 4 3 2 1

29 我经常把汉语和英语进行一些相关的比较 5 4 3 2 1

30 我经常把生词和以前学过的相关知识联系起来 5 4 3 2 1

31 我运用构词法知识（如分析词根、词缀）来猜测词义 5 4 3 2 1

32 向老师和同学请教如何记单词 5 4 3 2 1

Appendix III
Vocabulary Test One (pre-test)

姓名 __________ 年龄 __________ 性别 __________ 班级 __________

本试题共有 40 题，请从 A, B, C, D 四个选择项中选出一个最佳答案，并把答案写在词汇测试答题纸（一）上。

1. ambition	A 情感	B 志向	C 歧义	D .理由
2. abuse	A 逗笑	B 滥用	C 捏	D 惊奇
3. bare	A 稀少	B 赤裸的	C 关心	D 票价
4. bay	A 射线	B 路线	C 湾	D 抵达
5. cent	A 分币	B 送	C 帐篷	D 弯腰
6. coast	A 吹嘘	B 海岸	C 烧烤	D 祝酒
7. dam	A 果酱	B 坝	C 咒骂	D 绳索
8. Deceive	A 收到	B 欺骗	C 接待	D 值得
9. emit	A 散发	B 遗漏	C 褪色	D 迁移
10. exert	A 专家	B 施加	C 拖	D 组成
11. file	A 英里	B 文件	C 开火	D 电线
12. folk	A 折叠	B 人们	C 旗帜	D 水平
13. grace	A 年级	B 葡萄	C 优雅	D 种族
14. generate	A产生	B.感激	C.应用	D.积累
15. horizon	A问候	B.眼界	C.边界	D.艰苦
16. hostile	A主人的	B.敌意的	C.厌恨的	D.空白的
17. indifferent	A不同的	B.劣等的	C.冷漠的	D.极限的

18. initial	A最初的	B.决定的	C.繁重的	D.光亮的
19. luxury	A平静	B.奢侈品	C.流动	D.贫乏
20. leisure	A愉快	B.闲暇	C.财富	D.确信
21. Marvelous	A巨大的	B.奇迹般的	C.大理石的	D.仁慈的
22. mutual	A相互的	B.匹配的	C.剩余的	D.另外的
23. neglect	A仰视	B.疏忽	C.考虑	D.延迟
24. naughty	A溺爱的	B.偏袒的	C.淘气的	D.私人的
25. justice	A正义	B.判断	C.刚才	D.陪审
26. journey	A航海	B.度假	C.行程	D.瞬间
27. knot	A结	B.靶子	C.亲属	D.织布机
28. kid	A开玩笑	B.敲击	C.热切的	D.愚蠢的
29. thereby	A然而	B.因此	C.并且	D.虽然
30. remedy	A补救	B.悲剧	C.能量	D.策略
31. case	A案件	B.地窖	C.追赶	D.阶段
32. deserve	A保留	B.预定	C.值得	D.观察
33. immense	A巨大的	B.浓厚的	C.开销	D.集中的
34. swallow	A阴影	B.寡妇	C.枕头	D.燕子
35. blade	A刀片	B.褪色	C.十年	D.入侵
36. scrape	A刮	B.逃跑	C.葡萄	D.形状
37. define	A提炼	B.定义	C.着重	D.合并
38. famine	A饥荒	B.女性	C.纪律	D.引擎
39. switch	A抓住	B.开关	C.观看	D.土地
40. volume	A栏目	B.最小	C.音量	D.汽油

Appendix IV
Vocabulary Test Two (post-test)

姓名 __________ 年龄 __________ 性别 __________ 班级 __________

本试题共有 40 题，请从 A, B, C, D 四个选择项中选出一个最佳答案，并把答案写在词汇测试答题纸（一）上。

1. triumph	A 修剪	B 整齐	C 胜利	D 缠绕
2. tense	A 感觉	B 时态	C 拉力	D 物质
3. utilize	A 利用	B 执行	C 鼓励	D 结合
4. undertake	A 强调	B 销售	C 承担	D 忧愁
5. vanish	A 渴望	B 消失	C 活跃	D 渐趋
6. vibrate	A 摇摆	B 替代	C 压迫	D 调查
7. widespread	A 普遍的	B 直立的	C 时新的	D 斜侧的
8. withstand	A 经受	B 倒下	C 行走	D 担保
9. yawn	A 打哈欠	B 小艇	C 庭院	D 码数
10. yell	A 叫喊	B 产生	C 遭受	D 拷打
11. zone	A 区域	B 骨头	C 孤独	D 语调
12. zip	A 拉链	B 肋骨	C 臀部	D 小费
13. qualify	A 使合格	B 数量	C 性质	D 计算
14. queue	A 糕点	B 长队	C 疑问	D 奇怪
15. restrain	A 抱怨	B 忍受	C 抑制	D 获得
16. atmosphere	A 大气	B 球体	C 某地	D 到处
17. breed	A 超出	B 成功	C 出血	D 繁殖

18. neglect	A 树立	B 感染	C 影响	D 忽视
19. dialect	A 方言	B 工程	C 角度	D 物体
20. contest	A 抗议	B 竞赛	C 征服	D 消化
21. complicated	A 狡猾的	B 意外的	C 复杂的	D 习惯的
22. diagram	A 电报	B 方案	C 千克	D 图表
23. planet	A 行星	B 字母	C 壁橱	D 小号
24. parcel	A 包裹	B 迷惑	C 骆驼	D 标签
25. spot	A 场所	B 射击	C 打结	D 有污点的
26. ribbon	A 丝带	B 地平线	C 尼龙	D 纽扣
27. clap	A 击掌	B 陷阱	C 帽子	D 代沟
28. lag	A 滞后	B 小毯子	C 拖拉	D 贴标签
29. compress	A 忏悔	B 压缩	C 出版	D 沮丧
30. actress	A 女演员	B 地址	C 会议	D 进程
31. elaborate	A 解释	B 绝望	C 谦虚	D 最后
32. hostile	A 主人的	B 使命	C 敌视的	D 同时
33. fertile	A 肥沃的	B 纺织	C 手机	D 子弹
34. angle	A 天使	B 角	C 丛林	D 单一的
35. kettle	A 牛群	B 定居	C 水壶	D 战役
36. principle	A 原则	B 校长	C 紫色	D 例子
37. idle	A 理想的	B 懒散的	C 白痴的	D 捆绑
38. miracle	A 奇迹	B 圈子	C 循环	D 三角形
39. eagle	A 急切的	B 鹰	C 挣扎	D 角度
40. humble	A 原木	B 数字	C 卑微的	D 瘸的

List of Abbreviations

CECR	College English Curriculum Requirements
CET-4	College English Test Band Four
CC	Control Class
EC	Experimental Class
EFL	English as a Foreign Language
IH	Input Hypothesis
L1	First Language
L2	Second Language
SBI	Strategy-based Instruction
SD	Standard Deviation
SILL	Strategy Inventory for Language Learning
SLA	Second Language Acquisition
VLS	Vocabulary Learning Strategy
VLST	Vocabulary Learning Strategy Training

Chapter 2
阅读法在大学英语写作教学中的应用

2.1 大学生的英语写作现状

根据现行大学英语教学大纲，本科学生在学完大学英语四级课程后要具备初步的写作能力。因此，在全国大学英语统一考试中，写作部分的目的就在于检测考生用英语进行书面表达的能力。作文最能体现出学生的综合英语水平，所以它自然就成了教学活动及考试（平时考试，全国四、六级统考）的一个重要部分。根据 10 年来全国英语四、六级统考的成绩来看，有相当多的考生未能达到初级的写作能力要求，平均得分在 5 分线上徘徊，得高分者实在少之又少。究其原因：其一，内容方面。不少考生没有认真审题，提笔就写，结果不是偏离主题，抓不住重点，就是深入不下，扩展不开。逻辑思维混乱，结构杂乱无章，主题内容陌生；其二，语言方面。最突出的问题是词不达意，不合句法。不少考生常用汉语表达习惯代替英语表达习惯，比如把这个句子“他们认为自己是幸福的”译成“They think themselves are happy”。仅以英语单词与汉字对上号，结果往往就只有汉语意思，而不合乎英语句法。

2.2 阅读和写作的关系

2.2.1 阅读和写作相对独立而又相互依赖， 互相促进

阅读是人类的一项重要的思维活动，它利用视觉读取由文字所记载的信息，使人们在不受时空限制的条件下进行广泛的交流。实际上，阅读是

一个复杂的双向交际活动，是一个人和书充满意义的互动过程。读者在阅读过程中，运用头脑中的图式，与作者进行积极的相互作用，达到创造性的理解。基于此种观点，当注意到阅读和写作之间的关系时，他们吃惊地发现阅读和写作几乎是两个相同的过程，共同拥有关键的认知机制。1994 年谢薇娜具体地阐述了两者的关系：写作实际上是模拟阅读的过程，写作过程也就是模拟读者阅读的过程；而阅读也是模拟写作的行为，因为读者在阅读的过程中，必须揣摩写作者的意图，扮演写作者的角色，理解写作者的意图。司托茨基（Stotsky）1987 年在综合了有关阅读与写作关系的调查后指出：写作活动对阅读理解非常有用。反之，通过阅读来提高写作的方法也证明是有效的。两者相互间关系的研究和实验都表明，阅读经验似乎始终与写作能力有关系，或者说始终影响着写作能力。由此可见，阅读与写作是两个相对独立而又相互依赖、相互作用的过程，二者是能够互相促进，共同提高的。

2.2.2 从语言发展的内在规律看，阅读和写作两项技能紧密相连

在语言学习过程中，大量的语言输入固然重要，但是如果学习者只是一味追求获得语言知识而忽视运用，那么他们掌握的仅仅是大量彼此毫无联系的、孤立的语言形式。当真正使用语言时，仍会感到束手无策。重视语言输出，强化输出练习是语言学习的有效途径。因为，语言知识需要反复循环才能得以巩固，大量的语言材料必须经过多次强化才能在记忆中牢固保持。英语阅读与写作同属英语书面语言的学习与运用的范畴，读写能力同属文字思维能力，二者息息相通，联系紧密。语言学习必须有大量的语言输入。阅读的过程是学习者自外而内获取语言知识即输入的过程。没有语言知识的输入，语言运用就成了无本之木、无源之水。克拉申（Krashen）在 20 世纪 80 年代提出了自然输入法，他认为学生只要接触大量可理解输入（听、读语篇），运用能力便会自然产生。在篇章层面上的大量可理解输入能使外语能力全面提高，这符合我们的常识与直觉，通过有

目的的大量阅读，学生从中学习、掌握语言知识，获取所需信息，并将这些信息记录，把所获知识转化并储存。而写作则是学习者将所学知识自内而外地再现过程，也就是输出过程。正所谓：“读书破万卷，下笔如有神”。

2.2.3 写作能有效地促进语言知识内化

有意识地接触到大量语言材料，从中学习写作技巧，获取写作经验与素材，开阔思路，扩大知识面，丰富思想与情感，增进观察与分析能力，学习用英语运思行文的技巧。写作能扩大学习者所用语言的范围，有助于提高学生运用语言的准确性，提高他们用英语自由表达思想的能力。通过大量的阅读和写作实践，学生可以反复练习所输入的语言知识，使之逐渐消化、吸收、深化，从而把显性语言知识转化变为隐性语言知识，并形成自己的语言生成系统，促进语言使用的自动化。

2.3 教学策略

为什么很多考生感到写作难，不是找不到话说，就是表达不清楚，我认为有两个主要原因：第一，阅读得太少；第二，没有掌握写作的技巧。找出了问题的症结，那么在今后的写作教学中我们应该注意对学生在知识、能力和技巧方面的培训。

2.3.1 激发学生的阅读动机，培养学生的阅读技能

设定明确的阅读目标对激发学习者的主观能动性和参与意识极为重要。国内外对外语阅读动机的研究表明：每一个阅读者都有一定的目的，并且具有其独特的阅读风格和方式，阅读目的和方式会随着阅读进程而发生变化。教师的任务在于激发学生阅读的动机。在学生开始阅读前，教师首先要使他们感到所读材料有用，阅读此材料有助于他们获取赖以解决疑难问题的信息。教师应引导学生为确定的目标而阅读。这种有目标的阅读可以将他们的注意力和兴趣集中到与目标任务相关的信息上，提高学生的

阅读兴趣，激发他们强烈的求知欲望，提高他们对阅读文章的理解和学习效率。一个高效率的阅读者，不仅要具备丰富的语言知识（词汇、词组、句型、语法等），还要在篇章层面上分析、理解文章内容，注重文章段落、中心句（ topic sentence）所提供的信息，结合文章的上下文，抓住重点，获取所需信息。与此同时，一个高效率的阅读者还需熟知、培养、综合运用不同的阅读方法、技巧和策略，对所读内容进行分析、归纳和总结，切实提高阅读能力。

2.3.2 在阅读中学习写作

我们知道在外语学习中，听和读就是输入，说和写即是输出。只有达到足够的输入量，量的积淀达到一定程度才能保证有较好的输出能力。古人说："熟读唐诗三百首，不会作诗也会吟。""读书破万卷，下笔如有神。"这两句话都道出同一道理："Writing is often learned from reading"。因此，我认为从阅读入手学写作，是提高写作水平的捷径。平时积累的素材越多，考试时选择的余地就越大，才有可能选出最具代表性和典型性的材料写进自己的文章，使文章既有深度和力度，又具强烈的说服力，而不至于使文章内容贫乏、空洞，甚至找不到话说交白卷得零分。在获取信息和扩大知识面的同时，我们还应该在阅读中学习语言表达。既然我们写的是英语作文，就不能用中文的方式去构思表达，机械地将中文意思译成英文，那种不伦不类的中国式英语只能使人误入歧途。

2.3.3 掌握写作技巧

作文的评分原则及标准是从内容和语言两个方面进行综合评判，那么无论是什么题型的作文，只要抓住内容和语言两大要素，掌握其训练技巧，我们就可能写出高水平的文章。

（1）认真审题

审题是写作的第一步，也是最关键的一步。它的目的在于确立思想内容，这在很大程度上关系到整篇文章的成败，切不可忽视。审题时最好草拟一个提纲，构思出文章的大概轮廓，罗列出先写什么，后写什么。经过这样的通篇考虑、统筹安排，写出的文章起码不会偏离主题，思路清楚有条理。

（2）精心选材

审好题，有了主题句，不等于文章写成了，必须有丰富的素材充实和发展提纲，从而充分地阐述文章的中心思想。因此，接下来就要确定表现内容的材料，围绕主题句尽情发挥，就好像是有了骨架之后还应有血有肉才成其为生灵，有了树干之后还应有枝丫绿叶才显得茂盛。

（3）语意连贯

思路的连贯与文字的连贯是密不可分的。作文应考虑语篇的整体性，我们可以根据上下文的关系，正确使用关联词（如表转折的、表先后次序的、表结论的、表原因、效果的、表举例或补充说明等），这样不仅可以把独立的各段的思想自然地连贯起来，还可以把句子间的衔接连贯起来。

（4）做好遣词和造句

写作中能熟练运用基本词汇，用词妥帖，在选择词汇时尽量做到：第一，用词要准确，认真区别同义词，注意介词组成的固定搭配及不同含义；第二，用词要精练，避免重复和累赘。第三，用词要具体，不要下大包围，给人模糊的印象，比如句子“ Friendliness is the salesman’s best asset”不如“A smile is the salesman’s best asset”更具体。

写作时能熟练运用各种基本句型并能灵活变换句式，为了避免句型单一，我们可以通过简单句、并列句、主从复合句、排比句、倒装句或陈述句、疑问句、祈使句、感叹句等多种句式变换来使文章内容生动、清楚，通过正确运用标点符号、并列连词（and，but ，or，for）、主从连词（because，although，if，when）等来调节句子的长短。

2.4 结论

只有阅读和技巧是不够的，我们还必须动手培养实际的写作能力，进行大量的练习。从写好句子开始，逐步写好段落、写好篇章。可以创造性地写作，也可以模仿范文写作。在大量的写作练习中，有意识地将平时积累的东西运用起来，用技巧指导写作，在大量的写作练习中发现规律，反复修改，不断提高。

参考文献

[1] 大学英语教学大纲 (修订本)(高等学校本科用)[M]. 上海：上海外语教育出版社，1999.

[2]Krashen S.The Input Hypothesis:Issues and Implications[M]. NY:Longman,1985.

[3] 肖澜，唐树成 . 作文写作技巧训练 [M]. 成都：成都科技大学出版社 ,1991.

[4] 赵雪芹 . 阅读在大学英语教学中的作用 [J]. 外语界 ,2001(1).

[5] 陈立平 . 从阅读与写作的关系看写作教学中的范文教学 [J]. 外语与外语教学 ,2001(4).

Chapter 3
任务教学法与英语写作教学

3.1 引言

现今社会信息技术日益普及，社会对高素质人才的英语交际能力提出了较以往更为苛刻的要求，英语写作已成为外语教学大纲中至关重要的一个教学内容。但在多年的英语教学中，我们过多地重视听说能力和阅读能力的培养，却忽视了写作能力对培养其综合语言能力的重要影响。面对当前社会对语言学习者的新要求，教师应该打破传统的英语写作教学方法，培养学生的实际写作能力。

3.2 理论基础

近几年来，大量的研究者教材设计者和教育改革家呼吁语言教学向任务型教学发展 (Prabhu，1987 ; Nunan ，1989 ; Long and Crookes，1991) 。任务型语言教学的研究始于 20 世纪 80 年代的英美国家，强调学生从被动学习到主动学习，使学生成为英语课堂教学的真正主人。Nunan(1989) 以为，交际型任务是一种涉及学习者理解、运用所学语言进行交流的课堂活动，学生的注意力主要集中在语言的意义上，而不是语言的形式。Long(1989) 认为，任务是一项为自己或为他人而完成的有偿或无偿的工作，是人们在日常生活中所从事的有目的的活动。Skehan(1996) 则认为任务是一项活动，在这项活动中，意义是主要的，所以应在交际的环境中，通过任务的合理设计和控制，在任务完成的过程中，使注意力得到合理的分配，从而使语言得到持续平衡的发展。

3.3 任务型教学在大学英语写作课堂的运用

3.3.1 教学模式

任务型教学是以培养学生综合语言能力为目标，强化语言实际应用的过程，以充分体现语言的交际本质。学生在任务驱动型活动中是主体，是课堂的主人，这就意味着学习是学生自己的责任，学生需要明确自己的目标和实现目标的手段。学生在完成各种各样的任务中达到学习语言的目的，同时在完成任务过程中学习人际交往，建立和维持某种人际关系，形成和发展自己的学习动机，决定自己的学习途径和手段。在任务型教学中，教师摆脱了传统的课堂中心地位，其定位是多向的，既是策划者，也是指导者，促进者，监控者和帮助者。具体而言，在任务型教学活动中，教师在确立每个课堂教学的目标和学生需求这一前提下，坚持由易到难，由简到繁，层层深入的原则，形成一个个任务链，营造一个轻松的学习环境，促进学生自己学习。

任务型教学主要把课堂分为三个阶段：前期任务，中期任务和后期任务。前期任务主要是设计一些引发学生学习兴趣的“热身”活动，根据不同的写作目的、不同的学习对象以及不同的内容主题设计组织不同的写作准备活动；中期任务包括写作、报告和评价，主要是围绕整个写作课堂任务设计多个小型任务，构成任务链，学习单元中任务的设计由易到难，层层深入，学生以个人和小组形式完成，随后以报告、讨论和辩论等形式展示其任务成果，在此阶段中，写作是第一个环节，而报告和评价两个环节必须根据教学的实际需要灵活安排，或先报告再评价再报告；后期任务在于学生根据课堂任务内容以个人或小组形式完成写作任务，师生共同对任务执行的过程、状态及结果进行评价分析，老师给予及时有效的反馈，教师可对学生的写作进行讲解性的归纳总结，鼓励和表扬学生的闪光点。

3.3.2 大学英语写作课中运用任务教学法需要注意的几个问题

任务型教学对教师提出了更高的要求，它需要教师以崭新的教学理念、完整的知识结构、反思教学的研究方式，通过有价值的课堂任务设计，为学习者创造更好的学习氛围，教师要具备很好的课堂组织能力。但是，由于教师自身能力素质的高低或对任务型教学理解不够正确，在实际的课堂教学过程中应该注意以下几个问题：

（1）要充分考虑学生的英语学习实际，灵活地安排任务

在教学实践中，不少教师错把任务型教学完全夸大理解为以学生自我为中心，忽视了对学生进行一些很有必要的知识传授、语言训练及任务交代等一些进行任务型教学的必备工作，便让学生仓促接受写作“任务”，致使学生从一开始就难以开口或无话可说。受应试教育的影响，我国大学生还不具备很强的学习独立性，还需要老师的引导和指示。因此，教师应充分考虑学生们的实际情况，设置贴近学生实际的情景模式，使他们在有目的的学习中提高写作能力。

（2）避免任务型教学活动流于形式，要注意科学的分工和管理

任务型教学过程中，小组活动是其主要的教学活动方式，但在实际教学过程中，有些教师进行的小组活动仅仅是停留在表面形式上，只是为完整教学过程，缺乏科学的管理和必要的分工。教师的分组要充分考虑组员之间的写作水平差异，保证每个学生能积极主动地参与活动，在发挥各自的特长的同时，相互学习，相互借鉴，取长补短。

（3）避免任务环节的实施过程程序化，增强其灵活性

在英语写作中进行任务型教学时，不少教师为了追求任务环节的完整性，常常会出现简单机械地按部就班，缺乏有针对性和灵活性的错误。任务型写作教学以学生为中心，重视人与人的交往互动与协调，有助于提高学生的综合素质，但同时又不完全否定写作知识、范文的作用。写作过程、写作时间、写作环节根据写作任务的性质，在不断地变化、调节，因

而它的课堂模式并不是单一的，且具有多样化的特点，教师应充分认识这一点，以丰富多样的教学形式调动学生的积极性。

3.4 结论

学生写作能力的提高会使其它语言技能得以加强和巩固。除了学生的自身努力，写作技能也需要教师的精心教学。任务型教学在大学写作课堂的应用，鼓励学生主体参与，通过完成写作中一系列递进的任务活动来培养和提高学生的写作能力和技巧证明是行之有效的。同时在写作教学中用任务型理念不仅提高学生的语言运用能力，而且通过任务型教学活动中的各种分工与合作活动，使学生学会共同生活，学会学知，学会做事，学会发展，为他们的可持续发展打下坚实的基础，也提高了他们的综合素质。这应该是我们大学老师必须达成的一项共识。

参考文献

[1] 程静英 . 英语写作教学分析 [J]. 外语教学与研究，1994(2):12-181.

[2]Prabhu. Second Language Pedagogy[M].Oxford :Oxford University Press,1987.

[3]Nunan.Designing Tasks for the Communicative Classroom[M]. Cambridge:Cambridge University Press,1989.

[4]Long and Crookes.Task-based Syllabus Design[J].TESOL Quarterly, 1991,26/1:27-551.

[5]Long.Task Group,and Task-Group Interaction[J].University of Hawaii Working Papers in English as a Second Language,1989(8):1-261.

[6]Skehan.A Framework for the Implementation of Task based Instruction[J].Applied Linguistics,1996,17/1:39-591.

[7] 廖晓青 . 任务型教学的理论基础和课堂实践 [J]. 中小学外语教学，2001(11) :12-151.

[8] 余广安 . 任务型教学 [J] 中小学外语教学，2002(6):5-91.

[9] 全新版大学英语 . 上海 : 上海外语教育出版社，2001.

Chapter 4
文化差异对英语听力的影响及其对策

4.1 引言

语言离不开文化，文化依靠语言，英语教学是语言教学，当然离不开文化教育。随着我国对外交往与民族接触日益迫切的需要，英语教学要重视交际能力的培养和随之而来的要求对所属文化有所了解的呼声越来越高。听力理解是语言学习中的一项艰巨任务，需要更多地对其进行分析和指导。在英语学习过程中，许多中国学生只重视语言本身的学习，而忽视了对于文化背景的了解。在听力理解过程中，许多学生听懂了每个单词和每个句子，但却依然不能正确地理解整篇的听力材料，其中一个很重要的原因就在于他们不了解中西方文化的差异。本文将对听力理解的过程加以分析，并进一步剖析文化差异及其对听力理解的影响，最后就如何利用文化背景来提高听力理解的水平提出几点对策。

4.2 文化因素在提高听力理解水平中的作用

语言与文化是相互依存的：语言是文化的载体，文化是语言的内容。因此语言的学习过程也是对英语国家文化的了解和掌握过程。语言中有神话、历史典故演变而来的习语，也有关于宗教、政治等社会生活的交谈。人们日常生活中的大部分信息都是在与人交谈中传递与获得的。这些信息也正是英语学习者所要听的重点。对这些文化背景知识的缺乏无疑将干扰学生的听力水平与理解能力。成功的听力理解取决于听者的语言知识和背景知识的相互作用，这两者缺一不可。不同文化背景的语言学习者，由于接受的文化教育的不同，对文章理解是有所差别的。然而在语言教学中，我们往往仅重视语言形式的讲解而忽视语言形式的社会意义的阐释，忽视了语言在实际场合的运用及文化背景差异的比较。其结果是学生在听力过程中，很大程度上依赖语言知识，对词语倾注了很大的注意力，竭力去记住每一句话的意思，并且孤立地去理解每一句话，似乎听懂了句子却找不到答案。究其原因不在语言本身，而在于不熟悉文化背景知识或知识面过窄。因此只有具备一定的文化意识和文化积累，了解文化背景知识，才能准确的理解文章内容。语言是文化的载体，要搞好听力必须使学生具备一定的英美历史和语言文学知识。同时，还需了解和熟悉一些英美国家人民的生活习惯、文化背景、风土人情及生活方式，如果这方面知识贫乏，就会影响听力。

4.3 文化差异对英语听力影响的原因分析

听力理解是一个复杂的过程，从语音的听辨到心理词汇提取，再到句法、语用的分析及语篇的连贯性，在大脑记忆的配合下，最终完成对句子或语篇的听力理解过程。我们就从听力理解的过程角度，分析一下文化因素对听力的干扰。

4.3.1 语言文化问题

有些学生刚开始学习英语时就没有很好地掌握单词的正确发音。英美英语语音差异，英美英语除了在词汇上有差异，在语音上也有很大的不同，有些读音差别还相当大。我国英语教学大多采用英国语音教学体系。近年来，随着对外开放，美音教材逐渐增多，有些学生因不熟悉英美语音差异，就产生了听力障碍。

4.3.2 心理因素的问题

听力理解过程也是很复杂的大脑心理活动过程。心理学家认为，当人的情绪处于紧张焦虑的状态时，就容易产生恐惧的心理，从而影响所听的内容。另外，外部环境也有一定的影响，如在教室、语音室与户外听的效果不一样，户外会受到多种因素的制约，从而影响听力。

4.4 英语教学中存在的问题

（1）听力教材缺乏充分有效的背景知识介绍。听力教材中虽然有关于英美文化，地理，背景知识的介绍，但是这些介绍内容单一，针对性差。比如，以前我们使用的大学英语教材内容和现实生活不够贴近，而且看起来显得有些枯燥，不具有足够的吸引力，很多同学在进行听力活动时根本就不看这些背景知识。

（2）教师的教学过程缺乏背景知识的导入。教师在进行听力教学的过程中，往往把重点放在词汇和语法上。大多数教师认为学生只要理解了词汇和语法，听力材料就很容易做了。所以在教学的过程中，老师们宁愿把时间花在讲解词汇和语法上，也不愿花一点时间在介绍背景知识上。

（3）学生们自己在听力的准备过程中忽略了学习文化背景知识。学生从高中过渡到大学以后，学习方法还没有得到改进，去适应大学学习方式。学生还没有意识到文化背景知识的欠缺会影响听力理解的效果。他们仍然认为听力考查的是词汇和语法，因此在准备听力的过程中就忽略了文化背景知识的学习。

4.5 对利用文化差异提高听力水平的几点建议

4.5.1 改变教师的教学观念，加强文化背景知识的传授

从素质教育的要求来看，现代教育培养出的人，应是适应国际竞争要求的现代人，应该善于吸取其他民族的优秀文化，提高本民族的文化素质。英语教学也应适应这一要求，如英语教学大纲指出的那样，帮助学生“正确认识世界，增强对英语国家文化的了解”。既然语言是文化不可分割

的一部分，同时又担负着传达文化的任务，所以一个语言教师同时也就是个文化教师。但是，教文化必须适度，不能脱离语言教学，必须为英语教学服务。大多数教师认为教学的目的在于使学生顺利地通过各种考试。教师就是要通过听力教学提高学生的听力水平，真正提高学生“听”的能力。而不是一切以考试为中心，而应加强文化知识的传授，提高学生真正驾驭语言的能力。老师还应利用丰富多彩的活动增强学生的文化背景知识。例如在过圣诞节的时候，老师可以把大家聚集起来一起装扮圣诞树，让大家互赠礼物，有的同学扮成圣诞老人在长统袜里装礼物，一起唱圣诞歌，一起吃中国所谓的“年夜饭”。如果有那么一次仿真活动的话，学生们一定会对西方的圣诞节印象十分深刻，更多的了解西方文化。

4.5.2 增加文化背景知识的习得

从目前的教学环境和条件来看，掌握一定的西方文化背景知识，可通过课堂教学过程和课外学生自学两方面入手。课堂教学上教师应注意选择内容涵盖面较广的材料，补充有关政治、经济、文化、科学等各领域知识，帮助学生扩大知识面。此外教师还应鼓励学生在课外进行大量的阅读，博览群书，增加信息量和文化背景知识。另外，电脑与网络的发展也为英语学习者创造了极为便利的条件。比如，对电脑接触得越多，就越能发现自己的词汇量不足，激励他们多学新的单词；利用互联网可以远隔重洋和说英语国家的人交朋友，利用网络语音视频聊天，发电子邮件交笔友等等；还可以去国内外英语学习网站或论坛搜集学习资料，交流心得。

4.5.3 加强听力技能的培养

教师应针对学生缺乏听力技能的现象，有计划地注重对学生进行听力的培养。根据上下文猜测词义的技能即根据上下文，利用场景和对话者的言语、语音、语调、语境、逻辑推理或经验常识进行联想、揣摩、预测、判断等，从而达到理解所听材料的目的；捕捉重要信息的技能即抓住关键词，掌握主题，提高长期记忆效果；记忆所听内容的技能即指导学生运用简略符号做笔记，记关键词句(如时间、地点、年代、数字、关键词等)，以提高短期记忆效果。基本语法知识对于听懂英语的重要性也是不言而喻的。由于英语中同音异义和近音异义的词非常多，在没有现成听写记录可供参考，完全由自己独立听写的情况下，没有一定的语法知识做后盾，即使你掌握了所有的同音词和近音词，还是没有办法确定取舍，把录音正确地听写出来，因此还要加强语法的学习。

参考文献

[1] 王永杰 . 谈英语教学中加强文化背景知识教育 [J]. 中国成人教育 ,2007(4).

[2] 桂诗春 . 新编心理语言学 [M]. 上海 : 上海外语教育出版社 ,2004.

[3] 王瑛 . 文化背景知识与外语教学 [J]. 南京人口管理干部学院学报 ,2000(4).

[4] 张慧军 . 论外语教学中的文化因素 [J]. 西北工业学报 ,2001(3).

[5] 贾明舫 . 非语言性因素对英语听力理解的影响及对策 [J]. 清华大学教育研究 ,2003(12).

[6] 蒋祖康 . 第二语言习得研究 [M]. 北京 : 外语教学与研究出版社 ,1999.

[7] 孙丹 . 英语听力理解中的文化干扰与对策 [J]. 科技信息 (科学教研),2007(19).

[8] 傅睿 . 利用文化背景知识提高英语听力教学的效率 . 双语学习 ,2007(6).

Chapter 5 大学生英语写作中“Chinglish”的现象分析

5.1 引言

由于思维与语言密切相关，中国学生不可避免地把中国的思维习惯运用到英文写作中去，写出的作文是“中文的思想 + 英文形式”的蹩脚英文 . 本文将对大学英语写作中“Chinglish”的产生根源进行分析，从而有针对性的找到具体有效的方法来避免其对学生写作的影响。

5.2 英语“Chinglish”现象分析

5.2.1 认知心理学理论

皮亚杰 (JeanPiaget) 的发生认识论：皮亚杰是现代认知心理学的奠基者。皮亚杰认为同化 (assimilation) 就好像消化系统将营养物吸收一样，是个体把刺激纳入原有的格局之内，同化不能使格局改变或创新。当刺激进入大脑时，个体就根据已有的格局对它同化。但是同化并不总能成功，因为个体所具有的格局是有限的，并不是包罗万象的。在这种情况下，个体要么建构一个新的格局，要么对原来的格局进行修正。这两种作用方式被皮亚杰称为顺应 (accommodation)。在英语学习过程中，如果同化的程度多了，顺应的成分就相应减少，也即意味着受汉语的影响大，这样做的结果就是，所学的英语带有中国腔，“Chinglish”就这样出现了。

5.2.2 英汉思维差异的影响

语言是思维的主要工具，是思维方式的构成要素。思维方式的差异，正是造成语言差异的一个重要原因。中国学生英语写作中遇到的困难，除了语言知识和技能外，更主要的是源于中西方思维模式的差异。英汉语篇思维的差异有许多方面的表现，从以下两点进行阐述：

（1）直线式和螺旋式

受中西方各自重综合和重分析的思维习惯影响，英汉语篇分别呈现出直线式和螺旋式的逻辑特征。所谓直线式就是由中心意思展开，或层层推演或逐项分列，后面的意思都由前面的语句自然引出。而汉语的螺旋式以八股文的“起、承、转、合”为典型：先宣称主题之重要，继而进行反复的论述，最后回归到主题并对它再三强调。

（2）形合和意合

中西方思维差异的又一表现是构思方式和语言组织方式的悟性和意合与理性和形合的不同。句子衔接方式有三种：句法手段、词汇手段和语义手段，通过前两种手段实现的衔接被称为形合，后一种手段的衔接被称为意合。因此，形合与意合之别也就是语篇的显性连贯和隐性连贯的不同。汉语以意合和隐性为特征，仅靠词语和句子内含意差别。西方人由理性分析而执着于主客区别，以“人”这个主体为主语，或以事物这个客体为主语，视需要而定。

5.2.3 母语负迁移

“语言迁移”的概念是Lado在他的著作《跨文化语言学》中提出来的，他认为，在学习第二语言时，学习者广泛地依赖已经掌握的母语，并经常把母语中的语言形式、意义和与母语相联系的文化迁移到第二语言中，又分为“正迁移”和“负迁移”。母语和第二语言的相同之处对学习第二语言带来的积极意义就是所谓的“正迁移”；母语和第二语言的差异对第二语言学习所引起的干扰被称为“负迁移”。

5.3 应对策略

产生中式英语的原因是多方面的，但最根本的原因是一种误解。那么，如何很快跨越这个阶段、达到写出地道的英语并能熟练运用英语呢？我认为可以从以下几方面抓起：

5.3.1 提高词汇学习

熟练运用英语基本单词是提高英语综合水平不可缺少的条件，这一点要给予充分重视。在学习英语单词时，除知道词义外，还要学会正确使用单词，举一反三，遇有一词多义或同义词的情况时，应注意其用法异同，学会比较，学会宏观上增加自己的词汇量。

5.3.2 语法要加强训练

语法是组词造句的规则。语法概念模糊不清，中英文混淆不清，一张口一下笔就会出差错。一些语法知识，必须经过来回的反复的练习，让它在自己头脑里生根。事实证明，只有这样做，对语法知识学透学精，只有这样做，才能克服中式英语。在练习和运用英语中去学习语法，做有针对性的练习，让学生达到对语法知识点的反复，是语法教学中的一个必不可少的环节。

5.3.3 培养语言能力

语言是交际工具，学习英语的目的是学习者掌握知识和基本技能并能运用英语进行交际。但如何使学生正确地使用英语进行交际就显得更加困难。因为，我国英语教学是在非自然的外语情境中进行的，受母语影响很重；正确使用英语进行交际不仅以语言知识技能为基础，还要了解所学语言国家的社会文化、风土人情、生活习惯。为了克服或满足上述要求，就必须培养学生的语用能力。例如，英语教学中同时加大英语语言文化的学习，因为语言反映社会现实。利用英语录像和电影进行教学，然后组织讨论。通过阅读了解外国的社会、文化、历史、地理乃至人情风俗等方面的知识，真正认识并掌握英语自身的语言规律及其表达习惯，从而讲出或写出地道的英语。

参考文献

[1] (瑞士) 皮亚杰 . 发生认识论原理 [M]. 北京 : 商务印书馆 , 1997.

[2] 连淑能 . 论中西思维方式英汉语言文化对比研究 [C]. 上海外语教育出版社 ,2004.

[3] 张玉玺 . 英语写作中 Chinglish 的成因分析 [J]. 中国环境管理干部学院学报 ,2006(2).

[4] 李雪红 . 浅析中式英语产生的原因 [J]. 合肥工业大学学报 (社会科学版),2005(4).

[5] 马庆林 . “中式英语”成因之认知分析 [J]. 西北大学学报 (哲学社会科学版),2003.

Chapter 6
背诵在大学艺术、体育类学生英语学习过程中的作用

6.1 引言

交际法教学在中国目前英语教学中非常流行，但是它并不完全适合中国的外语教学，难以产生明显的教学效果，尤其是对大学艺术、体育类学生。课堂内，仅靠有限的输入要产生大量的交际活动是不可能的，如果强迫学生在没有足够输入的情况下进行交际，则必然会产生大量不规范的输出。另外，艺体类学生高中阶段英语基础就比较差，大学入学英语成绩本来就比其他专业学生低，若采用交际法教学，势必会影响其大学英语学习。因此对于这类大学生，采用传统的背诵式语言学习方式不失为一个好的策略。陈琳教授指出："在没有语言环境的情况下，外语是不可能'习得'的，只能'学得'，必须下艰苦的功夫。我一向主张要背。不仅儿童，成人更加要背。"（陈琳，1999：1）张维友教授说："回想起来，我学英语在很大程度上得益于过去的'死记硬背'，无捷径可走。"(张维友 ,2002 :1) 胡文仲教授也讲道："要学好外语，……要充分发挥青年人记忆力强这个优势，多背一些对话和课文。有的教学法家反对背诵，我认为外语应该多背，……"（胡文仲，1989：1）当今以计算机为基础的多媒体教学手段，在大学英语学习与教学中广泛应用，对大学英语教学产生变革性的影响。但在多媒体教学条件下，传统背诵法是否还有必要？本文通过一些实验数据，来揭示背诵在大学艺术、体育类学生英语学习过程中的作用，期望能以此为现代大学英语教学提供某些理论依据。

6.2 理论基础

应用语言学家 Krashen（1987：21-25）第二语言习得理论认为语言习得是通过语言输入来完成的，教学的主要精力应放在为学生提供最佳的语言输入上。背诵输入符合 Krashen 的语言输入理论，通过背诵输入加强学生对所学语法知识的理解，学会用地道的英语表达自己的思想，摆脱母语的负面影响，最终提高英语写作能力，使其语言输出规范化。

背诵式输入可提高英语学习者的语感。加拿大语言学家 Bialystok（1978：28）的第二语言学习的理论模式将外语习得者的语言知识主要分为显性语言知识和隐性语言知识两种。显性语言知识指学习者意识层中的所有目标语的语言知识，包括语音、语法词汇等知识，这些知识存在于学习者的意识层中，可以清晰地表达出来。隐性语言知识指那些内化了的语言知识，他们存在于学习者的潜意识层中，使得学习者不一定能清晰地表达出来；但能不加思索地使用语言，这就是人们常说的语感。语言学家 Bialystok 的第二语言学习的理论模式给我们的启示是，“一个人的隐性语言知识越多，他熟练使用目标语的程度就越高”(马广惠，1997：9)。

而背诵输入加强了对学生语言知识的积累和巩固，因而能将显性的语言知识转化为隐性的语言知识（曹怡鲁，1999：2），学生的语感也因此而形成，这势必能促进其语言习得。随着背诵输入的不断增加，学生对所学的目标语语言现象的敏感度也会不断增强，隐性语言知识将不断得到扩展，语感也将不断增强。

6.3 问卷调查

6.3.1 研究问题

本调查试图让艺体生回答以下五个问题：

（1）你认为背诵对提高英语有用吗?

（2）你更喜欢背诵词汇，句子，还是文章？

（3）你的英语老师是否要求背诵并且定期检查背诵？

（4）你的背诵材料来源于哪里？

（5）最近一次期末考试英语成绩是多少？

6.3.2 调查对象

以下是参加本次问卷调查的人数及分布情况。

表 1　调查对象的人数及分布

音乐专业		体育专业		美术专业	
39		41		38	
二年级	一年级	二年级	一年级	二年级	一年级
22	17	18	23	26	12

调查对象全部来自本校音体美三个系的一二年级，一共有 118 名学生参加问卷调查。从以上图表中的数字可以看出，参加调查的学生分布是比较合理的。调查对象具有较大的代表性，因此调查获得的结果应该基本上能满足研究的需要：了解艺体生的背诵与英语学习的相关性。

6.3.3 调查工具及方法

调查工具为一份问卷，由 5 个小问题组成（详见附录）。问卷调查是笔者上课时随堂进行的。共收回 118 份问卷，均为有效问卷。

6.3.4 结果

由于我们的主要目的是想了解艺体生英语背诵与英语成绩相关性的一般情况，我们只对所获得的结果作总的归纳和分析，未对年级之间的区别进行具体区分。通过对所搜集资料的整理，我们得到如下结果：

（1）你认为背诵对提高英语有用吗？

在接受问卷调查的学生当中，认为背诵很有用及有用的百分比之和分别为 100%，100%，94.74%。因此，艺体类大学生对背诵作用是持肯定态度的。具体结果如下：

表 2　背诵对提高英语是否有用

	很有用	有用	无用	毫无用处	总计
音乐专业	21	18	0	0	39
百分比	53.85%	46.15%	0%	0%	100%
体育专业	24	17	0	0	41
百分比	58.54%	41.46%	0%	0%	100%
美术专业	20	16	2	0	38
百分比	52.63%	42.11%	5.26%	0%	100%

（2）你更喜欢背诵词汇，句子，还是文章？

在接受问卷调查的学生当中，三个专业的学生对于背诵内容的倾向有所不同。音乐专业的学生更喜欢背诵词汇（61.54%），依次为句子（25.64%）和文章（2.82%）。体育专业的学生喜欢背诵文章（48.74%）的比例大一些，依次为句子（26.83%）和词汇（24.39%），而美术专业的学生与音乐专业的学生比较相似，愿意背诵的内容依次为词汇（47.37%），句子（34.21%）和文章（18.42%）。可见，总的来说，体育专业的学生对背诵句子和文章比较感兴趣，而音乐和美术专业的学生则喜欢背诵词汇。具体结果如下：

表 3 更喜欢背诵词汇，句子，还是文章

	词汇	句子	文章	总计
音乐专业	24	10	5	39
百分比	61.54%	25.64%	2.82%	100%
体育专业	10	11	20	41
百分比	24.39%	26.83%	48.78%	100%
美术专业	18	13	7	38
百分比	47.37%	34.21%	18.42%	100%

（3）你的英语老师是否要求背诵并且定期检查背诵？

教师要求背诵且是否检查因教师和专业的不同而有所区别。体育专业的教师要求背诵且定期检查的比例最高，达 68.30%，而美术和音乐专业的比例分别为 36.84%、25.64%。在教师要求背诵但无定期检查的数据当中，三个专业的比例分别为 71.79%（音乐专业），55.26%（美术专业），31.70%（体育专业）。但总体来说，大部分教师都是要求学生去背诵英语的，其中教授体育专业的教师能够更多地去检查学生的背诵。具体结果如下：

表 4 是否要求背诵并且定期检查背诵

	要求背诵但无定期检查	要求背诵且定期检查	既无要求背诵又无定期检查	总计
音乐专业	28	10	1	39
百分比	71.79%	25.64%	2.57%	100%
体育专业	13	28	0	41
百分比	31.70%	68.30%	0%	100%
美术专业	21	14	3	38
百分比	55.26%	36.84%	7.9%	100%

（4）你的背诵材料来源于哪里？

从背诵材料来源的调查数据可知：三个专业的学生都有接近一半的人数认为背诵应以课文为主，课外材料为辅，它们的比例依次为 47.37%（美术专业），46.39%（体育专业）和 43.59%（音乐专业）。由此可见，学生们并不只是满足课文内容的学习和背诵，他们同时渴望学习课外知识，拓宽知识面。

表 5　背诵材料来源

	课文为主	课外为主	课外为辅 课文为主	课外为主 课文为辅	总计
音乐专业	15	4	17	3	39
百分比	38.46%	10.26%	43.59%	7.69%	100%
体育专业	14	3	19	5	41
百分比	34.15%	7.26%	46.39%	12.20%	100%
美术专业	16	2	18	2	38
百分比	42.11%	5.26%	47.37%	5.26%	100%

（5）最近一次期末考试英语成绩是多少？

在接受调查的学生当中，成绩优秀人数（≥ 80）的比例依次为 48.78%（体育专业），10.53%（美术专业）和 7.69%（音乐专业）。由此可见，体育专业学生的成绩优秀人数大大高于其他两个专业，接近总人数的一半。具体结果如下：

表 6　最近一次期末考试英语成绩

	≤59	60–69	70–79	≥80	总计
音乐专业	1	19	16	3	39
百分比	2.56%	48.72%	41.03%	7.69%	100%
体育专业	1	6	14	20	41
百分比	2.44%	14.63%	34.15%	48.78%	100%
美术专业	0	12	22	4	38
百分比	0%	31.58%	57.89%	10.53%	100%

6.3.5 讨论

依据以上的问卷调查结果，我们试对结果进行如下分析和解释。

（1）背诵的作用

调查结果显示：艺体类学生对背诵的作用持肯定态度，但是他们对背诵内容的种类持有不同的看法，大部分音乐专业和美术专业的学生仅仅喜欢背诵词汇，却忽略了句子和文章等其他材料的背诵；而体育专业的学生则恰恰相反，更喜欢背诵句子和文章。而在英语期末考试中，体育专业学生的成绩明显好于其他专业的学生。因此，我们可以做出推测：背诵文章、句子等篇章材料要比仅仅背诵词汇更有利于提高英语成绩。

（2）背诵的材料来源

问卷调查的结果表明，大部分艺体生都认为背诵应该以课文内容为主，同时增加一些课外材料。这反映了学生在英语学习过程中，学好课文内容的同时，更想增加课外知识的学习，拓宽知识面。

（3）背诵的要求及检查情况

从问卷调查的数据得知，教授艺体类学生的英语老师能够要求学生去背诵英语，但是在定期检查学生的背诵方面，部分教师做的还略有不足。

学生学习英语的情况，从根本上来说，取决于学生学习英语的态度，即内因。内因是决定因素，但是，外因对内因也有一定的促进作用。这就需要教师对学生进行督促和指导，发挥教师对学生学习的外因作用。例如，教授体育专业的教师更多地会检查学生的背诵，因而他们的英语成绩明显好于其他两个专业。教师应该定期检查学生的背诵，给与他们一定的指导，最终使学生能够增强语感，学好英语。

6.4 结论

根据以上的调查数据的相关讨论，我们可以得出以下的结论和建议：

6.4.1 背诵的作用

艺体类大学生认为英语背诵对他们英语水平的提高有促进作用。

6.4.2 背诵的材料来源

艺体类大学生认为背诵应以课文内容为主，同时增加一些课外材料。因此教师应选择与课文内容密切相关，文笔流畅，语言优美的段落篇章让学生背诵，同时查找适合学生背诵的课外材料让学生去背诵，发挥教师的指导作用。

6.4.3 背诵的要求及检查情况

英语背诵归根到底由学生自己来完成，他们是背诵的主体。但是，教师应该督促他们进行背诵，给予一定的指导。背诵更应该以句子和文章为主，篇章记忆会更好地促进学生的英语水平提高。（何家宁，1998）如果孤立地背诵词汇表中的词汇，收效就很小，“因为这种做法实际上把每一个外语的语词和母语的语词等同起来，而且把它从语言和语境中孤立开来。”（桂诗春，1988：192）

参考文献

[1]Bialystok E. A Theoretical Model of Second Language Learning[J]. Language Learning, 1978(28).

[2]Krashen S. Principles and Practice in Second Language Acquisition[M]. Hertfordshire: Prentice Hall International (UK) Ltd, 1987:21-25

[3]Nunan,D. The Learner-centered Curriculum[M]. Cambridge: Cambridge University Press,1998:137.

[4] 曹怡鲁 . 外语教学应借鉴中国传统语言教学经验 [J]. 外语界，1999(2).

[5] 陈 琳 . 英语专家如是说（专栏）[J]. 英语学习，1999(6):1.

[6] 丁言仁 . 背诵课文在英语学习中的作用 [J]. 外语界，2001(5).

[7] 邓郦鸣 . 注重背诵输入克服写作中的负迁移 [J]. 外语教学，2001(4):43-44.

[8] 桂诗春 . 应用语言学 [M]. 长沙：湖南教育出版社，1998.

[9] 胡文仲 . 英语的教与学 [M]. 北京：外语教学与研究出版社，1989.

[10] 何家宁 . 词汇呈现方式对词汇记忆影响的实验研究 [J]. 山东外语教学，1998(2):60-63.

[11] 何家宁 . 关于大学生英语背诵的调查报告 [J]. 山东外语教学，2006,(1).

[12] 龙献平 . 背诵强度与英语学习成绩的相关性研究 [J]. 西安外国语学院学报，2006(1).

[13] 刘欣 . 兴趣. 参与. 活动—英语专业课通用教学模式 [J]. 外语教学，1997(2):43.

[14] 马广惠 .Bialystok 的语言学习模式 [J]. 国外外语教学，1997(1):8-9.

[15] 张维友 . 英语专家如是说（专栏）[J]. 英语学习，2002(1):1.

Chapter 7
英语专业学生学术论文写作中因果连词运用研究

7.1 引言

Halliday 和 Hasan(1976) 在 Cohesion in English 中谈及到了英语的衔接与连贯，他们认为：言者在语篇的组成过程中，通过使用篇章中语言与结构成分的接续性，实现了篇章的统一与紧密。这些连续性的语言手段被称为衔接手段，分别为指示、替代、省略、连接、词汇衔接五种手段。这些语篇连贯的衔接手段，在篇章的紧密衔接、语义连贯等方面发挥着重要的作用。因此，国内外学者和研究者对多样文化和社会背景下的英语学习者连词的使用情况进行了卓有成效的研究。Mauranen（1993）研究了在芬兰国家中的学生对文本中连词的使用情况，认为：此国家学生在英语习作中显著的少用关联连接词，更多地运用词汇衔接手段。同样，Altenberg et al.(1998) 对比了法国和瑞典两国学生在习作中的英语语言连词的运用和分配情况，结果发现学生错用英语联结词的情况很普遍。Crewe（1990）研究了香港大学英语习得者在英语写作中连词的运用情况。研究研究显示：香港的英语学习者同样出现学生在英语写作中误用和过多使用了连接词。我国学者潘王番、冯跃进（2004）对我国非英语专业学生在研究生作文写作中，使用对比语料库的方式，探讨了英语连接词的使用状况，也呈现出过连接词使用过少的错误现象。前人的大量研究表明，不管哪个国家的英语习得者，都出现了连词使用的差错现象，这是英语学习的难点。因此，能否正确、合理并恰当地使用英语因果连词，很大程度上决定了英语学习者的写作质量。本文选择逻辑语义关系中的因果连词作为研究对象，探索英语专业的学生在英语习作语篇中因果连接词的使用情况，以期对大学英语教学与研究及教师教育等有一定的帮助。

7.2 设计方案

7.2.1 研究问题

根据 Quirk(1985) 和邢福义（1997）从语法、语义和功能的视角进行分类，将因果连词分为连词或连词性短语、副词或副词性短语、和介词性短语三类。然本文采用 Kennedy(1992:68) 的分类方法进行统计和分类。

词的属性	词汇功能	例证
连词或连词性短语	结果	It follows that, so
	原因	As,for, because, since, now that
副词或副词性短语	结果	As a consequence, as a result, hence, so, therefore, thus
介词性短语	结果	As a consequence, as a result
	原因	Because of, due to, for fear of, in response to

本次研究主要解决以下两个问题：

（1）与英语国家学生写作语料相比较，中国大学英语专业学生的英语习作中因果连词的运用情况所展示的特点。

（2）英语专业大学生英语写作与非英语专业大学生学术写作进行对比，其因果连词分布所表现出的差异。

7.2.2 研究步骤

针对英语专业大学生英语写作与非英语专业大学生学术写作的差异，

笔者按照搜集到的文本进行归类，电脑分析，和对比分析等程序。自己根据教学及科研需要自行设计了小型语料库 A1 和 A2，本语料汇集和整理了学生英语习作实际样本。本文作者采用“cluster sampling”的方法，以某地方本科院校外文学院的各个年级学生为参考班级，每个年级随机选取了 3 个班级的文本语料 A1，总共 245 篇习作，总字数为 8 万字符，写作题目为“Time is precious”。同样，我们在此校随意选取了各个年级的非英语专业大学生的英语习作语料 A2，总共 276 篇习作，总字数也为 8 万字符，作文题目同样是“Time is precious”。

利用检索软件“Wordsmith Tools 4”检索出文本中所包含的因果连词，然后通过人工检索的方法排除不适合本研究的明显不是因果联结意义的词汇，以连词“as”为例，此词语除了表示因果关系之外，还可以表示伴随，时间先后顺序，因此这类关联词可以排除。

7.3 分析研究

我们按照 Kennedy(1992:68) 的分类方法进行统计和分类，本文作者使用检索软件“Wordsmith Tools 4”检索出文本中所包含的因果连词，然后通过人工检索的方法排除不适合本研究的明显不是因果联结意义的词汇，对此语料库中的词汇的出现频率列统计表格如下：

因果连接词汇	频率			
	英语专业A1		非英语专业A2	
	实际频率	8万词相对频率	实际频率	8万词相对频率
as	24	5	13	17.8
because	946	193	128	162
Due to	25.6	6.1	22.4	29.2
for	8.8	18.4	21.6	28

因果连接词汇	频率			
	英语专业A1		非英语专业A2	
	实际频率	8万词相对频率	实际频率	8万词相对频率
hence	11.2	2.3	0.8	1.0
Now that	5.6	1.12	0.1	0.1
since	66	1.35	13.5	17.7
so	1511	309	195	255
therefore	132	26.7	43.9	58.2
thus	122	25.1	23.1	30.2
thereby	0.8	0.15	0	0

通过数据调查和分析，中国英语专业学生已经可以有效并且合理地使用因果连词。他们通常使用“so，because”等来表达因果关系，可是从他们的语料来看，有些连接词存在误用现象，例如：

I bought an apple，so my sister got home.

很明显，“so”之前和之后的小句在语义连接上不存在因果关系，所以这是错误的。

Because I recall the companions in the company，so I encourage all the members of my companions to celebrate my birthday.

此句中，因果连接词同样出现误用现象。

7.5 结论

研究表明，与英语国家大学生写作语料库相比，在中国英语专业大学生的议论文写作中，因果连词的使用呈现过多使用，so 和 because 使用比率过高的特征，与非专业大学生英语写作相比，英语专业学生写作中因果连接词更多样化，这说明我国英语专业学生对因果连接词的把握比非专业学生稍好。

在今后的专业英语写作教学中，英语教师应当对因果连接词使用频率过高和多样性不足的问题予以重视，并针对问题采取相应的教学策略。

参考文献

[1]Altenberg, B. &M. Tapper.The Use of Adverbial Connectors in Advanced Learner's Written English[M]. London and NewYork: Longman, 1998.

[2]Crewe, W. J. The illogic of logical connectors[J].EFL Journal,1990(44):316-325.

[3]Halliday,M. A. K. &R. Hasan.Cohesion in English[M]. Beijing: Foreign Language Teaching and Research Press, 1976.

[4]Kennedy. Expressing causation in written English[J].RELC Journal, 1992,23(1):68.

[5]Mauranen, A.Cultural Differences in Academic Rhetoric:A Textlinguistic Study[M]. Frankfurt: PeterLang, 1993.

[6]Quirk, R.A Comprehensive Grammar of the English Language[M]. London and New York: Longman, 1985.

[7] 潘王番 , 冯跃进 . 非英语专业研究生写作中连接词用法的语料库调查 [J]. 现代外语，2004(2):157-162.

[8] 邢福义 : 汉语语法学 , 东北师范大学出版社 ,1997.

Chapter 8
The Motivation Approach in College English Learning and Teaching

8.1 Introduction

It was not until the 1970s that lexical research became a subject of discussion among linguists. Numerous writings and studies on L2 vocabulary acquisition have emerged. Some of these works focus on teaching techniques. The essence of learner vocabulary acquisition is through the cognitive method of metaphor; this study inscribes that metaphor is not only a linguistic phenomenon in our daily life, but the human thought process is metaphorical in nature. Metaphor is a closely related thought process in the human mind. It is a lind of a cognitive perspective for us to study English learners' vocabulary learning and vocabulary competence in my viewpoint.

The metaphor, concerned with the cognitive views, helps us to better understand the abstract meaning of metaphor in language. In the past few decades, in the process of the teaching and learning of vocabulary, the learners' interest is never aroused to pay attention to grammar, reading or writing. Cognitive linguists have understood the process of metaphor and continue to shape the abstract meaning of language. It is also widely recognized that metaphorical thinking is a part of the cognitive process of the conceptual world of human thought. And this metaphorical thinking allows us to understand and describe new experiences in the world with relatively few words.

However, the current situation of English teaching in China is far from satisfactory. In many high schools, English classes are to a large extent teacher-centered and text-oriented grammar translation methods. Few students and students interact. Therefore, when high school students attend college, many of them have grammar, vocabulary, and writing skills, and their oral and listening skills are low. Cognitive linguists have understood the process of metaphor and continue to shape the abstract meaning of language. It is also believed that metaphorical thinking is part of the cognitive process of the conceptual world of human thought. And this metaphorical thinking allows us to understand and describe new experiences in the world with relatively few words(Huang, 2006).

With the development of the global economy and the advent of the information age, as a tool to communicate with the outside world, English is becoming more and more popular in China. Some students want to make more progress in English learning in the new era. In practical English classrooms, teachers will try their best to help them improve their useful skills to communicate with foreigners.

At the same time, the written test is designed to examine how college students better make a great mastery of English according to the Syllabus for CET-C60 and Syllabus for CET-VI (2004). Therefore, in teachers'minds, the important goal is to help students pass the exam at the end of the term. This is partly due to the fact that many college English teachers use the same traditional model with a greater emphasis on the use of English rather than the use of language. To make matters worse, the traditional model ignores the ability to develop problem-solving, and students' critical thinking does not help cooperative learning capabilities, these are the future of career. The teaching process should be guided under the Syllabus for College English (2001: 1).

According to this syllabus, English learners are required to improve their overall English communication skills. In order to adjust their teaching methods for the newly revised Syllabus, more and more college English teachers are beginning to read modern teaching methods and try to apply them to daily classroom activities. The most prominent problem is that although students master a large number of English words, phrases and grammar, but they are familiar with the topic of writing, but still can not express their ideas clearly and accurately in English. In view of the limitations of traditional one-way teaching methods, the English proficiency of college graduates can no longer meet the needs of a fast-growing society. The Ministry of Education of China amended the 2005 Syllabus for College English Courses.

Exchange is mainly from interaction. Interaction means the receipt and presentation of information. In order to promote the interaction of another language, we must encourage our students to enthusiastically take part in some interactive activities to make their interests and attention attractive to them, making the interaction natural and attractive.

With the development and depth of China's reform and open policy, it is more necessary to cultivate the young's will to acquire many varied cognitive as well as physical skills. These skills necessarily include second language acquisition—English learning. In fact schools are created as artificial arrangements in which we require our children to carry out all kinds of activities which would not occur to them spontaneously in their young lives. Most Chinese parents realize the importance of English learning and force their children to learn however young they are. In this syllabus, learners are required to improve their overall English communication skills. In order to adjust their teaching methods for the newly revised Syllabus, more and more college English teachers are beginning to read modern teaching methods and try to apply them to daily classroom activities. In view of the limitations of traditional one-way teaching methods, the English proficiency of college graduates can no longer meet the needs of a fast-growing society. The Ministry of Education of China amended the 2005 Syllabus for College English Courses.

A study of motivation, therefore, is crucial for a teacher. Without the means of encouraging the children learning, understand their "appetites" , in the widest sense of the world and nature, being sensitive to their interests, the teachers' would be impossible.

It costs our more efforts because we do not have enough time to focus on the fluidity and coherence of the entire composition, leading to a lack of efforts for fluent, accurate and customary composition. The most obvious problem is that although students have leaned various English words, phrases and grammar and also are familiar with the content meaning of the passage, but they still can not convey their ideas to anyone clearly and accurately in English. In addition, it is a fact that in the process of writing, there are often some ideas initially in their head for Chinese, then find out the corresponding English words one by one in Chinese words, and finally they together arrange them verbatim based on the construction of English sentences grammar.

However, in China, classroom interactive experiments have been tried, mainly in primary and secondary schools, while for the college English teachers and students, a bit of cheating interactive research theory and technical analysis, some researchers in a thorough manner to enhance the practice of teaching And learning mode. Therefore, this article tries to study the interactive ways in college English teaching and explore a new learner-centered teaching mode. In fact, many reserchers and scholars have made great contributions to college English teaching, using the interactive approach and achieved some success.

Theorists in the study of motivation generally concerned themselves with four basic questions representing different states in the processes of motivated behavior. They are: what initiate action, what direction does this action take, how strong is the action and why does the action terminate? Action is meant to be no only the obvious movement, but also the mental action.

Students who are motivated to learn have a positive and positive attitude towards learning, and strive to learn English well. They have clear goals and aspirations, and their grades are higher than those who do not have the motivation to learn. Those students usually regard learning English as a boring burden for them in their college life. Indeed, motivation is a fundamental element of language learning and no teacher can pay no attention to the student's motivation. In language learning, motivation is not only a strong desire to learn and acquire knowledge in any research feild, but also to promote students' enthusiasm and willingness to learn English. It's like a car's engine and steering wheel that lets students get bored and interested. It is an inherent force that can drive and uphold students' English learning. Gardner pointed out that the motivation of foreign language learning includes four aspects: the goal, hard work, the desire to achieve the goal and attitude (Jia Guanjie, 1996). Therefore, it is necessary to understand the motivation more deeply and the author turns to the next one.

People are always motivated. They may not have the motivation to do what we want them to do, but they can not really say that they have no motive. In psychology, motivation is a force that motivates and guides people toward their goals (Paul Eggen & Don Kauchak, 1994, p427). Like a force moving objects, power will move a person. More intuitively, if the individual is a machine, motivation is like an engine that drives and guides the individual's behavior. Motivation has three important functions: Motivating us (ie: turning the key, starting the motivation engine) leads us (ie, and helps us to choose the behavior that best suits our goals) (Don Hamachek, 1989, p262.) In summary, Motivation is an internal state that arouses the individual's desire for a goal and maintains their efforts in a certain direction and time.

The fact is that people who speak English have different ways of thinking when expressing their thoughts and show different styles. For example, English-speaking people tend to be straightforward, speak the most important messages at the beginning of writing, while those in Chinese do the opposite. Therefore, in order to write a well-organized English essay, Chinese students can learn and remember vocabulary, which is the general direction of discourse. Students who are motivated to learn have a positive and positive attitude towards learning, and strive to learn English well. They have clear goals and aspirations, and their grades are higher than those who do not have the motivation to learn. Those students usually regard learning English as a boring burden for them in their college life. Indeed, motivation is a fundamental element of language learning and no teacher can pay no attention to the student's motivation. In language learning, motivation is not only a strong desire to learn and acquire knowledge in any research feild, but also to promote students' enthusiasm and willingness to learn English. It's like a car's engine and steering wheel that lets students get bored and interested. It is an inherent force that can drive and uphold students' English learning. Gardner pointed out that the motivation of foreign language learning includes four aspects: the goal, hard work, the desire to achieve the goal and attitude (Jia Guanjie, 1996). Therefore, it is necessary to understand the motivation more deeply and the author turns to the next one.

R. Garden introduces four components in the Motivation of learning foreign language: purpose, diligence, desire and attitude. Working hard does not mean having strong motivation. Similarly, having desire or correct attitude to study does not necessarily reflect motivation. Only combining desire to success and correct attitude and hard working together can students have a real motivation .

R. Gardner and W. Lambert postulated two kinds of MLFL. One is integrative motions, with which people want to become a member of this target language speaking community. So they should not only learn the language, but receive their culture style. The other is instrumental motivation. People of such motivation of learning English have their actual purpose, such as find a better profession or improve their social status. Gardner also stated that students' attitude to target language can influence their study effect. And if students with integrative motivation can get positive support from their parents, they are sure to make progress.

Brown defines the interaction in more detail: Interaction is the collaborative exchange of thoughts, emotions, or ideas between two or more people that have any interplay. The theory of communicative competence emphasizes the importance of interaction because humans use language to "negotiate" meaning in different contexts or, simply, get an idea from your mind and then into the mind of another, and vice versa Also (Brown, 1994: 159). CLT distinguishes itself from other approaches because it places more emphasis on students' communicative competence than language skills. Because of the the interactive approach I'm focusing on in this study which is primarily based on CLT. Different scholars can explain CLT in different ways.

J. Withall advocates "the interaction between learner's emotional and cognitive needs and environmental variables (including peer and teacher behaviors, educational products, and teaching facilities) with the help of mentors or peers" (Joriabanks 1991: 91).

From the above definitions and perspectives, it is not hard to come to the conclusion that interaction helps to express one's own thoughts and understand one's thoughts. Therefore, English teachers should always take interaction as an important concept. The theory of communicative competence emphasizes the importance of interaction because humans use language to "negotiate" meaning in different contexts or, simply, get an idea from your mind and then into the mind of another, and vice versa Also (Brown, 1994: 159).As Brown told us, "In an age of communicative language teaching, interaction is actually the heart of communication; that is the full meaning of communication (Brown 2001: 159)

Communicative Approach seeks to solve the role of teachers and students in the classroom. Dating back to the 1970s, major changes have taken place in the methods of language teaching in Western pedagogy. This specific language teaching approach is generally defined as "communicative language teaching." Teachers no longer dominate classes; on the contrary, learners have a great deal of autonomy because their initiative and creativity can be of great help to the learning process. CLT distinguishes itself from other approaches because it places more emphasis on students' communicative competence than language skills. Because of the the interactive approach I'm focusing on in this study which is primarily based on CLT. Different scholars can explain CLT in different ways. The CLT version associated with my research has the following four characteristics:

A. through interaction with the body, or through the work of pairs and groups, it is important for collaborative learning.

B. It thinks that language learning is learning to communicate in the target language.

C. It uses techniques such as "information gaps" to simulate the use of language.

D. It believes that intrinsic motivation will result from interest in tasks related to communication.

8.2 Types of Motivation

It would be safe to say that all theorists in the field of learning either explicitly or by implicitly argue that a motivated creature is more likely to learn than one which is not. Children need to satisfy their desire to explore and manipulate their surroundings; they need the approval of others; they pursue success. Incentive in the form of rewards, immediate knowledge of satisfying results, cooperate and self-competition. In practical teaching, most language teachers will agree that the motivation of the students is one of the most important factors influencing their success or failure of the teaching. Therefore it is important for teachers to find out how to effectively stimulate students in English learning and hoe to make up the language instruction.

Motivation can be classified into many types, and the main categories are intrinsic and extrinsic motivation. Intrinsic motivation is a response to the needs of the learner's internal needs, such as curiosity, the knowledge that needs to be known, the ability or the feeling of growth (Paul Eggen & Don Kauchak,1994, P428). It exists when someone is working, because they are eager to successfully complete a task, whether or not it has external value (Cheryl L. Spaulding,1992, p4). In other words, students are willing to learn new and interesting knowledge to satisfy their curiosity, need to understand and feel the ability and growth, thus stimulating intrinsic motivation. The purpose of their study is to enjoy the process, not praise or reward. Students with intrinsic motivation orientation learn English actively and tend to be interested in more challenging tasks. This has great value and importance to learning, because the intrinsic interest makes them self-start and self-perpetuating, and it can make the incentive mechanism go on for a long time.

In order to adapt English and the classroom setting to appeal to children, a teacher relies on two sources of motivation: extrinsic and intrinsic. But there is no clear distinction between these two motivations. For instance, reward in school such as praise, grades, and recognition are extrinsic motivation or incentives; Comparatively, extrinsic motivation is related to far-reaching success while intrinsic one is linked with short-term achievement.

Extrinsic motivation is when I am motivated by external factors, as opposed to the internal drivers of intrinsic motivation. Extrinsic motivation drives me to do things for tangible rewards or pressures, rather than for the fun of it. Most young learners have no stationary purpose in English learning and they are changeable in character, which makes incentives important in the way to stimulate them to proceed their learning. During the process of applying extrinsic motivation, there are two points that teachers must notice. Firstly, teachers have to apply immediate rewards. No longer the time between completing work and being told the verdict, particularly if it is favorable, there is of the results having a motivational impact on children. Secondly, the application of reward should be vary according to person and situation. Motivation can be classified into many types, and the main categories are intrinsic and extrinsic motivation. Intrinsic motivation is a response to the needs of the learner's internal needs, such as curiosity, the knowledge that needs to be known, the ability or the feeling of growth (Paul Eggen & Don Kauchak,1994, P428). It exists when someone is working, because they are eager to successfully complete a task, whether or not it has external value (Cheryl L. Spaulding,1992, p4). In other words, students are willing to learn new and interesting knowledge to satisfy their curiosity, need to understand and feel the ability and growth, thus stimulating intrinsic motivation. No longer the time between completing work and being told the verdict, particularly if it is favorable, there is of the results having a motivational impact on children. Secondly, the application of reward should be vary according to person and situation.

Intrinsic motivation is when I am motivated by internal factors, as opposed to the external drivers of extrinsic motivation. Intrinsic motivation drives me to do things just for the fun of it, or because I believe it is a good or right thing to do. Intrinsic motivation is more important than extrinsic motivation. Illustrate of children's motivation are desire for self-esteem, the need to satisfy curiosity, the need for approval and social need. Play is regarded as manifestation of the intrinsic motivation. The use of play in education has its origins in the belief that all children want to play and that learning will occur at the same time, as a bonus in a case. Carefully selected games are invaluable because they give students an opportunity to practice their language skills. Games are highly motivational because they are both fun and challenging. In addition, they use meaningful and useful language in real situations. They can also encourage and enhance cooperation.However, long periods of unstructured practice are wasteful and unnecessary. As most students and teachers know, learning has its enjoyment, but it also involves hard work.

In English learning, intrinsic motivation and extrinsic motivation are important, inseparable and complementary. Intrinsic motivation is the intrinsic motivation for students to move forward and they are also driven by their own curiosity and interest. However, in the real teaching process, not all students are automatically inspired to put this or that task into practice, or learn this or that topic. Sometimes, a good result, failure and the threat of praise can move students from an inactive state to an active state. Most young learners have no stationary purpose in English learning and they are changeable in character, which makes incentives important in the way to stimulate them to proceed their learning. During the process of applying extrinsic motivation, there are two points that teachers must notice. Firstly, teachers have to apply immediate rewards. Intrinsic motivation drives me to do things just for the fun of it, or because I believe it is a good or right thing to do. Intrinsic motivation is more important than extrinsic motivation. Illustrate of children' motivation are desire for self-esteem, the need to satisfy curiosity, the need for approval and social need. Play is regarded as manifestation of the intrinsic motivation. The use of play in education has its origins in the belief that all children want to play and that learning will occur at the same time, as a bonus in a case.

8.3 Primary Principles of Motivation

Conventionally, most learning settings have been structured as if all learners possessed similar characteristics (Morgan & Fonseca, 2004). A phenomenal discovery in the arena of education in the 21st century is that students in the same classroom possess substantially different learning profiles. As a result, the need for recognizing the individual needs of students has become a major issue of consideration in designing teaching and instructional methodologies. The need for differentiated instruction has even been more pronounced in foreign language teaching contexts. Non-intelligence factors, especially motivation and attitude, have been shown to play a crucial role in fulfilling the individual needs of language learners. These factors raise the awareness of students' individual learning styles by arousing their potentialities in learning a target language and by enabling students to be in charge of their own learning.

H. Douglas Brown(1994) pointed out seven principles of interaction, which are the basis of the theoretical foundation for building language classroom interaction. They are automaticity, intrinsic motivation, strategic investment, adventure, language and cultural communication, language communication and communicative competence. These principles are elaborated by brown as follows:

1) Automaticity

2) The Intrinsic Motivation Principle

3) Strategic Investment

4) The Language-Culture Connection

5) Interlanguage

6) Communicative Competence

A great deal of research has been done on communicative competence. According to Trenholm and Jensen, communication skills are an ability to communicate in an effective and socially appropriate manner. The need for differentiated instruction has even been more pronounced in foreign language teaching contexts. Non-intelligence factors, especially motivation and attitude, have been shown to play a crucial role in fulfilling the individual needs of language learners.Teachers should value vocabulary, but don’t ignore other important components of communicative competence. Teachers should also ensure that students have the opportunity to speak English fluently without having to think about small mistakes all the time.

8.4 Ways to Arouse Students’ Motivation

Motivating students encompasses not only leading them to English, but also arousing their thirst for knowledge and understanding (Lins, 2006). Unlike other subjects, English learning has individual attributes that require learners to remember, practice, and communicate more. In this regard, English teachers have a duty to boost their students’ willingness to participate actively in the language learning process. There are various ways through which students can be motivated: utilization of various fascinating activities, new techniques such as technology, setting expectations and use of rewards, creation of a positive learning environment, and cooperative activities (Kong, 2009).

The use of a variety of fascinating activities can be an effective way of arousing students’ potentialities in learning English. Unlike other subjects, English learning involves learning listening, speaking, reading, and writing capabilities by memorizing a great deal of vocabulary grammar and practicing more in and outside class (Nakata, 2006). Given this, blending English learning with recreational activities (such as games, songs, and role-playing) makes the learning process more interesting, which in turn helps in the maintenance of motivation. The use of new techniques also plays an integral role in stimulating extrinsic motivation (Paton, 2009). These techniques include computer assisted language learning (CALL) and the use of technology (the internet, audio, captioned videos, and so on).

In a similar vein, Mao (2011) argues that the utilization of multi-media technologies has turned out to be a widespread phenomenon against the backdrop of tremendous technological advancement. Students are willing to participate in English learning, combine English and entertainment, and realize the fun and fun of English learning, which is the key to keep motivation throughout the course. Games are popular in English teaching, especially in primary schools. Several scholars have extensively demonstrated the role of technology in the language classroom (e.g. Gu, 2009; Lins, 2006; Nakata, 2006). Computers, projectors, podcasts, mobile devices, and e-readers can all play an instrumental role in the teaching and learning of English as they provide an interactive and motivating environment for learners of all ages.

Using moderate challenge to attract students to arouse their curiosity about English learning, to stimulate their intrinsic motivation for learning, motivational and the characteristics of language learning, it is effective and practical. The use of a variety of fascinating activities can be an effective way of arousing students' potentialities in learning English. Unlike other subjects, English learning involves learning listening, speaking, reading, and writing capabilities by memorizing a great deal of vocabulary grammar and practicing more in and outside class Language learning with other students all-round development of subject is a little different, they need a lot of words, sentences and grammar through memory, practice, and speak more in class, to fully develop the students' four skills in listening, speaking, reading and writing. Students are willing to participate in English learning, combine English and entertainment, and realize the fun and fun of English learning, which is the key to keep motivation throughout the course. Games are popular in English teaching, especially in primary schools. As Aydan Ersoz explains:

Carefully selected games are invaluable because they give students an opportunity to practice their language skills. Games are highly motivational because they are both fun and challenging. In addition, they use meaningful and useful language in real situations. They can also encourage and enhance cooperation.

Guessing game, gap filling, and chain story games are all practical and fun to use in English learning. Role-playing, song and summer English camping trips are also effective. Some real situational discussions and innovative activities are encouraged at a higher level, such as creating ads. Various interesting activities encourage students to invest as much time and energy as possible, and to enhance learning motivation.

Using some technology in teaching, teachers have more choices and ways to stimulate students' intrinsic motivation, such as CALL (computer-assisted language learning), multimedia, using the network and education software. Through examinations, cooperative activities and homework, teachers can provide a more comprehensive and positive feedback or evaluation of students' performance. At the same time, as teachers, don't forget to give more effective and appropriate rewards, which must explain why students should get it; Avoid harsh criticism, which lowers motivation and rewards for students, so that students may rely on rewards as a reason for learning rather than knowledge itself.

These methods are innovative, interesting, practical and effective, has the rich and colorful pictures and vivid sound, abundant information and effective interaction, arouse the students' curiosity and interest, and promoting the students' intrinsic motivation. With an intrinsic motivation, many students can start self-learning at school or at home, effectively improving their listening, reading and writing skills.

On the basis of extrinsic motivation theory, high expectation and proper reward are the effective methods for motivating students to learn English. Sometimes, our expectations of people lead us to treat them in a way that we expect them to do well. Motivated students need to be complemented by external energy, such as teacher's high expectations, praise and some rewards. Studies have shown that teachers' expectations influence student performance -- higher expectations can improve student performance. "I know that if you can solve these problems, you can solve them." Now let's get started. I'll help you if you have some problems. These words show the teacher's emotional support and confidence in students' ability, so that students can show a special introversion and shy personality in class, and try to overcome the expected problems. In addition, in the classroom, teachers can ask students to answer the question more often, these problems are more complete, more accurate, and to give more time to reply, and give more encouragement to inspire their motivation. Through examinations, cooperative activities and homework, teachers can provide a more comprehensive and positive feedback or evaluation of students' performance. At the same time, as teachers, don't forget to give more effective and appropriate rewards, which must explain why students should get it; Avoid harsh criticism, which lowers motivation and rewards for students, so that students may rely on rewards as a reason for learning rather than knowledge itself. Climate is important because it creates an environment that encourages achievement and motivation.

From Maslow's hierarchy theory, motivation and demand, and the characteristics of English learning, a relaxed and positive learning atmosphere should provide the conditions for students to learn English. In a friendly atmosphere, students can feel safe, their understanding and challenge and learning motivation can be improved. In learning English, students need a lot of practice to speak in class, so as to realize some of the rules, to ensure that they make full use of the practice time, make them feel safe and comfortable at the same time,and avoid they are criticized and ridiculed. At the same time, teachers should allow students to discuss widely without being afraid to express themselves differently from others. When students make mistakes, teachers use "it's a good experience" to describe their growth opportunities. When you finally get it, you'll make great progress. With more smiles and encouragement, teachers and students can become friends. Later, before starting classes and activities, teachers should learn to tell students what and why the interpretation of the study is, promotes the student's self-study consciousness, let the students in the process of learning English is more clear and positive. Secondly, it is not easy or difficult for teachers to put forward tasks that are neither too easy nor too difficult, because difficult tasks hinder their attempts. It is easy to generate boredom and reduced ability and self-efficacy tasks for students because of the easily obtained tasks. In cooperative and interactive activities, students can effectively and satisfactorily remove fear of failure in the process of communicating and exchanging information effectively, and solving problems through high emotion and hard work. In this case, students who are unwilling and afraid to express themselves are attracted to share their thoughts. This kind of approach is suitable for high level students to communicate in English.When students are dealing with these tasks, teachers should always be prepared to give supportive help.

The best level of cooperation is to make students feel safe and excited. Therefore, more and more teachers use cooperative activities in English teaching instead of competition, which is also relatively effective. In cooperative activities, students can effectively reduce fear of failure, communicate and exchange information effectively, and solve problems through high emotion and hard work. In this case, students who are unwilling and afraid to express themselves are attracted to share their thoughts. This method is suitable for high level students to communicate in English. For example, group discussions and projects, which are complex and challenging, are a great way to enable students to collaborate with peers. As teachers, it is more effective to provide help and commentary in time, or to ask students to self-evaluate their own projects. This enables students to focus on their learning process and let them see their progress. Self-evaluation gives students a sense of accomplishment and a sense of responsibility to learn.

The most important thing to learn English is to use target language to communicate with others, but not all learners actively use English, especially when they fail in English learning. We can use more methods to let the students to use English, have fun in learning English, to succeed in learning English, and we are more likely to make our students in need and faith based on the theory of motivation and success. Hamachek makes impact on the failure of the school to do a lot of research, almost without exception, believe that success will often encourage students to improve the level of their expectations, failure will often lead to lower their expectations (1972). Language educators have thus been compelled to rethink their teaching methodologies in order to cater for the personal needs of their students. This explains why new techniques such as the use of technology or group discussions are increasingly finding their way into the language classroom. According to Gardner (2010), pursuing predesigned curriculum does not always fulfill student needs—customizing teaching strategy is now the way to go.

This can be achieved by providing more opportunities to participate in student activities to gain more freedom and self-determination. For example, a teacher can take five minutes in each class for students to do the "today I am a teacher" activities, which gave the students a chance to convert their role to teacher, let them to teach other students in the classroom of English as a feeling of success. In these five minutes, students can decide what to teach, such as reviewing, teaching new words and telling stories.

Today, the language classroom features learners with diverse abilities and academic needs. According to Mao (2011), these differences are mainly brought about by factors such as age, ethnic background, and beliefs. This implies that what works for one student may not work for another student in the same classroom. Language educators have thus been compelled to rethink their teaching methodologies in order to cater for the personal needs of their students. This explains why new techniques such as the use of technology or group discussions are increasingly finding their way into the language classroom. According to Gardner (2010), pursuing predesigned curriculum does not always fulfill student needs—customizing teaching strategy is now the way to go.

The other way through which students can be motivated is the use of appropriate rewards and setting expectations (Kong, 2009). At times, our expectations about others make us treat others in a manner that makes them react just as we anticipated them to. Students need to be reenergized by an external force such as teacher praise, rewards, as well as teacher's high expectations. Literature demonstrates that teacher expectations have a significant influence on learner achievement—the higher the expectation, the better the performance (Gardner, 2010; Nakata, 2006; Lins, 2006). Together with positive feedback and positive reinforcement, rewards and expectations stir up students' desire to acquire knowledge.

Creating a positive learning environment entails building an atmosphere that supports both motivation and achievement. In such an environment, students feel secure, ultimately enhancing their sense of understanding as well as their learning motivation (Sheorey, 2006). When learning English, students require plenty of practice, especially in terms of speaking. In this regard, implementing some measures to ensure that they make adequate use of their practice time without experiencing criticism or mockery when they make mistakes creates a safe and comfortable climate for learning. Educators should also create an environment where students can freely express their differing opinions (Paton, 2009). This stretches to viewing mistakes as opportunities for warm remarks and more encouragement. It is also important for teachers to provide tasks that are neither too easy nor too complex for students, since too easy tasks yield boredom and decreased feelings of self-efficacy, while too complex tasks discourage students from trying (Dornyei, 1994).

Cooperative activities can also be an effective way of stimulating student motivation. These activities mainly take the form of group discussions or accomplishing tasks together with peers. Language educators are increasingly using cooperative activities to teach English as opposed to competition, which is fairly effective as well (Gu, 2009). Cooperative activities are effective in that they minimize the fear of failure since reluctant and fearful students are encouraged to participate and share their perspectives. This method is often appropriate for students at an advanced level (Paton, 2009). Cooperative activities enable students to take control of their learning and to be each other's coaches.

8.4.1 Interaction Patterns

In interactive classroom, there are two kinds of interactive modes: interaction between teachers and students and students' interaction.

1) teacher-student interaction

The relationship between teachers and students in interactive classroom is very different from that of traditional classroom. In traditional language classes, students only listen to teachers, take notes and passively accept knowledge. There is little or no information exchange. The only answer the student gives is to answer some questions or read the text. The teacher plays only one knowledge bearer, or the so-called "sage on the stage" .

2) Student-Student Interaction

Apart from the interaction between teachers and students mentioned above, the interaction between students is also indispensable to improve the language learning of learners. What's more, the interaction between students and students helps to cultivate students' critical thinking ability, cultivate students' positive personality, and form the habit of collaborative learning.

8.5 Factors of Learning Motivation

Motivation can be explained as the interaction between behavior, environment, cognition and individual factors. Personal factors play a very important role in the study of personal English. Here, let's focus on four personal factors: arousal, needs, beliefs, and goals.

Paul Eggen and Don Kauchak (1994) explains:

Arousal is a physiological and psychological response to the environment, including anxiety and curiosity. Anxiety is a kind of awareness of common anxiety and tension, and curiosity motive is based on such a view, namely students from the surprise, difference of optimal (intermediate) or incongruous happy activities, each of which can induce excitation (p438, 439).

As the teacher handed out the papers, the students sat nervously, curious about the contents of the test, with raised blood pressure, shortness of breath and sweaty hands. This time, the students were alert and alert. They are aroused, their motives are at a high level. The optimal level of arousal is required to achieve optimum status. So proper arousal can help motivate motivation.

Need is a lack of what is necessary or needed. In maslow's hierarchy of needs, he divides demand into two categories. The bottom four are called scarcity requirements, and the first three are called growth needs. People are likely to shift to higher demand before meeting lower demand. His work has an important impact on education. In the classroom, the students are potentially embarrassing so not actively learning, until they are in a safe and relaxed environment study, they will need the relevant ability motivation is innate need of mankind, inspire the main tasks and skills. The need for achievement drives students to achieve their goals. Students who have high performance requirements tend to be subject to challenging assignments, high grading standards, clear feedback, and opportunities to try again. In contrast, students who need to avoid failure avoid challenging tasks and experience anxiety during testing. Realizing these differences can help teachers have different needs for different students, so that education students are more effective.

The third factor that influences people's motivations is their belief. An optimistic belief in one's ability to learn in English can help students improve their learning motivation. In the progressive understanding of the belief in ability, one can insist that the ability can be improved by working hard. Although students tended to be influenced by teachers' ability to participate in activities, they had an optimistic view of their abilities, which increased their self-confidence initially. They also have a strong reaction to failure and self-doubt. The association theory is the attribution theory, which attempts to systematically describe the success and failure of students in classroom situations. Therefore, the teacher can help students attributed their success to ability and effort, while failure is a bad luck and task difficulty, and provide them with more opportunities to experience success, this is in order to establish an optimal belief of learning ability, and improve the learning motivation.

Students' goals affect their motivation and effort in English learning. With the goal of learning, students have a purposeful study and work hard to learn English. They are concerned with mastering language and completing tasks, rather than worrying about failure or comparing themselves to others. It is effective to help students set realistic and appropriate goals in their studies.

8.6 Conclusion

Foreign language students want teachers who can encourage them to speak more of English in and outside class as well as teachers who can rectify their mistakes without attacking their ego. This explains why throughout history the role of the teacher has shifted from a being a stringent disciplinarian to a facilitator (Bain et al., 2010). Being a facilitator entails accepting mistakes as integral elements of the language learning process. When a teacher is more of a facilitator than a strict instructor, students develop a positive attitude, which consequently arouses their potentialities in English learning.

To sum up, motivation is the most important factor influencing English learning and an important way to motivate students to learn English. The methods mentioned above are relatively effective for students' motivation and support in English learning. Sometimes a teacher is more like a salesman, and he has to convince and convince his customers (ie, students) that he has what they need and what works for them (in Kripa, 1988). As a teacher, to gain more knowledge of education psychology, especially the incentive theory and effective method, and puts forward to become an excellent “salesman” to encourage and support the students to learn English is very necessary and useful new technology. This empirical study is based on brown’s six interactive principles to motivate college students to study foreign languages.Being a facilitator entails accepting mistakes as integral elements of the language learning process. When a teacher is more of a facilitator than a strict instructor, students develop a positive attitude, which consequently arouses their potentialities in English learning.The results of the study support the hypotheses that incorporating the interactive approach into Chinese college English classrooms can help Chinese college students: 1. cultivate their interest and motivation to learn English well; 2. learn to think critically and work collaboratively; 3. improve their performance of English.

In short, motivation is fatal, and the way to motivate students to learn English is more important to English learning. The methods mentioned above are effective in motivating and supporting students in English learning. Sometimes, a teacher is more of a salesman, and he has to convince and convince his customers (ie, students) that he has what they need and what is useful for them (in Kripa, 1988). Attitude, which is an outcome of chronologically cultivated values and beliefs, is also a critical ingredient of success or failure in the language learning classroom. Therefore, the Interactive Approach, which has a strong theoretical foundation and mature theoretical system, owns its robust feasibility and plasticity.As a teacher, to obtain more knowledge of education psychology, especially the motivation theory and effective method, and use new technology to motivate and maintain students’ English learning, it is very necessary and useful. This empirical study is based on the six interactive principles of brown, to motivate college students to study foreign languages. The results of the study support the assumption that interactive integration into Chinese college English classrooms can help Chinese college students: 1. To cultivate students' interest and motivation to learn English well; 2. Learn to think critically and collaborate; 3. Improve their English.

There is a great deal of literature demonstrating that motivation, particularly the use of assorted fascinating activities, emerging techniques, setting expectations and use of rewards, creation of a positive learning environment, and cooperative activities, plays an instrumental role in foreign language learning. Attitude, which is an outcome of chronologically cultivated values and beliefs, is also a critical ingredient of success or failure in the language learning classroom. Therefore, the Interactive Approach, which has a strong theoretical foundation and mature theoretical system, owns its robust feasibility and plasticity. It focuses on the learner, attaches importance to the learning environment, and pays attention to cultivating the interests and motivations. So it can make up many disadvantages of the traditional teaching approaches and become an important theory in college English teaching.Anyway, the researcher does hope that this study may make contributions to the future research in this field.

Reference

[1] 贾冠杰 . “1+1>2”外语学习模式 [D]. 北京大学出版社 ,1996.

[2] 孔哲琼 . 大学英语学习负动机影响因素研究 [D]. 北京：华北电力大学 , 2009.

[3] 孙建军 . 非英语专业大学生英语学习负动机个案研究 [J]. 东北师范大学硕士论文 ,2011.

[4]Bain, S. et al. Learning Aptitudes, Attitudes, Attributions, and

Achievement of Postsecondary Students Identified as Gifted. Journal of Advanced Academia, 2010, 22, 130-156.

[5]Brown, H.D. Teaching Principles: An Interactive Approach to Language Pedagogy. [M] New Jersey: Prentice Hall Regents,1994.

[6]Brown, H.D. Teaching by Principles: An Interactive Approach to Language Pedagogy [M] Foreign Language Teaching and Research Press,2001.

[7]Brown, J.S.,&Collins, A., and Duguid, P. Situated cognition and the culture of learning. Educational Researcher, 1989:18.32-42. [EJ 386 603]

[8] Cheryl L. Spaulding. Motivation in the classroom. The United States: McGraw-Hill, 1992.

[9] Don Hamachek. Psychology in teaching, learning, and growth. The United States: Allyn and bacon,1989.

[10] Dornyei, Z. Motivation and Motivating in the Foreign Language Classroom. The Modern Language Journal, 1994, 78:273-284.

[11] Dornyei, Z., & Schmidt, R. Motivation and Second Language Acquisition. University of Hawaii, Manoa: Second Language Teaching & Curriculum Center,2001.

[12]Gardner, R.C. & Lambert, W.E. Attitudes and Motivation in Second Language Learning [M]. Rowley, Mass.: Newbury House, 1972.

[13]Gardner, R. C. &Trembley, P.F. On motivation, research agendas, and theoretical frameworks [J]. Modern Languge Journal, 1994, 78(3): 359-368

[14]Gu, M. The Discursive Construction of Second Language Learners' Motivation: A Multi-Level Perspective. New York: Peter Lang Publishing, 2009.

[15]Joriabanks,K.M. The Foundations of Students' Learning[C]. UK:Pergamon Press,1991.

[16] Kong, Y. A Brief Discussion on Motivation and Ways to Motivate Students in English Language Learning. International Education Studies, 2009, 2,

145-149.

[17] Kuhlemeier, H., Van Den Bergh, H., & Melse, L. Attitudes and Achievements in the First Year of German Language Instruction in Dutch Secondary Education. Modern Language Journal, 1997, 80, 494-508.

[18] Kripa K. Gautam. English language teaching: a critical study of methods and approaches. New Delhi: Harman, 1988.

[19] Lins, T. (2006). Motivation and Second Language Learning. Norderstedt: GRIN Verlag.Mantle-Bromley, C. (1995). Positive Attitudes and Realistic Beliefs: Links to Proficiency. The Modern Language Journal, 79, 372-386.

[20] Mao, Z. A Study on L2 Motivation and Applications in Reading Class in Senior High School. Theory and Practice in Language Studies, 2011, 1, 1731-1739.

[21] Morgan, J., & Fonseca, M. Multiple Intelligence Theory and Foreign Language Learning: A Brain-based Perspective. International Journal of English Studies, 2004, 4, 119-136.

[22] Nakata, Y. Motivation and Experience in Foreign Language Learning. New York: Peter Lang Publishing, 2006.

[23] Paton, A. Teaching English to Speakers of Other Languages: A Teacher Education Handbook. New York: McGraw-Hill, 2009.

[24] Paul D. Eggen, & Don Kauchak. Educational psychology: classroom connections. The United States: Macmillan, 1994.

[25] Saul Kassin. Psychology The United States: Prentice-Hall,1998.

[26] Sheorey, R. Learning and Teaching English in India. Delhi: Sage Publications, 2006.

[27] Yoshiyuki Nakata, Motivation and Experience in Foreign Language Learning [M]. Peter Lang Pub, Inc. 2006.

Chapter 9
Research of Listening Strategies in Non-English Majors' College English Learning

9.1 Introduction

One important objective of language teaching is to develop the communicative competence of learners. Whenever language proficiency is addressed in the English classroom, both language and content area teachers face problems regarding the use of English as the students' medium of communication particularly the students' inability to express themselves orally. It has been observed that when learners are asked to explain, discuss, converse or ask questions in English, they frequently stop speaking because they hardly know what to say.According to Nunan, listening is the Cinderella skill in second language learning. Listening comprehension, as one of the most frequently used language skills, has been playing an important part in language learning and daily communication. With the implementation of *College English Curriculum Requirements* in 2004 and the reform of CET-4 and CET-6 (College English Test-Band Six) issued by the Ministry of Education, the cultivation of college students' listening and speaking abilities under current circumstances has become an important task for Chinese English teachers.

9.2 Language Learning Strategies

9.2.1 Definition of Learning Strategies

What is a learning strategy? Since 1975, various theorists have contributed to the definition of language learning strategy. Different models have been proposed to categorize and create a hierarchy of strategies on the basis of how they relate to the learner and the task and how they are employed in the learning process.

Definition of Language Learning Strategies

In Oxford Advanced Learner's English-Chinese Dictionary, the term strategy is defined as "a plan that is intended to achieve a particular purpose." It is also defined as "A particular plan for gaining success in a particular activity, e.g., in a war, a game, or a competition, or for personal advantage" in Longman Dictionary of Contemporary English (1998). Some people think that language learning strategy is defined as the competence that people try to communicate with others. It is well known that since the 1970's, studies on learning strategies have begun. In the past decades, the researches on language learning strategy have been on the rise. The following are the definitions given by some famous researchers.

Definitions of learning strategies (Ellis, 1994)

Source	Definition
Stern 1983	'In our view strategy is best reserved for general tendencies or overall characteristics of the approach employed by the language learner, leaving techniques as the term to refer to particular forms of observable learning behavior.'
Weinstein and	'Learning strategies are the behaviors and thoughts that a learner

Source	Definition
Mayer 1986	engages in during learning that are intended to influence the learner's encoding process.'
Chamot 1987	'Learning strategies are techniques, approaches or deliberate actions that students take in order to facilitate the learning, recall of both linguistic and content area information.'
Rubin 1987	'learning strategies are strategies which contribute to the development of the language system which the learner constructs and affect learning directly.'
Oxford 1989	'Language learning strategies are behaviors or actions which learners use to make language learning more successful, self-directed and enjoyable.'

The definitions of learning strategies are very clear and different from each other. However, these definitions also reveal several problems (Ellis, 1994). Oxford (1989) considers the strategies as learners' behaviors. However, Weinstein and Mayer (1986) refer to them as learners' physical and mental behaviors and then the exact characteristics of the behaviors are given more concerns. Stern (1983) makes a distinction between 'strategies' and 'techniques'. The former are defined as universal methods to learn language. The latter consist of forms of language acquisition performances which are clear in language learning. The third problem is whether these learning strategies are thought of as conscious and subconscious.

9.2.2 Classification of Language Learning Strategies

A variety of researches focused on the language learning strategies. In these researches, the language learners were given instruction on how to use strategies. However, few researches were conducted to make the detailed classification of strategies.

When it comes to the classification of language learning strategies, Skehan (1989) concentrates on three fields. The first field is the students' ability to incorporate themselves into the learning environment. Naimen et al. (1978) refer to 'an active task approach', which is evident in such behaviors as seeking out and responding positively to learning opportunities and engaging in practice activities. 'Classification/verification', which Rubin (1981) puts at the top of her list of strategies, also belongs to this area. This strategy includes checking the examples of word usage, arranging words in a sentence to check understanding, looking up words in a dictionary, and paraphrasing a sentence to check understanding. Wong-Fillmore lists two strategies that fall into this area: 'get some expressions' and 'make the most of what you have got.' The second field is about the learner's 'technical predispositions'. The third general area involves the learner's capacity to evaluate. For example, Naiman et al. and Rubin both refer to the importance of monitoring.

However, the early taxonomies differ in a number of ways, reflecting the particular subjects that researchers worked with (Ellis, 1994). Thus Rubin and Naimen et al., who elicited information from adults, emphasized the importance of learners reflecting on their own learning and of conscious analysis, while Wong-Fillmore, who studied 5 ～ 7-year-old Spanish-speaking children in play situations, emphasized the social aspects of learning. For example, Rubin lists "memorization" and "deductive reasoning" among her strategies, while Wong-Fillmore indentified "join a group" and "count on your friends" as important. These differences also seem to reflect whether the setting is a formal or informal one, raising the possibility that the learning strategies involved in classroom and naturalistic acquisition may not be the same.

The following studies have been endeavoured to identify broad classes of learning strategies.

Rubin's (1987) classification of language learning strategies is listed as follows.

Rubin's classification (1987)

Rubin (1987) classifies language learning strategies into three groups. The first group is the learning strategies, which "contribute to the development of the language… and affect learning directly". The learning strategies are categorized as cognitive and meta-cognitive strategies. Cognitive strategies refer to clarification/verification, guessing, deductive reasoning, practice, memorization, and monitoring. Communication strategies are the second group, which are used by a learner when he has difficulty communicating with others. The last group is social strategies, which include question to fellow students/teachers/native speakers, initiating conversations, listening to L2 media, etc.

O'Malley and Chamot's typology of learning strategies (Chamot, 1987)

Learning strategies	Definition
Meta-cognitive	
Advance organizers	Making a general but comprehensive preview of the concept or principle in an anticipated learning activity.
Directed attention	Deciding in advance to attend in general to a learning task and to ignore irrelevant distractors.
Selective attention	Deciding in advance to attend to specific aspects of language input or situational details that will cue the retention of language input.

Learning strategies	Definition
Self-management	Understanding the conditions that help one learn and arranging for the presence of those conditions.
Advance preparation	Planning for and rehearsing linguistic components necessary to carry out an upcoming language task.
Self-monitoring	Correcting one's speech for accuracy in pronunciation, grammar, vocabulary, or for appropriateness related to the setting or to the people who are present.
Delayed production	Consciously deciding to postpone speaking to learn initially through listening comprehension.
Self-evaluation	Checking the outcomes of one's own language learning against an internal measure of completeness and accuracy.
Cognitive	
Repetition	Imitating a language model, including overt practice and silent rehearsal.
Resourcing	Defining or expanding a definition of a word or concept through use of target language reference materials.
Directed physical	Relating new information to physical actions, as with response directives.
Translation	Using the first language as a base for understanding and/or producing the second language.
Grouping	Recording or reclassifying and perhaps labeling the material to be learned based on common attributes.
Note-taking	Writing down the main idea, important points, outline, or summary of information presented orally or in writing.
Deduction	Consciously applying rules to produce or understand the second language.
Recombination	Constructing a meaningful sentence or larger language sequence by combining known elements in a new way.
Imagery	Relating new information to visual concepts in memory via familiar easily retrievable visualizations, phrases, or locations.
Auditory representation	Retention of the sound or similar sound for a word, phrase, or longer language sequence.
Key word	Remembering a new word in the second language by (1) identifying a familiar word in the first language that sounds like or otherwise resembles the new word, and (2) generating easily recalled images of some relationship with the new word.

Learning strategies	Definition
Contextualization	Placing a word or phrase in a meaningful language sequence.
Elaboration	Relating new information to other concepts in memory.
Transfer	Using previously acquired linguistic and/or conceptual knowledge to facilitate a new language learning task.
Inferencing	Using available information to guess meanings of new items, predict outcomes, or fill in missing information.
Social/affective	
Cooperation	Working with one or more peers to obtain feedback, pool information, or model a language activity.
Questions for classification	Asking a teacher or other native speaker for repetition, paraphrasing, explanation and/or examples.

In the above table, we can see that O'Malley and Chamot classify the learning strategies into three main kinds. Cognitive strategies are about learners' behaviors that tend to solve the problems in language learning. By using cognitive strategies, learners can analyze and transform the language learning materials. Learners tend to learn language with meta-cognitive strategies in cognitive process and also try to make an regulation on language learning. Social/affective strategies are about the approaches with which language learners choose to communicate with other people.

In Oxford (1990) a new taxonomy is presented, the general framework of which is shown in this table.

Learning Strategies	Direct strategies	Memory strategies
		Cognitive strategies
		Compensation strategies
	Indirect strategies	Meta-cognitive strategies
		Affective strategies
		Social strategies

Oxford's classification of learning strategies (1990)

In the above table, we can see that the subcategories of direct and indirect categories shown in the table have familiar labels. Direct strategies include memory strategies, cognitive strategies and compensation strategies. Memory strategies help learners store and retrieve information. Cognitive strategies facilitate the understanding and production of a new language. Compensation strategies are used by learners to bridge large knowledge gap and use the language.

Cohen's classification of learning strategies (1998)

Theorist	Main Categories	Definitions or Subcategories	Examples
Cohen	learning strategies	identifying the material to be learned distinguishing the material from other material.	
		grouping	
		making repeated contact with learning material	
		committing the material to memory	
	use strategies	retrieval strategies	mental imaging
		rehearsal strategies	practicing
		cover strategies	producing simple language
		communication strategies	negative transfer

In Cohen's (1998) model, language learning strategies include those used for identifying the material that needs to be learned, distinguishing it from other material if needed, grouping it for easier learning, having repeated contact with the material, and formally committing the material to memory when it does not seem to be acquired naturally. For example, the strategies for learning the subjunctive in Spanish as a foreign language could include grouping together the list of verbs that take a subjunctive and memorizing them. The specific strategies for memorizing this group might involve the use of a keyword mnemonic.

Language use strategies include four subsets: (a) retrieval strategies, (b) rehearsal strategies, (c) cover strategies, and (d) communication strategies. Retrieval strategies are used to activate language material from storage through memory searching strategies such as mental linkages or sound association. Rehearsal strategies are used for practicing the target language structures and include both language learning and language use strategies. Cover strategies involve creating the impression that learners have control over the material when they do not. Examples of them are simplification, i.e., producing simplified utterances, and complexification, i.e., saying something by means of an elaborate and complex circumlocution, both of which are used to bridge knowledge gaps in the target language. Communication strategies focus on approaches to conveying meaningful and informative messages to the listener or reader. Intralingual strategies are such examples. These include overgeneralizing a grammar rule or vocabulary meaning from one context to another where it does not apply, and negative transfer, i.e., applying the patterns of a native or another language in the target language where those patterns do not apply.

9.3 Listening Comprehension Strategies

9.3.1 The Importance of Listening

Language learning depends on listening. The listening skill is not only a rule of language but also acquisition second language skill (Vandergrift, 1997). Listening provides the aural input that serves as the basis for language acquisition and enables learners to interact in spoken communication. Listening is the ability to identify and understand what others are saying. It is used most frequently. According to Feyten (1991), in daily communication, people allot 45% of time in listening, 30% on speaking, 16% on reading, and only 9% on writing. "Listening comprehension is viewed theoretically as an active process in which individuals focus on selected aspects of aural input, construct meaning from passages, and relate what they hear to existing knowledge (O'Malley et al. 1989: 418)." It has been estimated that students may receive as much as 90% of their in-school information through listening to instructors and to one another. In addition, the *College English Curriculum Requirements* in 2004 indicates that the goal of college English teaching is to develop students' ability to use English in an all-round way, especially in listening and speaking. And the listening comprehension parts have accounted for 35% of the total scores of CET-4. Therefore, it is essential for English teachers to help their students become effective listeners and more attention should be paid to listening comprehension in second language teaching and learning.

9.3.2 Listening Strategies

The Nature of Listening

Listening is an active not a passive operation. With this in mind I would like to emphasize three things:

The importance of understanding this concept of listening being an active engagement. That is, as a listener, the mind is actively searching for meaning.

The importance of what Krashen calls 'comprehensible input' (CI) or that 'we acquire when we understand what people tell us or what we read, when we are absorbed in the message.' Individual progress is dependent on the input containing aspects of the target language that 'the acquirer has not yet acquired, but is developmentally ready to acquire.'

This seems to imply the importance of ensuring that the language level is matched to the learners, which means teachers must understand their learners' abilities.Krashen advises that acquisition proceeds best when the acquirer's level of anxiety is low and self-confidence is high.This seems to enforce the importance of making the learning environment in our classrooms non-threatening.

Listening strategies are techniques, approaches or actions that students take in the listening process in order to facilitate the listening comprehension. The research on listening strategies can date back to 1980s in the west. Since listening strategies are important parts of learning strategies, on the basis of language learning strategies developed by O'Malley and Chamot (1990), which has gained considerable acceptability, listening strategies can also be classified into three categories: meta-cognitive strategies, cognitive strategies, and social/affective strategies.

Material selection refers to selecting the appropriate materials for listening task. Elaboration is to use prior knowledge from outside the conversational context and relating it to knowledge gained from the text to predict outcomes to fill in missing information.

In hearing cognitive strategies including prediction, repetitive, resource allocation, translation, notes, auditory representation, keyword listening comprehension cognitive strategies including: forecast, repeat, again package, translation, take notes, auditory expression, keywords, transfer, reasoning, selective listening, material selection and the elaboration. Prediction is to guess and predict the listening content based on the information provided by the listening material. Resourcing refers to the definition or extension of a word or concept by using the target language reference material. Translation refers to

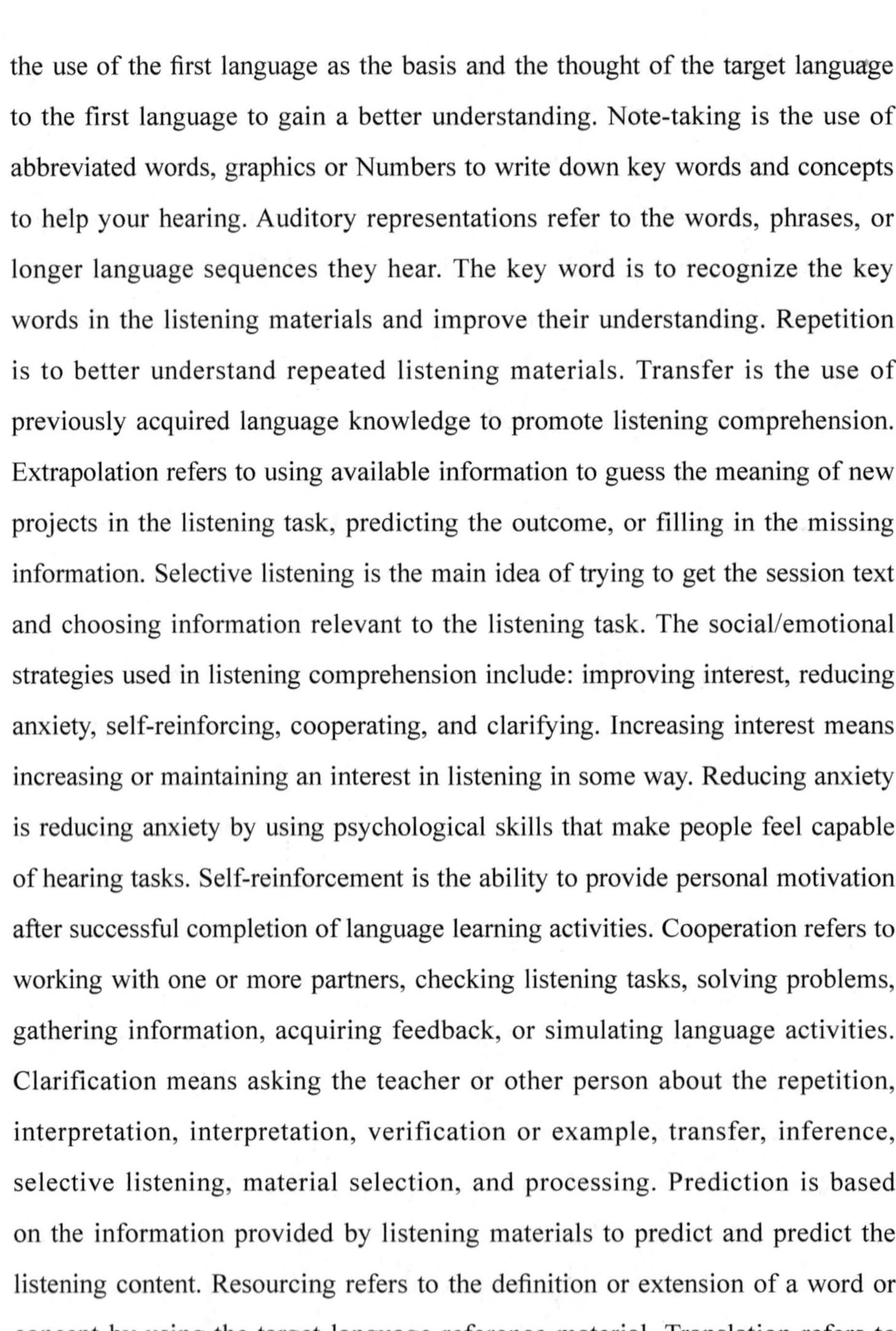

the use of the first language as the basis and the thought of the target language to the first language to gain a better understanding. Note-taking is the use of abbreviated words, graphics or Numbers to write down key words and concepts to help your hearing. Auditory representations refer to the words, phrases, or longer language sequences they hear. The key word is to recognize the key words in the listening materials and improve their understanding. Repetition is to better understand repeated listening materials. Transfer is the use of previously acquired language knowledge to promote listening comprehension. Extrapolation refers to using available information to guess the meaning of new projects in the listening task, predicting the outcome, or filling in the missing information. Selective listening is the main idea of trying to get the session text and choosing information relevant to the listening task. The social/emotional strategies used in listening comprehension include: improving interest, reducing anxiety, self-reinforcing, cooperating, and clarifying. Increasing interest means increasing or maintaining an interest in listening in some way. Reducing anxiety is reducing anxiety by using psychological skills that make people feel capable of hearing tasks. Self-reinforcement is the ability to provide personal motivation after successful completion of language learning activities. Cooperation refers to working with one or more partners, checking listening tasks, solving problems, gathering information, acquiring feedback, or simulating language activities. Clarification means asking the teacher or other person about the repetition, interpretation, interpretation, verification or example, transfer, inference, selective listening, material selection, and processing. Prediction is based on the information provided by listening materials to predict and predict the listening content. Resourcing refers to the definition or extension of a word or concept by using the target language reference material. Translation refers to the use of the first language as the basis and the thought of the target language to the first language to gain a better understanding. Note-taking is to write down keywords and concepts in the form of abbreviations, shapes or Numbers to help with hearing. Auditory representations refer to the words, phrases, or longer language sequences they hear. The key word is to recognize the key words in the listening materials and improve their understanding. Repetition is to better understand repeated listening materials. Transfer is the use of previously acquired language knowledge to promote listening comprehension. Extrapolation refers to using available information to guess the meaning of new projects in the listening task, predicting the outcome, or filling in the missing information. Selective listening is the main idea of trying to get the session text and choosing information relevant to the listening task. The social/emotional strategies used in listening comprehension include: improving interest, reducing anxiety, self-reinforcing, cooperating, and clarifying. Increasing interest means increasing or maintaining an interest in listening in some way. Reducing anxiety is reducing anxiety by using psychological skills that make people feel capable of hearing tasks. Self-reinforcement is the ability to provide personal motivation after successful completion of language learning activities. Cooperation refers to working with one or more partners, checking listening tasks, solving problems, gathering information, acquiring feedback, or simulating language activities. Clarifying means asking the teacher or others about the repetition, interpretation, interpretation, validation, or example of a listening material or task.

9.4 Computer Assisted Language Learning

CALL places a heavy emphasis on creating and using student centred materials that are interactive and individualized to create autonomous language learners. It can also be used as a way for students to review material outside of the classroom, especially for students who require additional learning supports.

In addition, the combination of face-to-face instruction and CALL, known as blended learning, is often the preferred method of second language acquisition rather than programs that only rely on CALL.

Creating suitable CALL software is extremely challenging, especially because the approaches to teaching languages are constantly evolving and, thus, development of these programs require a variety of people to achieve the learning objectives, including a subject matter specialist (SMS), programmer, graphic designer, sound engineer, and instructional designer.

In addition, effectively implementing CALL into language programs require a staff and centre that have technical know-how, and the ability to combine both traditional face-to-face instruction with the learning software. However, the development in web applications, with their notable shift from Web 1.0 programs that emphasized a one-way process to the current Web 20.0 programs that require more interaction and sharing between the computer, user, and other users and computers, has resulted in an explosion of applications that are serving as excellent CALL resources for language learners and instructors. These resources include, but are not limited to:video sharing and screen application tools animation tools discussion lists, blogs, wikis, and social networking

CALL refers to computer assisted language learning. There are various terms used by researchers to define CALL from different aspects which look different but actually refer to the same concept (Breatty, 2005:9):

CAI: computer-assisted instruction refers to learning on a computer, but not necessarily the language.

Computer-assisted learning is similar to CAI, which refers to learning any subject (including language learning) on a computer.

Computer aided language teaching, a term commonly used in North America.

CALT: computer assisted language teaching, focusing on teachers.

Network enhancement language learning refers to the network as the teaching medium.

Furthermore, CALL is incorporating Human Language Technologies (HLT) to aid language development and communication in multilingual societies, with a specific focus on the components of Natural Language Processing (NLP) such as parsing, speech synthesis and speech recognition. Speech Synthesisprograms are, for example, electronic dictionaries that utilize realistic voices that help learners hear how words are pronounced. Speech recognition programs, referred to as Automatic Speech Recognition (ASR),often provides a native speaker model that the learner is requested to imitate. Last, parsing is used to analyse the learner's input and diagnose errors.

One important question that surfaces in response to the impact and effectiveness of CALL is the perception that these applications are taking over the role of the instructor. In addition, although research on the effectiveness of CALL has demonstrated improvement in learners' spelling, reading, and writing, assessing speaking improvements is not as easy because of the complexity of, and the higher potential for error in using Artificial Intelligence (AI) programs to accurately evaluate speaking (Felix, 2008).

Lastly, as many instructors are not the technological savants that their younger students are today, another concern emerges over how to prepare language teachers to properly integrate these technologies into their classrooms, as well as how to improve the IT literacy of older learners so that they can also take advantage of these programs.

Although many different names have been adopted, computer assisted language learning (CALL) is the most commonly used term compared to other related acronyms. As for phone calls, the researchers also gave different definitions. Levy(1997:1) is defined as «applied research and research in language teaching and learning». In addition, although research on the effectiveness of CALL has demonstrated improvement in learners' spelling, reading, and writing, assessing speaking improvements is not as easy because of the complexity of, and the higher potential for error in using Artificial Intelligence (AI) programs to accurately evaluate speaking (Felix, 2008).

Computer assisted language learning in some degree is considered to be a kind of language teaching and learning method, in this process, the computer is used as a display of material, strengthen, and evaluation of auxiliary means, usually includes a large number of interactive elements (Davies, 2002). Beatty(2005:7) defines computer-assisted language learning (CALL) as «any process that learners use to improve their language ability». Compared with Davis's definition, levy's definition is clearer and more extensive, which has been accepted by most researchers.

Although the researchers defined the call from different aspects and named it in different terms, basically, the call refers to the tool that USES the computer as a secondary language to learn or teach.

In the mid-1990s, with the popularity of the Internet, it had a huge impact on language teaching and learning. It broke the barriers of time and space, make the language learners can at any time and any place communicate with other learners and speakers direct communication, make the teacher or a student with a small group of people, the whole class, or with many international discussion, share the information.

The main feature of the call is to shorten the distance between people, which can provide a lot of information and a real language environment. Phone environment, therefore, there can be a teacher of computer classroom, a students' autonomous learning room, or the students in their learning center, study at home or elsewhere. In short, in a telephone environment, computers are used as a tool for supporting language learning.

According to Oxford's taxonomy, there are two main types of language learning strategies: the direct strategies and the indirect strategies. Among the direct strategies are compensatory strategies that "enable learners to use the new language for either comprehension or production despite limitations in knowledge" . Computer assisted language learning (CALL) was developed in the 1960s to investigate how computers were applied in the process of foreign language teaching in the context of higher education. For several decades, computers have been explored as an aid to language teaching rather than teachers. With the development of digital technologies, cheap microcomputers became available. In the 1980s, microcomputer improvements enabled it to process audio, video, and graphics.

This fueled the burning desire of the researcher to investigate the learning and compensatory strategies that students employ in enhancing their English language proficiency, particularly their listening abilities. The present study aimed to identify the compensatory strategies frequently used by College of Industrial Technology (CIT) students in the Bulacan State University (BSU) and correlate them with student-related factors and their grade in English. The results of this investigation may help English teachers in enhancing their students' English language proficiency and eventually make them participating individuals in the language classroom as they use efficient compensatory strategies. According to Warschauer M. (1996: 14), the computer can serve a variety of uses for language teaching. It can be a tutor which offers language drills or skill practice; a stimulus for discussion and interaction; or a tool for writing and research.

Constructivism learning theory is a kind of philosophy to help improving students' practical thinking. The basic concept in this specific learning theory is experience - or the interaction with the atmosphere that is added to student education.

Funderstanding(1999) defines constructivism as a philosophy of learning. The premise is that by recalling on our experience, we form our own categorization of the world we live in. Each of us has our own «rules» and «mental models» that we use to understand our reflections. Therefore, learning is simply the process of adapting our mental model to the new experience.

Constructivism learning theory holds that people generate knowledge and derive the meaning from the knowledge based on the experience. Two significant concepts in constructivism learning theory to create personal knowledge construction are adaptation and assimilation. Assimilation leads individuals to integrate new experiences into old experiences. This allows individuals to produce new concepts, rethink their previous misconceptions, evaluate what is significant, and ultimately change their perceptions into the true ideas. Accommodation, on the other hand, redefines the world and new experiences as existing mental faculties. The individual conceived of a unique way of running the world. When things don't work out in this situation, they have to adapt and realign the expectations of the results.

The constructivist perspective has two main trends: cognitive constructivism and social constructivism. Cognitive constructivism focuses on the conceptual reorganization of individuals (Piaget, 1977). It insists that knowledge is a restructuring and rehasals of experience, which cannot be taught, but is unique to everyone (Candy, 1988). In the cognitive perspective, students actively construct their own cognitive style to achieve effective results by restoring the consistency of their individual experience world (Fosnot, 1996:34).

Piaget was a philosopher from Switzerland. He was also a natural scientist that was famous for the work that he did studying cognitive development and learning theories encompassed in his view of «genetic epistemology». At the young age of eleven he attended high school at Switzerland Latin wherein one of his short pieces was the start of his scientific career.

Piaget was a philosopher from Switzerland. He is also a natural scientist, known for his research on cognitive development and learning theory, whose view is «genetic epistemology». When he was 11 years old, he went to high school in Switzerland, where a short story was the beginning of his scientific career.

Piaget's constructivist theory has influenced the learning curriculum, because teachers must develop a curriculum plan to improve students' logical thinking and concept growth. Teachers must emphasize the important role of experience or the relationship to the atmosphere that has been added to students education. For example, teachers must keep in mind the basic concepts, such as the persistence of objects, when building cognitive structures.

Constructivism learning theory holds that people generate knowledge and derive the meaning from the knowledge based on the experience. Piaget's theory covers learning theory, teaching approaches and the education reform. The two key elements of creating a new knowledge structure are accommodation and assimilation. Assimilation leads individuals to integrate new experiences into old experiences. This allows individuals to produce new concepts, rethink their previous misconceptions, evaluate what is significant, and ultimately change their perceptions into the true ideas. What tends to work best is material that engages as many of our students as possible, making them interested and satisfied because at the end of the day, language learning is hugely affected by feelings or the affective filter (Krashen, 2003). Accommodation, on the other hand, redefines the world and new experiences as existing mental faculties. The individual conceived of a unique way of running the world. When things don't work out in this situation, they have to adapt and realign the expectations of the results. In addition to learning theory, Piaget's constructivist theory also explains how learning happens, rather than focusing on factors that affect learning. The role of the teacher is very important. In this theory, the teacher did not act like the coach, but acted as a helper, and their role was to help students understand themselves. This will divert attention from teachers and classes to students and their studies. The resources and curriculum that this learning theory must initiate have taken a very different approach to traditional learning. Teachers have to start asking, not telling them. In this case, the moderator does not answer questions that match only their courses, but instead must allow students to draw their own conclusions, rather than being told. At the same time, teachers constantly engage in dialogue with students, according to the students' learning needs, according to the students' needs, to create a learning experience for the new direction. Under the Piaget's theory of constructivism, teachers have to challenge students, making them effective critical thinkers, and not just a «teacher», is also a teacher, consultants and trainers.

In Piaget's theory, learning is seen as building meaningful representation on the basis of previous experience, and understanding the process of new experiences by adjusting existing mental models. In his view, the learner is an active thinker, seeker, questioner, and intellectual constructor.

The three most critical components in English language teaching are learners, materials, and teachers. These three elements must interact to ensure the success of the whole teaching/learning process. When dealing with weak learners but strong materials and an experienced teacher, a positive result from the teaching process can be certainly expected. But, how can this be achieved?

Different researchers define autonomous learning from different perspectives. Therefore, it is difficult to give a satisfactory definition. Here is a list of different western scholars who have different understandings of themselves.

In constructivism learning theory, teacher's role is very important. In this theory, the teacher did not act like the coach, but acted as a helper, and their role was to help students understand themselves. This will divert attention from teachers and classes to students and their studies. What tends to work best is material that engages as many of our students as possible, making them interested and satisfied because at the end of the day, language learning is hugely affected by feelings or the affective filter (Krashen, 2003). The resources and curriculum that this learning theory must initiate have taken a very different approach to traditional learning. Teachers have to start asking, not telling them. In this case, the moderator does not answer questions that match only their courses, but instead must allow students to draw their own conclusions, rather than being told. At the same time, teachers constantly engage in dialogue with students, according to the students' learning needs, according to the students' needs, to create a learning experience for the new direction. Under the Piaget's theory of constructivism, teachers have to challenge students, making them effective critical thinkers, and not just a «teacher», is also a teacher, consultants and trainers.

As for teaching materials, no one expects teachers to generate reams of new material for each class; instead, we are encouraged to supplement course books with commercially produced material or suggested activities on teaching websites. What tends to work best is material that engages as many of our students as possible, making them interested and satisfied because at the end of the day, language learning is hugely affected by feelings or the affective filter (Krashen, 2003). Satisfied students are more motivated and are more likely to stay in their courses and actually benefit. My students are engaged and entertained but also challenged. This is when real learning takes place.

But what does it mean to succeed at language learning? Some teachers believe it means to exercise one's abilities when practicing a certain skill. Others believe it means to perform and compete in an academic learning context. Both are correct but in all situations the burden is on the learner, as self-appraisal is essential. Our students need to ask themselves: Do I understand a native speaker professor delivering a lecture? Am I able to take accurate and complete notes in class? Do I get the main points of an academic reading or article? The above independent study shows that autonomous learners should strive to set learning goals, and make clear their progress in language learning, make careful selection and use of learning strategies, monitoring and learning. The main purpose of this study is to explore the use of listening strategies in the context of the current Chinese context. If learners can access the computer after class, they can use vocabulary tests and dictionaries to check the pronunciation of the new words they encounter in their reading. This is especially useful for learners who are not familiar with all the sound on the chart. Encourage your learners to record their pronunciation of new words in and out of the classroom in their vocabulary notes. Network autonomous hearing is a new form of listening teaching. At the beginning of each semester, the Internet provides students with basic requirements, listening materials and exercises. During the semester, students will learn new knowledge and adjust themselves to meet these requirements. They can teach themselves online and improve their listening. If they have any difficulty, they can ask their English teacher for help, or discuss BBS with teachers and classmates via email or online discussion.

9.5 Studies on Listening Strategies

9.5.1 Studies on Listening Strategies Abroad

L2 voice perception, Wilson and Iacoboniused fMRI study the neural responses of adult monolingual English speakers to familiar (native) and unfamiliar (non-native) phonemes. Their research results show that the moving region in the distinction between native and non-native phoneme plays an important role, more interestingly, motor system constantly trying to hearing non-native phoneme perception, which leads to greater, therefore may be more expensive sports activities. It is also important that these studies provide evidence for the development of the cerebral cortex as a function of language ability. More specifically, in the Japanese native speakers, compared with native English speakers, in perception recognition/r/and/l /, more apparent in the related activity in the brain, and as the participants in the L2 (English) to complete a goal task, compared with the L1 (Chinese). One thing to note here is that the participants in both studies were late bilinguals. In addition, in the study of Gandour et al., the activation of differences in brain regions of participants with lower L2 levels was also demonstrated. These findings have important implications for understanding the impact of L2 speech characteristics on L2 listening ability, especially in less proficient listeners.

A second language (L2) listening comprehension is various, multi-level skills involved in operating a variety of components, including but not limited to phoneme - level of consciousness, word recognition, lexical access, morphological and syntactic processing, activation of prior knowledge, the use of context information, all interact to produce a final said. There are not many studies looking at how and how these factors explain L2's hearing performance.

Not much, a key work is Vandergrift (2003), the result is a group of teenagers (14 to 15 years old) English L1 speakers learn French in Canada in L2 listening L1 and L2 proficiency together account for about 39% of the L2 listening ability, the former explanation about 14%, which is about 25%. Put forward a series of practical teaching lower-level processing efficiency in L2 listening to technology development, including centralized analysis target script, the word positioning tasks, dictation dictogloss, exposure to the «A» level through the materials attached scripts, and various other remedial exercises. However, most of these technology is only applicable to the auditory text repeated exposure, sometimes will have different speed control, in the end their main purpose is to provide learners' accumulation and classification of acoustics, phoneme, syllable, morphology and lexical information. Another expedition L2 proficiency in the study of the contribution of L2 listening ability is Mecartty, the result from the university level of English learning Spanish native speakers of the multivariate regression analysis results show that vocabulary knowledge rather than grammar knowledge have significant effect on listening comprehension, explained 14% of the total variance.

In general, extensive study of the influence of L1 literacy and L2 proficiency L2 reading with similar results considering L2 listening: although the L1 reading ability and L2 read successful L2 performance plays an important role, which makes a bigger contribution in the beginning readers, and L1 literacy predictive value becomes larger and more advanced learners' second language reading level. The importance of specific components of the level of reading ability, reading ability as a whole, the study found that rooted in automaticity and suggests that the concept of working memory capacity, the reader once it reached a certain degree of bottom-up processing capabilities, including processing, such as spelling, pronunciation and vocabulary more attention resources can be assigned to a top-down processing. The exact level of bottom-up processing is a function of L2 reading ability, task type, task complexity, and L1 - L2 language relationships.

Listening and reading are processes of acceptance, sharing a large number of component processes, such as decoding, parsing, and meaning building. Indeed, the research achievements of L2 listening research shows that the contribution of the basic L2 processing skills, such as recognition of phoneme - level and the efficiency of word segmentation, at the start of a bigger audience than advanced counterparts, especially in connected speech. The use of a series of research results to straps - tegies said that although the skilled use of a wider range of audience cognitive and meta-cognitive strategy, the specific strategy to self adjusting their listening comprehension process, such as questioning and monitoring to understand, and have higher self own hearing problems, low skills peers may depend on the bottom-up processing such as ci of lexical access and online translation. From Graham, the study found that, there is a medium level of teenagers (16 to 18 years old) learn French, English native speakers to reflect their own hearing problems, it shows that the difficulties they hearing seems to be due to the lack of understanding of the characteristic of the pronunciation and intonation, it is essential to the accurate perception of French. The Goh report says that less skilled listeners have significant difficulty in identifying phonemes and word levels than more skilled listeners. These views and these views mentioned above, are strongly suggests that, along with reading, bottom-up processing become more easy, there will be more attention resources are assigned to the top-down processing.

Put forward a series of practical teaching lower-level processing efficiency in L2 listening to technology development, including centralized analysis target script, the word positioning tasks, dictation, dictogloss, exposure to the «A» level through the materials attached scripts, and various other remedial exercises. However, most of these technology is only applicable to the auditory text repeated exposure, sometimes will have different speed control, in the end their main purpose is to provide learners' accumulation and classification of acoustics, phoneme, syllable, morphology and lexical information. Neuroimaging studies cited above, however, provide reliable empirical basis for the effectiveness of educational technology to develop fluent pronunciation accuracy/to establish a reliable production, rather than accept, phonology of L2, especially to L2 pronunciation ability of L2 users aren't rich.

A series of related research is induced by imitating test (EIT) or verbal response (EOR) test, the purpose is to explore the validity and reliability of these measurements, as an effective assessment tools, especially the L2 proficiency in spoken English. These tests require participants to listen and repeat as accurately as possible, usually after a short silence, and some sentences either stay the same or increase the length; They have a significant impact on L2 speech ability. Cox and investigate the effect of several factors on the oral Davis: use automatic speech recognition (ASR) system of EOR scores, and other tests in the test score of listening, reading, writing and grammar, English L1 L2 users have different background. Although their results showed that all variables were significantly correlated, the highest correlations were found between EOR performance and hearing tests. However, their scores were based on the correct number of repeated words, rather than being identified by the ASR system, rather than the actual quality of the stimulus. However, their conclusion is that «listening ability is an important part of conversational oral English and can be processed and repeated in the second language»; As mentioned above, the reverse is also true: repetition can be a prerequisite for hearing or a common premise.

Murphy (1985) studied the listening strategies of college students who took English as a second language in 1985. He found that more skilled listeners used a wider variety of strategies than an unskilled audience. Cox and Davies examined effects on speaking proficiency of several factors: EOR scores calculated by an automatic speech recognition (ASR) system and scores on listening, reading, writing, and grammar as measured by other tests, among English L2 users with various L1 backgrounds. Although their results indicated significant correlations for all the variables, the highest correlation was found between EOR performance and the listening test. They use reasoning, draw conclusions, often self-describe, and interact more actively with the text rather than low-skilled listeners. Unskilled listeners tend to focus too much on text or their own world knowledge. A growing number of skilled listeners are distinguished by the frequency of their strategies

Vandergrift (2003) investigated the listening strategies of seventh-grade French students and studied the differences between skilled listeners and unskilled listeners. He found that the more metacognitive strategies are used by skilled listeners. They are better able to control their hearing through the use of understanding monitoring. In addition, more skilled listeners were asked to clarify questions, while less skilled listeners used more translations. A range of research findings on the use of listening strategies has indicated that while skilled listeners make use of a wider range of both cognitive and metacognitive strategies, in particular of strategies to self-regulate their listening process, such as elaborating questioning and monitoring comprehension, and have higher self-awareness of their own listening problems, less skilled counterparts are likely to rely on bottom-up aspects of processing such as word-by-word lexical access The study also showed that good language learners are good at implying good strategies to tasks they are doing in the learning process. In the end, the author discusses the new model of the skilled listener and the teaching process of developing listening skills.

In the above studies abroad, listening comprehension strategies are developed by learning strategies. Subjects at different levels of language used language as their second language. In addition, various listening materials were used in the study, and the research was mainly focused on metacognitive strategies and cognitive strategies.

9.5.2 Studies on Listening Strategies at Home

In China, many researchers have made great progress on the research of listening strategies, hoping to contribute to English teaching in China. The following is some important research on the strategy of listening comprehension in China.

Liu's study (1996) showed that the listening strategies used by students were significantly different from those used by students without background knowledge. In addition, the former is much better than the latter in listening tasks.

Wang's listening classroom strategy training (2000) pointed out that strengthening strategy training is a necessary and indispensable approach to help students improve their listening comprehension. The essence of strategy training is to help students find problems in the listening process, then take effective measures, and timely monitor and assess their own listening performance. In the process, the teacher is not the instructor, but the instructor. More importantly, tactical training may improve learners' autonomy. Wang (2002) conducted another study, through the quantitative method to investigate 178 Chinese non-English major students' listening strategy use, found that: 1) the order of listening strategy use frequency is: focus, focus and social/emotional, vowel dependence, form metacognitive strategy; 2) the listening strategy has a positive effect on the hearing results, but the degree is limited. 3) there is a difference between effective audience and ineffective audience. Effective listeners tend to use more social/emotional, monitoring, reasoning and strategy, grammar and ineffective listeners tend to use more dependent on «mother» and the new vocabulary strategies. Ma(2002) investigated the effect of non-intellectual factors on hearing in ESL listeners. The study revealed the cognitive process of listening comprehension in Chinese students and analyzed some major factors of listening comprehension. The results of this study indicate that second language listening level is affected by many factors, and there are significant correlation between the audience listening proficiency and pronunciation, vocabulary, cultural background knowledge and psychological factors of king. Wang (2006) conducted a survey of non-english major students use listening strategies to distinguish between top students and the underachiever. He found that there were significant differences in the use of metacognitive strategies and cognitive strategies. In addition, the first year of university is a key period to cultivate students' awareness of strategy. The metacognitive strategy should be noted.

9.6 Conclusion

This paper studies many empirical researches on autonomous listening learning based on the web-based autonomous learning environment. With the development of college English teaching reform, this topic has attracted more and more researchers' attention.

Brett(1996) studied the influence of multimedia on listening skills and learning effects through the use of multimedia. He found that learners believe they can make great progress in English Learning from multimedia, which is a good independent learning experience. Brett surveyed his hearing in a computer-based multimedia environment in 1997. The results showed that when using multimedia, the learner's performance was more effective than audio or video.

Through a survey about non-english major students, Lin (2006) made a research about the web-based autonomous learning environment of English listening teaching proposing that the experimental group performed better than that of control group in the final testing advantage; The experimental group USES the learning strategy more frequently than the control group, indicating that under the good influence of web-based self-access environment students are more willing to use the learning strategy to a certain extent. There was a positive correlation between high achievers' listening performance and learning strategies, but there was no significant correlation between them. Different audiences adopt different listening strategies, while the high achievers use a wider range of listening strategies compared with those in the middle and low achievers. Therefore, the research indicates that listening strategy training should be included into English teaching to improve the effect of the web-based autonomous learning mode.

Wei(2006) studied the application of listening strategies for second-year students in their extracurricular English activities. It found that most students were not exposed to a lot of efficient language input. The barriers to their listening comprehension include vocabulary, followed by memory, background and grammar. In addition, students tend to overlook the application of predictive strategies. Xiao and Zuo (2006) discussed how to improve the efficiency of autonomous learners through the strategy training under the Internet multimedia environment. They compared the «autonomous learning classroom» and «classroom teaching» between the differences in listening strategies, and the differences between good listener and lousy listeners, found that audience in the «autonomous learning class» more frequently use social/affective strategies than those in the «classroom teaching» , especially the cooperation strategy. There are significant differences between good listeners and poor listeners in «autonomous learning classrooms.» Good listeners are better at planning, monitoring, and self-evaluating the study process than the bad listeners. Listening strategy training should be integrated into English listening teaching.

In the network teaching and learning environment, all of the research about listening strategies pointed out the following findings: (1) the students in the traditional learning mode or in the web-based learning environment, is the most commonly used cognitive strategies (Lin, 2006; Li, 2006). Cox and Davies examined effects on speaking proficiency of several factors: EOR scores calculated by an automatic speech recognition (ASR) system and scores on listening, reading, writing, and grammar as measured by other tests, among English L2 users with various L1 backgrounds. Although their results indicated significant correlations for all the variables, the highest correlation was found between EOR performance and the listening test. Metacognitive strategies are the least commonly used in these three types, and are more obvious in web-based self-learning environments (Lin,2006; Li, 2006; Wei, 2006). (2) Students who are good at listening use listening strategies in the online learning environment to promote the frequency of listening comprehension more than the lower level listeners.

It can be seen from the literature review that both researchers and teachers at home and abroad recognize thesigniicance of hearing, and they study a lot of listening, many of which are related to listening strategies. However, the study of listening strategies rarely mentions whether there is a gender difference in the use of listening strategies in online learning environments. In recent years, a variety of web-based language learning systems have been provided by many foreign language publishers. In this study, the author studies the listening strategies of non-english majors in the online learning environment, with a view to the implications for listening teaching and listening learning.

Reference

[1]Beatty, K. Teaching and Researching Computer-assisted Language Learning, Longman, 2003.

[2]Brett, P. A. Comparative Study of the Effects of the Use of Multimedia on Listening Comprehension 1997. Retrieved July 11st, 2010 from http://faculty.ksu.edu.sa/yousif/Research%20Papers/The%20effects%20of%20using%20multimedia.pdf.

[3]Candy, P. C. On the Attainment of Subject-matter Autonomy. Developing Student Autonomy in Learning. London: Kogan Page, 1988.

[4]Chamot, A.U. Learning Strategies in Language Learning. New York: Present Hall, 1987.

[5]Chamot, A. U., S. Barnhardt, P. E. L-Dinary. & J. Robbins. Methods for Teaching Learning Strategies in the Foreign Language Classroom. In R. Oxford. Language Learning Strategies around the World: Cross-cultural Perspective: 175-187. Honolulu: University of Hawaii, 1996.

[6]Cohen, A. O. Strategies in Learning and Using a Second Language. London & New York: Longman, 1998.

[7]Ellis, R. The Study of Second Language Acquisition. Oxford: Oxford University Press,1994.

[8]Feyten, C. The Power of Listening Ability: An Overlooked Dimension in Language Acquisition. Modern Language Journal, 1991,75:173-180.

[9]Fosnot, C. T. Constructivism: Theory, Perspective and Practice. New York: Teachers College Press, 1996.

[10]Funderstanding. 1999. About Learning/Theories. Retrieved March 20,

2010, from http://www.funderstanding.com/theories.html

[11]Krashen, S. D. Principles and Practices in Second Language Acquisition. Oxford: Pergamon, 1982.

[12]Levy, M. Computer-Assisted Language Learning: Context and Conceptualization. Oxford: Clarendon Press, 1997.

[13]McGarry, D. Learner Autonomy 4: The Role of Authentic Texts. Dublin: Authentik, 1995.

[14]Murphy, J. M. An Investigation into the Listening Strategies of ESL College Students. Paper presented at the 19th Annual TESOL Convention, New York, 1985.

[15]Naiman, N., M. Frohlich, H. Stern, and A. Todesco. The Good Language Learner. Research in Education Series No7. Toronto: The Ontario Institute for Studies in Education, 1978.

[16]O'Malley, J. M., & Chamot, A. U. Learning Strategies in Second Language Acquisition. Cambridge: Cambridge University Press, 1990.

[17]O'Malley, J. M., Chamot, A. U., Stewner-Manzanares, G. Russo, R. P., & Kupper, L. Learning Strategy Applications with Students of English as a Second Language. TESOL Quarterly, 1985,19 (3): 557-584.

[18]O'Malley, J. M., Chamot, A. U. & Kupper, L. 1989. Listening Comprehension Strategies in Second Language Acquisition. Applied Linguistics, 1989, 10 (4): 418-437.

[19]Piaget, J. Equilibration of Cognitive Structures. New York: Viking Press, 1977.

[20]Oxford, R., Nyikos, M., & Ehrman, M. Reflections on Sex Differences in Use of

[21]Language Learning Strategies. Foreign Language Annals, 1988, 21(4): 321-329.

[22]Oxford, R. L. Use of language learning strategies: A synthesis of studies with implications for strategy training. System, 1989,17, 235-247.

[23]Oxford, R. Language Learning Strategies: What Every Teacher Should Know. New York: Newbury House,1990.

[24]Oxford, R. Gender Differerces in Language Learning Styles: What Do They Mean? In J. M. Reid (Ed.). Learning Styles in the ESL/EFL Classroom. Beijing; Foreign Language Teaching and Research Press, 1995.

[25]Rubin, J. Learner Strategies: Theoretical Assumptions, Research History and Typology. In Wenden, A. & Rubin, J.(eds.) Learner Strategies in Language Learning. Englewood Cliffs, N . J: Prentice Hall, 1987.

[26]Skehan, P. Individual Differences in Second-language Learning. London: Edward Arnold, 1989.

[27]Stern, H. H. Fundamental Concepts of Language Teaching. Oxford: Oxford University Press, 1983.

[28]Thompson, L. & J. Robin. Can Strategy Instruction Improve Listening Comprehension? Foreign Language Annals, 1996,29 (3): 331-342.

[29]Vanergrift, L. Orchestrating Strategy Use: Toward a Model of the Skilled Second Language Listener. Language Learning, 2003,53 (3): 463-496.

[30]Vanergrift, L. The Strategy of Second Language(French) Listeners: a Descriptive Study. Foreign Language Annals, 1997, 30 (3): 387~409.

[31]Warschauer, M. Computer Assisted Language Learning: an Introduction, 1996.

[32] 李冬梅 . 近十年来国内英语听力理解研究述评 . 外语界，2002（2）：30-34.

[33] 李建华 . 大学英语网络教学改革探索 . 外语教学与研究，2006（1）：61-65.

[34] 林莉兰 . 网络自主学习环境下学习策略与学习效果研究 - 英语听

力教学改革实验 . 外语研究，2006（2）：39-45.

[35] 刘绍龙 . 背景知识与听力策略—图式理论案例报告 . 现代外语，1996（2）：80-91.

[36] 教育部高等教育司 . 大学英语课程教学要求（试行）. 上海：上海外语教育出版社，2004.

[37] 王宇 . 策略训练与听力教学 . 外语与外语教学，2000（8）：61-64.

[38] 王宇 . 关于中国非英语专业学生听力策略的调查 . 外语界，2002（6）：5-12.

[39] 韦建辉 . 大学生自主听力策略调查分析 . 高教论坛，2006（4）：116-120.

[40] 文秋芳 . 英语学习成功者与不成功者在方法上的差异 . 外语教学与研究，1995（3）：61-66.

[41] 文秋芳 . 英语学习策略论 . 上海：上海外语教育出版社，1996.

[42] 肖婧，左年念 . 网络多媒体环境下如何从学习策略上提高听力自主学习效率 . 外语电化教学，2006（3）：74-77.

Chapter 10
The Lexical Approach in College English Learning and Teaching

10.1 Introduction

In learning L2 lexicon, adult learners after the puberty period have a strong tendency to search the L2 translation equivalent for a target L2 word. Tanaka & Abe called this strategy "the search translation equivalent (or STE) strategy" . Given a new word in context, the teacher typically explains its meaning in L1 (i.e., Japanese). Writing is one of the four basic skills of language application. Both teachers and students spend a lot of time to improve their writing. The results, however, did not seem satisfactory. The statistics of CET-4 and CET-6 show that the writing level of college students is stagnant, the overall performance is still at the same level, and their overall learning performance shows that they need a further improvement in language study.

The teacher may ask students the meaning of the word, and be satisfied if the answer is given in Japanese. With the word governance and compliance, for example, the teacher explains their meanings by referring to their Japanese equivalents. In a vocabulary test, students are asked to say the meaning of governance or compliance, and expected to give their Japanese equivalents (i.e., touchi for governance, and houreijunshu for compliance). This type of instruction is called "translation-based instruction (TBI)" , which motivates and reinforces the learner's use of the STE strategy. Moreover, it is a fact that in the process of writing they tend to have some thoughts at first in Chinese in their mind and then try to find corresponding English words for Chinese words one by one, and finally they arrange them together word for word on the basis of grammar to construct English sentences. The most prominent problem is that although the students master a lot of English words, phrases and grammar, and also easily catch the main idea of the passage, they still can't express myself clearly and accurately in English. In addition, it is widely recognized that faced with the task of writing the Chinese students often have some ideas in their mind at first, then find out the corresponding English words and then translate Chinese words one by one, and finally they arrange them together based on the English word for word, sentence grammar.

10.2 What Is the Lexical Approach

For several decades, the earliest sociolinguistic research of speech events or among speakers of American English has mainly drawn attention on the way people in their society address one another. Particularly, when articulating language, people do more than just try to get another person to understand the speakers' thoughts and feelings. At the same time, both people are using language in subtle ways to define their relationship to each other, to identify themselves as part of a social group and to establish the kind of speech event they are in (Fasold, Falph, 2002: 1). Assuming that the learner's use of the STE strategy is inevitable because learning always depends on the pre-existing knowledge, we propose that focusing on "lexical core" minimizes the problems of semantic discontinuity and circularity.

Let us suppose that the teacher wants to teach the meaning of take to Japanese students. The question here is: Does a basic verb have multiple meanings as shown in a dictionary? The teacher may assume that a verb like take is highly polysemous, having a number of multiple meanings associated with it. This view is widely accepted, and if such is the case, then there is no way of avoiding the problems of semantic discontinuity and circularity in learning L2 vocabulary. If the verb take has 20 meanings, the teacher is most likely to present only some of them (a sample) in context. For example, the student will encounter the use of take in a sentence like “Let me take your temperature” or “Let’s take a picture of this statue.” The student will add “take one’s temperature” and “take a picture” to his list of collocations using take. However, at the same time, the student understands the meanings of the collocations on the basis of their Japanese equivalents: for example, “take one’s temperature” and “take a picture” will be understood as meaning “taion o hakaru” and “shashin o toru” , respectively. Here, Japanese hakaru and toru are totally different verbs, and the student naturally suffers the problem of semantic discontinuity. Yet the question is: Is it true that the verb take has a number of distinct meanings?

The emergence of vocabulary teaching method has attracted more and more attention and has exerted a great influence on the language learning and teaching of the whole world. It provides some eclectic methods for structural and communicative methods.

The term “lexical approach” was firstly coined by Lewis and his associates in 1993. It concentrates on developing students’ proficiency with lexis, or words and word combinations. It is mainly based on his idea that “a major part in language instruction is cultivating learners’ competence to comprehend and produce lexical chunks as unanalyzed wholes, and that these chunks become the raw data by which learners perceive patterns of language traditionally thought of as grammar” (p. 95). We argue that the idea expressed here, or what we call “the lexical core hypothesis” , is valid when it applies to verbal and prepositional polysemy, in that the meaning of a verb or a preposition is a function of the values of the arguments it takes. A preposition typically functions to relate two objects spatially. Moreover, the lexical approach places communication of meaning at the heart of language and language learning. This leads to an emphasis on the main carrier of meaning-vocabulary. This implies that teachers should try to draw students' attention to those fixed or semi-fixed words combinations and sentences, such as, "I'm sorry, I did not mean to make you jump," or "That will never happen to me," rather than individual words in glossary and the grammar in the process of language teaching.

The phrase "an apple in the box" can be expressed as: IN (X, Y), where the value of X is "an apple" , and the value of Y, "the box" , and the two objects are spatially related with the preposition in [+within the bounds of space]. The phrase "an apple on the box" , or ON (an apple, the box), expresses a different spatial relation between an apple and the box. A verb like take functions to relate two things to describe an event: "John took a picture of Mr. Fuji" is analyzed as "TAKE [+past]" (John, a picture of Mr. Fuji). In other words, a verb (or a preposition) does not have a set of determinate meanings; rather, its core meaning is semantically indeterminate, and the semantic disambiguation of the verb in an expression depends on the context in which it appears. Lexis rather than vocabulary are the basic units of language learning and teaching (p.96). In the application of lexical methods, Lewis(1993) clearly distinguishes between vocabulary and phrase. The former refers not only to those words, but also to the combination of words stored in our memory, while the latter is the storage of a single word that is traditionally defined. Vocabulary is not the basic unit of language learning and teaching.

Thus, core schema is not simply a static picture, or a static representation of the lexical meaning of take; rather, within one's mind, it functions in a dynamic and flexible way, which, in turn, makes it possible for an individual to produce a variety of context-sensitive senses. To explain this dynamic nature, we refer to cognitive operations such as schema-highlighting and schema-projection. As explained above, schema-highlighting is an operation of focusing on one aspect of the core schema. For example, highlighting or focusing on the source [S] aspect of taking, we have a sentence like "John took a plate from the table" . The same S-focused schema can be projected onto a more abstract situation to produce a sentence like "He took 7 from 17" .

The second language (L2) lexical evaluation has two main purposes: one is to measure the learner's vocabulary; The other is to measure the learner's vocabulary over a period of time (Bruton, 2009; Read, 2000). For any purpose, learners can regard some vocabulary learning as an increment of vocabulary learning (Barcroft & Rott, 2010. Schmidt,2010). Especially in the acceptance vocabulary test, learners may provide similar but inaccurate word meanings. Similarly, in carrying out effective vocabulary tests, learners may produce inaccurate spelling (or phonetic) forms of words. Part of the study is particularly common in assessing the learner's initial vocabulary learning gain (Barcroft & Rott, 2010) in experimental studies. Research on existing vocabulary learning shows that some people take part of the learner's knowledge into consideration (e.g. Barcroft, 2002, 2007). Others do not (for example, Hulstijn & Laufer, 2001; Minutes, 2008). Bruton (2007) argues that in the experimental study, from the acceptance of incidental vocabulary learning L2 reading evaluation should be considered part of the learning, because reading context may not be able to provide learners with enough vocabulary learning ability. Similarly, due to its progressive nature, the method of producing vocabulary learning should also include some vocabulary knowledge. The key point is, at the same time to investigate the efficacy of vocabulary learning tasks, computation part of vocabulary knowledge gain may influence across job vocabulary learning and the influence of learners' vocabulary knowledge acquisition. However, few studies have been devoted to this issue. Through experimental research, this paper discusses the differences in the learning of the vocabulary learning and the vocabulary learning of individual learners.

It is mainly based on his idea that "a major part in language instruction is cultivating learners' competence to comprehend and produce lexical chunks as unanalyzed wholes, and that these chunks become the raw data by which learners perceive patterns of language traditionally thought of as grammar" . We argue that the idea expressed here, or what we call "the lexical core hypothesis" , is valid when it applies to verbal and prepositional polysemy, in that the meaning of a verb or a preposition is a function of the values of the arguments it takes. This rule requires the use of the same pronoun in the case of equal rights. This is, you use the same pronoun, equal to the power they use to you. Since not all differences are related to power, the second semantic, that is, unity semantics, develops. In social order, two people can be equally powerful, but from different families, from different countries, and in different, if equally respected professions. In other words, there is a need to develop a common ground between people who have equal power. This is where unity comes in. Solidarity means sharing, intimacy, and intimacy between people. Americans tend to regard titles as trivial unless they give a clear idea of what kind of work a person does, what his responsibilities are. Chinese people always seem expected to let you know what they are, for example, "senior engineer" - a title that says nothing about what a person's functions are. For Americans it's what you actually do that counts, not where you fit on organizational chart. Your professional role defines you. This relationship is essentially reciprocal; If you are close to others, in the most natural situation, that person is very close to you. People use the same pronoun, no matter where the unity semantics apply. At first, according to Brown and Gilman, the unity of semantics only played a role in places that did not affect the semantic of power. The data from brown and gilman suggest that by the mid-20th century, unity had almost completely triumphed over power and became the dominant language of governance. The use of T and V pronoun is related to the choice of a person's name.

In our mind, a word or word concept does not stand alone in isolation of other words or other concepts, but rather it is linked semantically with others to produce a semantic network. Within the context of L2 acquisition, Crossley, Salsbury & McNamara point out that "connections between words allow newly acquired words to be easily assimilated within these networks because new words are not learned in isolation, but through links to already learned words" .Meara states that vocabulary is a network. Using association data obtained through a word association task, he analyzed how L2 learners' lexical knowledge is connected, and how it differs from the lexical networks of native speakers, using computer-based assessment tools. We can draw one conclusion from a series of studies done by and introduced in Meara that learning isolated words is one thing, and acquiring network knowledge is another. As a pedagogical implication, the teacher should help students store newly learned lexical items in a lexical network of already existing words.

However, the method of vocabulary does not ignore the function of grammar, still attaching great importance to grammar, and recognizing the generative elements of grammar, without «novelty and innovation becoming impossible» (Lewis,1997). Lewis (2000) proposed that when the speaker need create some novel things, syntax to promote the use of language, but only when we cannot find what we want to grammar ready-made mental lexicon.

Lewis(1993) put forward some principles of applying vocabulary teaching method to language teaching. Most fundamentally, «language is made up of grammatical vocabulary, not lexical grammar» (p.vii), which defines words instead of grammar as the center of language teaching. Other principles can be summarized as follows:

1) the grammar/lexical dichotomy is invalid, and the language consists of multiple words.

2) the core elements of language teaching are to raise students' awareness of vocabulary blocks and successfully cultivate their «block» language ability.

3) although the structural model is considered to be useful, the vocabulary and metaphor model are given the appropriate status.

4) collocation is the principle of organizing the syllabus.

5) the central metaphor of language is an organism; It's not an atomistic-a machine.

6) contextual factors are an important part of language teaching, rather than contextual factors.

7) grammar as an acceptance, involving perception of similarities and differences, is a priority.

Acceptance of skills, especially listening, is enhanced.

9) current - practice - producing examples are rejected, replaced by a paradigm of observation - hypothesis - hypothesis - experimental cycles.

In addition to the main principles mentioned above, Lewis(1997) put forward some Suggestions for organizing vocabulary teaching classes: «implement vocabulary: put theory into practice». The details are as follows:

1) the theme. Teachers should be aware of different types of lexical chunks in a thematic framework.

2) context Teachers are best to create an appropriate physical environment for language learning.

3) collocation It is an important feature of lexical method, and it is noted that collocation is a concentrated classroom activity.

4) concept. It is used to describe a general description of an event, for example, when comparing, apologizing or comforting, using specific words or phrases.

5) the narrator. In teaching, we should make full use of the method of «name», «narration» and «explanation».

6) metaphor. It is one of the most effective ways to determine a lexical block in a lexicon. It is too common in language to be despised.

7) it is obvious that changing the grammar will not produce pragmatic equivalents. Then, when a person is changed, the teacher should consciously look for the true counterpart.

8) speech segmentation. It is best to use the intonation of a word block because, from a psychological point of view, it is much easier to remember a piece of music than a random series of notes.

9) keywords. It suggests that teachers should emphasize the importance of the most common words in the language.

10) grammar. Teachers pay little attention to grammar, not ignore it completely.

In this experiment, the teaching activities and steps of «observe - hypothesis - experiment cycle» are adopted according to Lewis principle and the suggestion of applying lexical method. However, it is important to note that the use of lexical methods does not necessarily mean the upheaval of traditional teaching. In other words, traditional teaching methods and vocabulary methods can be combined to form college English reading and writing courses.

Due to the focus of this study, it is the effect of lexical approach to improve student's writing ability, through reading and writing course at the university of vocabulary method, to explain vocabulary teaching method on the teaching of reading and writing. Reading and writing are the same processes for both producers and recipients. Nattinger and DeCarrico(1992) proposed that «the process of writing effectively and the acceptance of reading can be taught through similar techniques and procedures».

The question is what form a lexical network takes specifically. There are different organizing principles of lexical networking. Words can be related in many ways. Miller & Johnson-Laird, however, note that "some efficient principles of organization exist in the lexicon in order to facilitate learning it" . The associative principle assumes that a set of words are triggered and evoked upon hearing a given word. Those words are linked with the target word in some ways, thus forming an associative network. For example, the word drum triggers a number of words or concepts such as "instrument [superordinate concept]" , "band [context]" , "loud [attribute]" , "trumpet [related concept]" , "play the beat [action]" , "Tom-Toms [part of the drum set]" , and "Elvin Jones [famous drummer]" , which will be clustered into an associative network. The thematic principle assumes that words are grouped by meaning referring to specific topics or fields such as cooking, stock market, nuclear energy, national election, desertification, globalization, and baseball.

A person who rarely hears English speakers is said to be director Smith, Jackson manager and morris principles. In English, can use only a few classes: doctor for those who are qualified in the health care industry is very common, and for those who are authorized to hear cases in the court trial. Professor for those who have made academic achievement. However, there are very few others. There are also few official titles in America, except for president, minister and etc. Americans tend to regard titles as trivial unless they give a clear idea of what kind of work a person does, what his responsibilities are. Chinese people always seem expected to let you know what they are, for example, "senior engineer" -- a title that says nothing about what a person's functions are. For Americans it's what you actually do that counts, not where you fit on organizational chart. Your professional role defines you. The American treat titles like "vice president for marketing" and "sales manager" as meaningful. Nonetheless they will not use them to address a person, even reduced to "manager" or "vice president" .

The lexical network model applies not only inter-lexically, but intra-lexically as well . In dealing with lexical polysemy, Lakoff represented the multiple senses of over in the form of intra-lexical network with the prototypical sense being the center of the network and other senses deriving from the prototype by means of cognitive operations such as metaphorical extension and profiling. As shown above, take is used in different situations, exhibiting different context-sensitive meanings. Those meanings are semantically related to each other and the lexical core of take explains how the different senses are related into a lexical network of word senses.

In addition, the authors and readers are actively involved in writing and explaining the process of written text. The text should be seen as a whole unit, rather than in a sentence or clause level, a series of separate pieces. There is no doubt that the text of the cohesive element is an important symbol of meaning, but if they were thought to have more global organization with discourse markers which has nothing to do with it. They will lead to the text and interpretation of inefficiency. L2 readers are usually bottom-up readers, that is, they build understanding through analysis and composite surface structures. In this case, the partitioning policy that they automatically use in the local language may not be operational in the L2 context. When blocks are blocked, information in short-term memory can be stored at once. Less storage means that fewer language data can be analyzed at the same time, resulting in redundant and context-prompt use.

Intra-lexical networking requires a common thread, that is, lexical core, which links the different usages of a word. By contrast, inter-lexical networking requires semantic differentiation among the related words. To differentiate the meanings of semantically related words, however, we need the lexical core of each word. Lexical core has both the uniting power and the differentiating power.

Therefore, teachers need to provide strategies to assist reading and writing students in a larger discourse. These strategies must be based on the elements of textual cohesion and coherence, must transfer the attention of students, in both local and global level, from a single project to a larger vocabulary form/ functional composites. The preposition on has different dictionary meanings associated with different situations. With the core meaning of on (i.e., [+contact]) as the common thread, the teacher asks to explore the meaning world of on. To start with, the teacher may use prototypical exemplars to introduce the usage of on. The teacher asks students to imagine the situations described by the following sentences.From the perspective of sentence, the lexical block has a lot of pressure on lexical study, and the students must follow it when analyzing the local structure of three steps: firstly identify the topic sentence, and then determine the progress of the sentence, finally draw out the topic sentence of progress (Nattinger & DeCarrico, 1992, p. 1992). In other words, the more students realize the characteristics of the topics in the written article, the more they can better understand the relationship between sentences and incorporate them into their works. Sentence level vocabulary block can be a sentence of coherent linear relationship between the signal clues, that is to say, the relationship with the former one sentence sentence is the relationship between the next sentence or affiliate of cohesion mode. If students were able to identify the cohesion and signal cues at the sentence level, they would apply the same principle to the boundary of the sentence and begin to focus on global cues to the consistency of the discourse. Therefore, the teacher should expose the students to the materials of the vocabulary blocks that are used as frequently as possible and use exercises to isolate the blocks.

From the perspective of process-centered discourse, Carrel (1987) argues that teaching ESL learners on the top floor of the rhetorical text structure, and teaching them how to pass through language means text organization plan, will make their writing more efficient, and reading more efficient. This shows that teachers can train students to identify and use top-level organizational structures and appropriate signalling devices. In addition, it can improve students' awareness of information flow through the mapping and hierarchical high-level discourse movement. Each top-level structure will display a vocabulary words equipment characteristics of the network, and combine the specific macro and micro model of organizers, and to cultivate their matching nature way to teach them.

The preposition on has different dictionary meanings associated with different situations. With the core meaning of on (i.e., [+contact]) as the common thread, the teacher asks to explore the meaning world of on. To start with, the teacher may use prototypical exemplars to introduce the usage of on. The teacher asks students to imagine the situations described by the following sentences.

Anyhow, lexical approach reflects a belief that the foundation of language learning and communication is not a grammar, function, concept or some other plans and teaching units, but the words and word combinations (Richards & Rodgers, 2008, p. 2008). It has received more and more attention and has exerted a great influence on the language learning and teaching of the whole world. It provides a middle ground between structural and communicative methods.

10.3 Literature Review

Lexical chunks are multi-word units of language. Some never change (like Good morning!) while others allow some substitution to convey different meaning (like Please pass the ___.) In The A- Z of ELT, Scott Thornbury suggests that lexical chunks or formulaic language might provide the 'raw material' for language acquisition. That is, "sequences that are first acquired as unanalyzed chunks (such as I don't know) may be later analyzed into their component parts. They are then capable of generating original phrases, such as I don't understand, You don't know, I know …, etc" .

Learning chunks is no more difficult than memorizing single words. In their paper, Language is a Complex Adaptive System, The Five Graces Group explains that "corpus analyses in fact verify that communication largely consists of prefabricated sequences" (p.6). Prefabricated sequences are lexical chunks that can often cause problems for our students. Combining lexical chunks (the raw material), pictures (content), and context (a situation), helps students learn language more effectively.

With the development of corpus linguistics and second language acquisition research results, the researchers and linguists at home and abroad, such as Michael Lewis (Michael Lewis Nattinger DeCarrio, paint, such as wang Lifei, prove the important role of lexical chunks in language learning and the effectiveness of the lexical approach in improving learners' language ability.

10.3.1 Research Abroad

The study of foreign lexical blocks has a great development, but it is still in its primary stage. At present, foreign research mainly involves three aspects: the process of lexical acquisition, the difference of vocabulary acquisition between learners, and the teaching of class vocabulary block (Wang Lifei & Zhang Dafeng,2006, p.19).

The acquisition of lexical blocks has been one of the key points of the SLA. On the one hand, some linguists have studied the process of children acquiring lexical chunks. Perera (2001), for example, observed four Japanese preschoolers and found that lexical chunks were a scaffold for language creativity. On the other hand, linguists also study the acquisition of lexical blocks of adults. For example, bardovie-harlig (2002) observed the acquisition of the future tenses of 16 adult learners using «will» and «going to». It was found that all students tended to use «will» to express future tenses, although the expression «going to» was earlier and more frequent in the input than the expression «will». Furthermore, there is no evidence that «will» is used as a lexical block. This finding challenges the concept of using this concept more frequently in the primary stage of language learning.

Researches indicate that 70% of the daily expressions express the metaphor processes originated from the conceptual metaphor, in the sense of which metaphor is the cornerstone of language. Teachers should first illustrate the necessity of learning fundamental vocabulary with strong interests and laid a solid foundation for the students. Meanwhile, teachers should also lay emphasis on the metaphorical meaning and help them have a good command of the denotations and connotations and have a clear idea of their relation.

“Polysemy” means that a word has many system-related meanings (Johnson), which is common in every language. The metaphor theory holds that a large number of polysemous words are not generated randomly in our language. It is the use of metaphorical usage, thinking and cognition in our language. On the basis of cognition, polysemy is regarded as a classification phenomenon. That is the relevance of the archetypal word, and relate it to each other's similarity. The archetypal meaning of a polysemous usually comes directly from our physical and concrete experience, while others derive from this core similarity. Learning chunks is no more difficult than memorizing single words. In their paper, Language is a Complex Adaptive System, The Five Graces Group explains that "corpus analyses in fact verify that communication largely consists of prefabricated sequences" . Prefabricated sequences are lexical chunks that can often cause problems for our students. Combining lexical chunks (the raw material), pictures (content), and context (a situation), helps students learn language more effectively. The mechanism of conceptual metaphor, which overlaps, as a conceptual system of cross-domain mapping, usually involves the understanding and experience of an immaterial or abstract thing or a physical or concrete thing. Let's look at the "ana1ysis" of English preposition "in" . Most Chinese college English learners may agree that "in" means "inner" or "inner" . They are always at a loss when dealing with a more complex "in" environment. In fact, "in" is a word of polysemy, and many meanings, "from the container metaphor. The container metaphor, as an ontological metaphor, refers to the traditional metaphor that we describe our bodies as containers to other objects. The container can be any object that we use to include things; It has internal and external; In our experience, almost everything can be regarded as a container; Almost everything can be contained in a container. We use containers to express our complex thoughts.

Recent research has shown that another important dimension of lexical decoding is reading fluency. Fluency factor is an additional component of the accuracy of lexical decoding process, which is a separable aspect of decoding quality. Fast coding and the measurement standard as decoding quality to express the fluency of the word decoding. The decoding speed is measured by the number of words that a person can read correctly in a finite amount of time

(Breznitz, 2001; Compton & Carlisle,1994; Green and royer,1994). Decoding speed leads to fluency in reading, including the general ability associated with information processing speed (Kail & Hall, 1994), and systems related to the reading decoding process (Breznitz, 2002a).The entire cognitive processing time relies on the SOP (Kail, 1991) of each factor and process of activity during the execution of a specific task. It has been suggested that some factors contribute to SOP, including the complexity and manner of the stimulus, the differential SOP (Kail, 1991) at each stage of the information processing system, and the basic SOP (Hale, 1990) of the information processor.

Teachers should first illustrate the necessity of learning fundamental vocabulary with strong interests and laid a solid foundation for the students. Meanwhile, teachers should also lay emphasis on the metaphorical meaning and help them have a good command of the denotations and connotations and have a clear idea of their relation.

ESL users typically performed better than English learners (lower error rates, and faster speed), but on the collocation of inconsistent, they still can make more mistakes, not consistent. Their research has shown that learners of different levels are affected by the ability of learners to use vocabulary blocks and group blocks.

Another study found that dyslexia was associated with failure to cope with the failure of the thographic process. Orthographic knowledge associated with the visual information of a word, it is a special kind of letters, it contains the vocabulary of form and order, which helps to spelling ability and the ability to identify the word visual patterns (Corcos & Willows, 1993; Wagner and buck,1994). In fact, one of the main features of adult dyslexia is the spelling. It is claimed that spelling errors and alphabetical order confusion are due to difficulty in handling and lack of orthographic knowledge (Brunswick et al.,

1999; Elbro, Nielson, & Peterson, 1994). Recent research has shown that another important dimension of lexical decoding is reading fluency. Fluency factor is an additional component of the accuracy of lexical decoding process, which is a separable aspect of decoding quality. Fast coding and the measurement standard as decoding quality to express the fluency of the word decoding. The decoding speed is measured by the number of words that a person can read correctly in a finite amount of time (Breznitz, 2001; Compton & Carlisle,1994; Green and royer,1994). Decoding speed leads to fluency in reading, including the general ability associated with information processing speed (Kail & Hall, 1994), and systems related to the reading decoding process (Breznitz, 2002a).

10.3.2 Research at Home

Inspired by the researches abroad, researchers and linguists at home have developed interest in the lexical approach and conducted relevant studies from different perspectives in recent ten years.Flipped classroom, as a revolution of the teaching methods, was pioneered by two American teachers John Bergmann and Aaron Sams. They combined real-time explanation and demonstration of PPT videos and put them on the Internet, which has aroused public attention. Since then, the flipped classroom model has been popularized at all American colleges and universities generally. In 2011, New York Times and Global Times published articles about Flipped Classroom and called it a great reform of classroom teaching models. According to different purposes, the studies at home mainly concern three areas: 1) the role of lexical chunks in language acquisition; 2) the learners' abiltiy of using lexical chunks; 3) the application of lexical approach in classroom teaching.

There are more and more researches on flipped classroom teaching mode. Song elaborated the process of flipped classroom English teaching, which provided us with a new method of teaching English. Zhang yuying (2008) found that there is a significant correlation between the ability to recognize the lexical block and the language ability. Wang wenyu and huang yan (2013) studied the relationship between the use of blocks and the quality of oral interpretation. The results show that the correct use of block can improve the quality of oral interpretation. Chen introduced the process of flipped classroom teaching mode, and pointed out the advantages and disadvantages of flipped classroom, which helped us better understand flipped classroom. However, in flipped classroom mode, it does not involve vocabulary teaching. Zhang introduced a lot of vocabulary teaching strategies, which is of great significance to vocabulary teaching. However, it pays more attention to teaching and neglects students' feedback. This does not involve the feasibility of these strategies, nor does it explore the impact of vocabulary teaching strategies.

By analyzing the generation of mind mapping, we can find that although the mind map is an external graphical expression, it contains profound knowledge precipitation. Therefore, it is obviously unrealistic to rely solely on students to complete mind mapping independently. The teacher should bear the main task of making mind map, and make the mind map making as less serious preparation. In specific preparation, they should adopt flexible, careful thinking, make relevant charts, strive for accuracy and content of the richness of knowledge into consideration, in order to attract students' interest in learning.

Specifically, in the process of making mind maps, teachers should clearly explain the logical relationship between words, and do not mislead students to misunderstand them. Yuan Ping and Guo Fengrong (2010) and Ding yangren and Qi yan (2005) found that the use of lexical blocks was highly correlated with the oral level. In addition, Ding Yangren and Qi Yan (2005) also found that the use of lexical blocks can improve learners' writing level. Zhang Yuying (2008) found that there is a significant correlation between the ability to recognize the lexical block and the language ability. Wang Wenyu and Huang Yan (2013) studied the relationship between the use of blocks and the quality of oral interpretation. The results show that the correct use of block can improve the quality of oral interpretation. Almost all of the above studies are about the relationship between the use of lexical blocks and verbal ability, but few studies have involved the role of lexical chunks in writing ability.

10.4 Conclusion

Research from home and abroad shows that lexical blocks play an important role in improving the language proficiency of learners, and vocabulary teaching methods can also be applied in classroom teaching. However, most researches focus on the role of lexical blocks in language learning and teaching, and there is not enough empirical research to study the application of lexical methods. Although there is some research methods applied in classroom teaching of vocabulary, most of them are concerned chiefly with comprehensive English ability and some of them focus on the writing ability, especially by applying the method of vocabulary study of non-english major college English reading and writing courses. Therefore, the purpose of this study is to explore the influence of vocabulary teaching methods on the writing ability of non-english majors, and how to use the vocabulary method to influence college English reading and writing courses. It is hoped that this study can provide an effective way for college English teaching.

Reference

[1]Bardovie-Harlig, K. A. New starting point? Investigating formulaic use and input in future expression. Studies in Second language acquisition, 2002,24 (2), 189- 198.

[2]Breznitz, Z. The Determinants of Reading Fluency: A Comparison of Dyslexic and Average Readers. In M. Wolf (Ed.), Dyslexia, Fluency and the Brain (pp. 245-276). Cambridge, MA: York Press, 2001.

[3]Breznitz, Z.. Asynchrony of Visual-Orthographic and Auditory-Phonological Word Recognition Processes: An Un- derlying Factor in Dyslexia. Reading and Writing, 2002,a15, 15-42.

[4] Brunswick, N., McCrory, E., Price, C. J., Frith, C. D. & Frith, U. Explicit and Implicit Processing of Words and Pseudowords by Adult Developmental Dyslexics. Brain, 1999, 122, 1901-1917.

[5]Carrell, P. Text as interaction: Some implications of text analysis and reading research for ESL composition. In U. Connor & R. Kaplan (Eds.), Writing across languages: Analysis of L2 text (pp. 44-55). Reading, MA: Addison-Wesley,1987.

[6]Compton, D. L., & Carlislie, J. F. Speed of Word Recognition as a Distinguishing Characteristic of Reading Disabilities. Educational Psychology Review, 6, 115-140, 1994.

[7]Corcos, E. & Willows, D. M.. The Processing of Orthographic Information. In D. N. Willows, R. S. Kruk, & E. Corcos (Eds.), Visual Processing in Reading and Reading Disabilities (pp. 163-190). Hillsdale , NJ : Lawrence Erlbaum,1993.

[8]Elbro, C., Nielsen, I., & Peterson, D. K. Dyslexia in Adults: Evidence for Deficits in Non-Word Reading and in the Phonological Representation of Lexical Items. Annals of Dyslexia, 1994,44, 205-226.

[9]Greene, B. A., & Royer, J. M. A Developmental Review of Response Time Data That Support a Cognitive Components Model of Reading. Educational Psychology Review, 1994, 6, 141-172.

[10]Hale, S. A Global Developmental Trend in Cognitive Processing Speed. Child Development, 1990, 61, 653-663.

[11]Hsu, J. Development of collocational proficiency in a workshop on English for general business purposes for Taiwanese college students. Unpublished doctoral dissertation, Indiana University of Pennsylvania,2002.

[12]Kail, R. Developmental Changes in Speed of Processing during Childhood and Adulescene. Psychological Bulletin, 1991,109, 490-501.

[13]Kail, R., & Hall, L. K. Processing Speed, Naming Speed, and Reading. Developmental Psychology, 1994,30, 949-954.

[14]Lewis, M. The lexical approach. Hove, England: Language Teaching Publications, 1993.

[15]Lewis, M. Implementing the lexical approach: Putting theory in practice.Hove, England: Language Teaching Publications,1997.

[16]Lewis,M.Teaching collocations. Hove,England: Language Teaching Publications,2000.

[17]MeCarthy, M. (1998). Spoken language and applied linguistics. Cambridge, England: Cambridge University Press.,1998.

[18]Nattinger, J. & DeCarrico, J. Lexical phrases and language teaching. Oxford, England: Oxford University Press,1992.

[19]Perera, N. S. The role of prefabricated language in young children's second language acquisition. Bilingual Research Journal, 2001,25, 327-356.

[20]Richards, J. C. & Rodgers, T. S. Approaches and methods in language teaching. Beijing, China: Foreign Language Teaching and Research Press,2008.

[21]Wagner, R. K., & Barker, T. A. The Development of Orthographic Processing Ability. Neuropsychology and Cognition, 1994,8, 243-276.

[22]Wiktorsson, M. Learning idiomaticity: A corpus-based study of idiomatic expressions in learners' written production. Unpublished doctoral dissertation, Lunds University, Sweden,2003.

[23]陈伟平.增强学生词块意识，提高学生写作能力.外语界，2008(3), 48-53.

[24] 丁言仁、戚焱.词块运用与英语口语和写作水平的相关性研究.解放军外国语学院学报，2005(3), 49-53.

[25] 王立非、张大凤.国外二语预制语块习得研究的方法进展与启示.外语与外语教学, 2006 (5), 17-21.

[26] 王文宇、黄燕.语块使用与口译产出关系的实证研究.外语电化教学，2013(7), 28-35.

[27] 原萍、郭粉绒.语块与二语口语流利性的相关性研究.外语界，2010(1), 54-62.

[28] 张玉英.二语学习者预制词块识别能力与二语水平的关联性研究.外语界，2008(3), 62-66.

第二部分
英语语言评价研究

Chapter 1
Invoking Implicit Evaluation: the Play of Graduation in News Text

1.1 Introduction

The news text always expresses the news reporters' attitude, as well as the media's stance and ideology. Fowler (1991) pointed out that the media tend to employ language resources, which are encoded with certain covert attitudinal denotation, to report the events happening besides us in order to coordinate the stance and align the readers. Martin's Appraisal System Theory (AST) provides a powerful analytic tool for evaluation analysis of news text. It consists of three sub-systems: attitude, engagement and graduation. According to Martin, the evaluation in the text is divided into the explicit and implicit evaluation. The explicit evaluation is regularly realized through the vocabulary with clear attitudinal meaning, while the implicit is expressed by some neutral semantic structure (but with attitudinal denotation) in the text. There are three approaches to realize the implicit evaluation (Martin & White, 2005): the lexical metaphor provokes the evaluation; the ideational meaning affords the evaluation; and the resources of graduation flag the evaluation. Graduation is the sub-system of Martin's AST, and it is central to the entire Appraisal system. Both attitude and engagement are always realized and mediated through the graduation. This paper aims to analyze the play of graduation in invoking the attitude and then explore the ideology and the stance in the news text.The news text, unlike other texts, tends to directly or indirectly convey the media's attitudes or thoughts with the implicit appraisal resources. Martin pointed out that graduation resource is the most significant approach to realize the implicit evaluation in the text and the scaling semantic meaning may flag the evaluation. This paper analyzed the role of graduation in English-language China Daily and then discussed the covert attitude encoded in the news text.

1.2 The Theoretical Framework of Analysis

The AST evolved from the interpersonal function of the Systemic-Functional Grammar (SFG). Many researchers (Martin & Rose, 2003; Jiang Wangqi, 2009; Wang Zhenhua, 2009) all focused on the discourse semantic characteristic of the AST. The classic theory of interpersonal meaning in SFG concentrated on the exchange function of the clause, which mainly concerns exchange of goods, services or information through the participants' interaction. Actually, the interpersonal function is realized through Mood and Modality systems. Mood and Modality belong to the category of the clause grammar, while Appraisal System belongs to the category of the discourse semantics.

The SFG focuses on the "inter" dimension of the interpersonal meaning, while the AST concentrates on the "personal" aspects of the interpersonal meaning. "Appraisal is concerned with evaluation-the kinds of attitudes that are negotiated in a text, the strength of the feelings involved and the ways in which values are sourced and readers aligned." (Martin & Rose, 2003:22) Martin's theory consists of three sub-systems: attitude, engagement and graduation. The attitude deals with our daily feelings, including emotional response, judgments of behavior and assessment of things. Engagement is mainly concerned with the source of attitudes. Graduation is the system about the scaling of attitudinal meaning and the intensity of engagement.

Force and Focus comprise the system of graduation, which is concerned with the scalability of meaning. Force refers to the cline (from low value to high value) of intensification and quantification, for example, a very smart guy, and I'm a little troubled. Focus is the cline from the core category to the peripheral category. The evaluated thing/person in the sharpening endpoint of the Focus cline possesses the typical attribute and the clear salience, for example, pure evil and a clear break, whereas, the appraised in the softening endpoint the Focus cline is vaguely concentrated on, for example, I'm feeling kind of upset.

1.3 Collecting Data

This paper studies the articles published in English-language China Daily within one week from May11th to 17th in 2015. The English-language China Daily is one of the longest-established and the most popular national daily newspaper published in China. It is, with no doubt, one of the most influential newspapers. The standard for the selection of news texts was as follows: articles of between 200-500 words in length, about "China news" published in the printed broadsheet. The news texts were selected at random, which cover such areas as politics, economy, culture, education and so on. The approach to the analysis of the collected data is an exploratory or interpretative approach. The aim of this analysis is to explore the role of the graduation in news texts in invoking evaluation according to AST.

1.4 Discussion: the Play of Graduation in Invoking Attitude

1.4.1 Analysis of Force

Force is classified into Quantification and Intensification according to the applied entities. Force covers assessments as to degree of intensity and as to amount. Assessments of degree of intensity can operate over qualities. (eg. slightly stupid, absolutely stupid), over processes (eg. It slightly upsets me and It greatly upsets me.), or over the verbal modalities of likelihood, inclination and obligation.

On the one hand, the term "intensification" is used to refer to this scalability of qualities and processes.

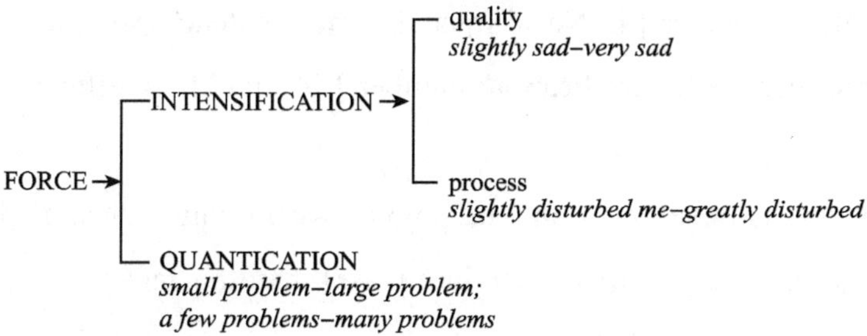

Figure 1. Force: intensification-quality and process (Martin & White, 2005:141)

On the other hand, we term the assessment of amount as "quantification", which refers to the evaluation of number, mass/presence, and extent of the entities.

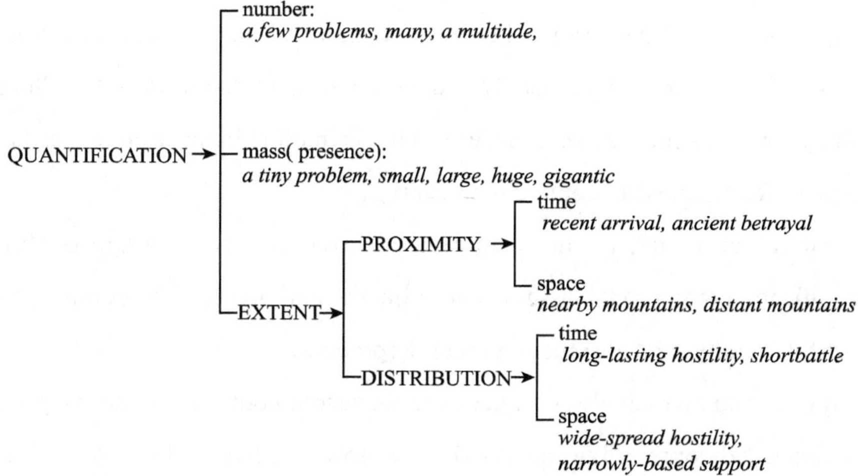

Figure 2. Force: quantification (Martin & White, 2005:151)

1.4.1.1 Quantification and Intensification

In English-language China Daily appear many examples of quantification and intensification, and then we analyze them according to the AST. At first, let's look at the application of quantification in the newspaper.

(1) The magnitude-7.9 [quantification: mass] earthquake on April 25 [quantification: extent: time], which had claimed more than 8,000 lives [quantification: number] in Nepal [quantification: extent: space] as of Sunday, killed more than 25 [quantification: number] in Tibet [quantification: extent: space].

(2) China is developing an amphibious assault ship whose displacement will be 1.5 times larger [quantification: mass] than the Japanese Izumo-class helicopter destroyer's 27,000 metric tons [quantification: mass].

The examples of mass, extent and number of quantification all appear in example (1). The mass magnitude-7.9 demonstrates the big scale of the earthquake. Equally, the number examples of more than 8,000 lives and more than 25, as well as the extent examples of in Nepal and in Tibet, also prove the destruction scale of the earthquake. Two examples of mass of quantification in example (2), 1.5 times larger and 27,000 metric tons, tell the readers that China's military force is stronger than Japanese. What is implied in this example is that it is unwise for Japanese to conflict with China.

Next, let's look at the examples of intensification in China Daily. Intensification refers to the assessment of quality and process, for example, very beautiful (quality) and absolutely upset me (process).

(3) The comparatively short deck cannot accommodate the fixed-wing J-15, and attack helicopters like the WZ-10 are slow and have a limited choice of weapons.

(4) Tourism quickly became a pillar industry of the province.

In example (3), comparatively is employed to modify the adjective "short", and it is to intensify the quality of the deck, but with the slightly weakening meaning, which implies that it is necessary to develop the military force in China to face the severe international situations. By contrast, the word quickly in example (4) functions to modify the verb "become", and belongs to the intensification of process. Quickly is the word encoded with the high value and as a result the utility of this word is to demonstrate the importance of tourism in China.

1.4.1.2 Isolating and Infusing Modes

According to the mode of evaluation, Force divides into two lexicalgrammar categories"isolating" and "infusing". The former refers that the graduation meaning is expressed by the isolated, individual item, while the latter refers that the up/down-scaling meaning of lexical item is expressed by its own semantic meaning as well as its isolated graduation meaning, for example, the prices skyrocketed. Both quantification and intensification have two kinds of mode: infusion and isolation.

(5) The country must be totally independent in food supply.

(6) The price of domestically produced corn···.

The above two examples are the isolating mode of Force, which function to intensify the quality and process respectively. The intensified denotation is expressed solely with the isolated meaning, with the exception of the ideational meaning. The following are the examples of the infusing mode of evaluation:

(7) China must resolve a host of technological and technical difficulties before it can develop a reliable short takeoff and vertical landing aircraft···.

(8) Eight teams of searchers are scouring nearly 40,000 hectares of forest for wild pandas in Southwest China's Yunnan province.

According to the infusing mode, the degree of intensity of meaning is conveyed by the scaling of one aspect of the single term. Therefore, A host of not only carries the meaning of amount, but also infused ideational meaning. In example (8), the word scouring carries the ideational meaning of "search for" and most importantly it also implies the intensity degree of the action.

1.4.2 Analysis of Focus

From the viewpoint of the experiential function, many things and entities are not scalable. The jazz is some kind of music, but from interpersonal semantic angle, the person makes a judgment about this kind of music according to their inclination, music knowledge and even their characters. The persons' different subjective inclinations leads to the distinct assessment of the jazz, and as a result, the scalability is possible to occur.

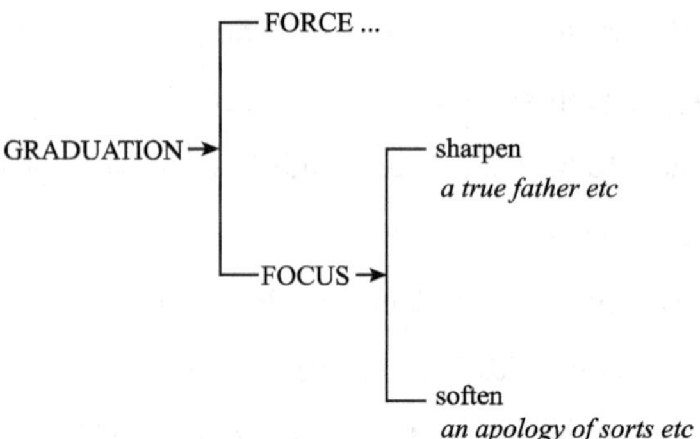

Figure 3. Focus (Martin & White, 2005:138)

(9) Some works featuring Chinglish translations have attracted the attention of linguists, Zhao said.

(10) The ultimate purpose is to ensure food security. But that does not mean that the country must be totally independent in food supply.

(11) So, while bribery in China may facilitate growth to some extent, it does not produce the kind of competitive business environment that supports long-term gains.

Chinglish in example (9) and to some extent in example (11) are exemplification of the softening Focus. Chinglish refers to this kind of Chinese learners' English that is different from the pure and standard English and belongs to the peripheral cline of prototypicality of English, which implies that the translation works are poor in quality. To some extent is also the example of softening Focus and have the low value of the intensity, with the implication that the bribery in China seemingly facilitate the growth, but actually is harmful to the economy development. The word ultimate carries the high value of the semantic meaning and tells the reader that the food safety is the high priority for the government.

1.5 Conclusion

The evaluation is central to the texts and utterances, and it is divided into explicit and implicit evaluation. Implicit evaluation functions to invoke the author's attitude. In this chapter, we have explored various means by which the news reporters can invoke attitude by scaling ideational meanings. By scaling ideational meaning writers subjectively position ideational meaning on a cline, implying a relative value (Hood & Martin: 2007, 758). So, is necessary to analyze the implicit evaluation encoded in the newspaper reflecting the author's attitude and stance.

Reference

[1] Fowler, R. Language in the News: Discourse and Ideology in the Press [M]. London: Routledge, 1991.

[2] Hood, Susan and James R. Martin. 2007. Invoking attitude: the play

of graduation in appraising discourse. In Ruqaiya Hasan, Christian M. I. M. Matthiessen and Jonathan Webster (eds.), Continuing Discourse on Language: A Functional Perspective. Volume 2. London: Equinox. 739-764.

[3] Jiang Wangqi. The appraisal System in Discourse Semantic [J], Foreign Language Teaching, 2009 (2): 1-5+11.

[4] Martin, J. R. & D, Rose. Working with Discourse: Meaning beyond the Clause [M]. London: Bookcraft Limited, 2003.

[5] Martin, J. R. & P. R. R. White. The Language of Evaluation: Appraisal in English [M]. London / New York: Palgrave Macmillan, in press, 2005.

[6] Wang zhenhua. Research Means of Discourse Semantics [J]. Foreign Languages in China, 2009 (6): 26-38

Chapter 2
Realization of Implicit Evaluation in News Text

2.1 Introduction

Any text conveys the evaluative connotation as well as the text author's attitudes, ideological states and feelings. News text is also no exception, because it also encodes the news media's direct or indirect viewpoint and displays the construal of the events happening in the world. Some linguists (Hodge & Kress 1979; Fowler 1991 ; Van Dijk 1988) pointed out that the news reports usually employ some implicit attitudinal resources to express the unrecognizable viewpoints in newspapers. With an aim to align the readers and maintain the social interaction, the journalists use these resources to instruct the readers to receive the value positioning. Now it is a tendency for the linguists to analyze the implicit evaluation resources in newspapers with the analytical model based on J. R Martin's Appraisal System Theory. Martin put forward three approaches that invoke the implicit evaluation: the provocation of lexical metaphor, the affording of the ideational meanings, and the flagging of the graduation. This paper tends to explore implicit evaluation by analyzing the reports in the English-language China Daily other than his three approaches.

Martin's Appraisal System Theory presents a powerful tool to decode the journalist's attitude or world view in news text. The evaluation in this Appraisal System can be further classified into explicit evaluation, which inscribes the attitude through the attitudinal vocabulary and implicit evaluation, which invokes the attitude through the use of non-core lexis. Martin (2005) pointed out that the implicit evaluation is realized by three approaches: lexical metaphor, the selection of ideational meanings, and graduation. However, the invoked attitude can be achieved by an amount of resources other than the above approaches. In this paper through the exploration of invoked attitude in the English-language China Daily, we find that the attitude is also invoked through grammatical metaphor, general noun as well as conjunction. It is of great significance to decode the journalists' or newspapers' viewpoints by exploring the implicit evaluation in the news text.

2.2 Implicit evaluation

Appraisal System Theory is founded and developed by the linguists of the Systemic-Functional Grammar (SFG) and … is concerned with various kinds of attitude and involved in the intensity of affections, as well as representing the values and aligning the readers" (Martin & Rose 2003:23). The Appraisal System Theory consists of three sub-systems: Attitude, Engagement and Graduation. The evaluation can be classified into explicit and implicit evaluation. The former is realized by words expressing the author's clear attitudes, such the words as happy, angrily and hate, While the latter is realized by the seemingly neutral (but with hidden attitude) semantic construction, which conveys the author's viewpoints. The 21st century has seen the fast development of the discourse analysis (Hunston & Thompson 2000; Martin & Rose 2003; Martin & White 2005; Hood & Martin 2007; Sook Hee Lee 2008) with the analytic powerful tool of the Appraisal System Theory. In China, some famous linguists (Li Zhanzi 2004b; Yang Xinzhang 2003; Liu Shizhu 2010; Liu Shisheng 2012) made further research about the application of Appraisal System Theory into the various discourses. The above analysis pays more attention to the explicit evaluation but less to the implicit evaluation, especially in the news texts. In the following discussion, we'll concentrate on the analysis of implicit evaluation in the newspapers.

2.3 Collecting the data

This is the study of 23 news reports published in the English-language China Daily within one week in March 2014. The China Daily is the most influential daily newspaper published in China. The purpose if this paper is to explore the realization of implicit evaluation in news reports and to decode the journalists' viewpoints. The criterion for the selection of the articles was as follows: articles about the Crimean crisis's news published in the printed China Daily. Those that form the corpus of the articles analyzed contain the events' description and comments in the news texts. The approach to analysis of the texts and interpretation of the collected data is an exploratory or qualitative and interpretative approach. The 23 news texts were analyzed and the implicit evaluation resources were recorded and tabulated. The texts conveying the implicit evaluation were then analyzed qualitatively in detail and explained the invoked attitude of journalists or the media.

2.4 Detailed analysis of implicit evaluation in news texts

2.4.1 Implicit evaluation realized through grammatical metaphor

Halliday (1994: 341-342) put forward the concept of grammatical metaphor and argued that the grammatical metaphor exists not only in lexical stratum but also in grammatical stratum. It is the incongruent form of language structure and aims to make a reconstruction of the semantic meaning through contraction of loose linguistic forms. Therefore, the metaphor contributes to the meaning potential of evaluation. Grammatical metaphor consists of ideational and interpersonal metaphors. Ideational metaphor is metaphorical construction of processes in the Transitivity System. According to the SFG, the ideational function is realized by the Transitivity System, which divides the human activities into the material, relational, mental, behavioral, verbal and existential processes. Fundamentally, the ideational metaphor is the transformation of two entities in six processes of the Transitivity System. The nominalization is the main form in the realization of ideational metaphor. By this device, processes (congruently worded as verbs) and properties (congruently worded as adjectives) are reworded metaphorically as nouns; instead of functioning in the clause, as Process or Attribute, they function as Thing in the nominal group (Halliday 1994: 349-352). For example,

(1) "The US ambassador's 'insults' were jeopardizing Moscow's willingness to cooperate with Washington on other diplomatic matters."

(2) "Preparation to become part of Russia-a process that could take months-are to begin this week if the referendum result is pro-Moscow."

In example (1) the nominalization structure "Moscow's willingness to cooperate with Washington on other diplomatic matters" can be transformed into the congruent form, that is, "Moscow was willing to cooperate with Washington on other diplomatic matters" . Actually the nominalization is the conversion of the adjective group into the nominal group. This conversion structure will instruct the reader to wonder whether Russia is willing to operate with the U. S diplomatically at the moment of Crimean crisis endangering Russian interests. The answer is very clear. In example (2), the nominal group of "Preparation to become part of Russia" is turned into its congruent form "Crimean people prepared to become part of Russia" . The clause of material process is converted into a nominal group, which implies that the proposition changes into the entity, with omission of the actor. The SFG insists that the actor is responsible for the action in the material process and imposes the certain influence on the subsequent goal. Therefore, the absence of the actor in this clause means the absence of initiator in the referendum, and then it is unrealistic to support or criticize the organizer in this situation. In this sense, the orderly and normal procession of this referendum is guaranteed, and the supportive attitude towards this referendum is implicitly expressed.

2.4.2 Implicit evaluation realized through general noun

Halliday & Hasan (1976) put forward the concept of general noun. It is one type of nouns, whose connotation needs identifying through the context. This type of noun is the contraction of the former textural information. On one hand, it realizes the cohesion of the information through contextualized semantic meaning. On the other hand, it also expresses the author's attitude and displays the implicit evaluative function, for example,

（3）"In a televised address to the nation, he said Crimea's vote Sunday to join Russia was in line with international law, reflecting its rights to self-determination. To back the claim, he pointed to Kosovo's independence bid from Serbia-supported by the West and opposed by Russia⋯."

In example (3), the general noun "claim" refers back to the Putin's utterance "Crimea's vote Sunday to join Russia was in line with international law" . The noun "claim" not only generates the cohesion between the two clauses, but also the comparison to the latter clause "Kosovo's independence bid from Serbia-supported by the West" . The anaphoric reference of the general noun displays the information transmission between two clauses, but encodes the construal of texts in the readers' minds.

2.4.3 Conjunction invoking the implicit attitude

The conjunction functions to connect the texts, and also implies the author's subjective attitude in the texts. Hunston & Thompson (2000: 9) pointed out that the more unobvious the evaluation is, the more likely it is to control and align the readers; the extreme example is the use of conjunction to imply the evaluative meaning. For example,

(4) "Chinese observers dismissed the possibility of a large-scale military conflict, although Ukraine said its forces would not withdraw from Crimea."

This example is the concessive structure, in which the conjunction "although" introduces the minor proposition, and the former clause is the main proposition. The main proposition is proposed and controlled by the author, while the minor proposition is subordinate to the main proposition. In this concessive-assertion structure, the main proposition cannot deny the minor proposition and then leads to existence of dialogic space between author and reader. The main proposition in example (4) is "Chinese observers dismissed the possibility of a large-scale military conflict" , and the minor proposition is "Crimean forces would not withdraw from Crimea" . Martin (2003) pointed out that the concessive structures in the texts actually instruct the readers to support the alternative proposition. Accordingly, we argue that the author in this report supports the main proposition: "The possibility of conflict explosion is minute, although Crimea is not to retreat."

2.5 Conclusion

The evaluation is the central part of the texts and utterances, and it is divided into explicit and implicit evaluation. Implicit evaluation tends to invoke the author's attitude, without the use of vocabulary containing the explicit attitude. This paper discusses the realization of the implicit evaluation in the English-language China Daily and also analyzes the appraisal function of these resources. The invoked attitude is realized by the linguistic resources with no clear attitude token, and the construal of the attitude depends on the understanding of the context and cultural backgrounds. It is of great significance to delve into the evaluative resources in the news texts.

Reference

[1]Fowler, R. Language in the News: Discourse and Ideology in the Press [M]. London: Routledge, 1991.

[2]Halliday, M. A. K & R, Hasan. Cohesion in English [M]. London: Longman, 1976.

[3]Halliday, M. A. K. An Introduction to Functional Grammar[M]. London: Edward Arnold, 1994.

[4]Hodge, R. & G. Kress. Language as Ideology [M]. London: Routledge, 1979.

[5]Hood, Susan and James R. Martin. Invoking attitude: the play of graduation in appraising discourse. In Ruqaiya Hasan, Christian M. I. M. Matthiessen and Jonathan Webster (eds.), Continuing Discourse on Language: A Functional Perspective. Volume 2. London: Equinox, 2007 : 739-764.

[6] Li Zhanzi. Evaluation and cultural model [J]. Foreign Languages Research, 2004b(2): 3-8

[7] Liu Shisheng. Discourse analysis under the perspective of appraisal system [J]. Journal of Tsinghua University, 2012(2): 134-141

[8] Liu Shizhu. The development of Appraisal System in China [J]. Foreign

Language and Foreign Language Teaching, 2010 (5): 33-37

[9] Martin, J. R. & D, Rose. Working with Discourse: Meaning beyond the Clause [M]. London: Bookcraft Limited, 2003.

[10] Martin, J. R. & P. R. R. White. The Language of Evaluation: Appraisal in English [M]. London / New York: Palgrave Macmillan, in press, 2005.

[11] Sook Hee Lee. An integrative framework for the analysis of argumentative/persuasive essays from an interpersonal perspective [J]. Text & Talk, 2008(28), 2.

[12] Thompson, G. & S. Hunston. Evaluation: An Introduction [A]. Hunston, S. & G. Thompson. Evaluation in Text: Authorial Stance and the Construction of Discourse [C]. Oxford: Oxford University Press, 2001, 1-27.

[13] Van Dijk, T. A. News Analysis: Case Studies of International and National News in the Press [M]. Hillsdale, New Jersey: Lawrence Erlbaum Associates Publishers, 1988.

[14]Yang Xinzhang. Evaluative methods in discourse [J]. Foreign Language and Foreign Language Teaching, 2003(1): 11-14

Chapter 3
隐性评价在新闻语篇中的体现

3.1 新闻语篇分析研究：评价系统理论视角

评价系统理论关注语篇中“所协商的各种态度，所涉及到的情感的强度，以及表明价值和联盟读者的各种方式。”评价可归纳为三大系统：态度，介入和级差。三大系统又可分为多个子系统。评价分为显性评价和隐性评价，显性评价（explicit evaluation）是指通过那些明显表明作者态度的词汇来表达，如“happy、angrily”和“hate”等。隐性评价（implicit evaluation）是通过那些貌似中性但却隐含着作者态度意义的语义结构来表达。运用评价系统理论分析新闻语篇，挖掘和探究媒体背后的态度和立场，越来越受到语言学家的重视。进入 21 世纪后，国内外学者也从不同方面探讨了评价系统理论在新闻语篇方面的应用研究，但是多集中于显性评价方面。媒体语篇通常会以含蓄的没有明显情感意义的隐性语言资源，来表达媒介集团的立场。王天华指出新闻语篇以隐性评价手段动态地建构新闻语篇和定位读者；张蕾和苗兴伟认为新闻语篇中的评价资源具有语篇建构功能；冉志晗认为英语新闻语篇的及物性结构具有隐性评价功能。因此，分析新闻语篇中的隐性评价资源，探究其背后隐含的态度，具有十分重要的意义。中国日报英文版 China Daily 是国内发行量最大的英文报刊，且具有较大社会影响力，因此本文以 2014 年乌克兰危机这一事件为例，以相关的新闻报道为语料基础，来分析隐性评价的体现形式，探讨其评价功能。

新闻语篇不同于其他语篇，通过对某一事件的报道传达着媒介集团的立场和观点。Fowler 指出媒体对发生在人们身边的新闻报道通常会使用一些隐性的，不易被读者识别的，隐藏在语篇字里行间中能传递一定态度的语言资源来协调立场和联盟读者。通过这些隐性表达方式，新闻语篇可引导读者接受其价值定位，建构双方主体间性关系，达到人际互动的目的。因此探究新闻语篇作者的态度以及媒体集团的立场和意识形态，对于建构和识解人际社会关系具有十分重要的作用。评价系统理论的诞生为新闻语篇的研究提供了强大的理论分析工具，近几年来运用此理论进行语篇分析研究，得到了国内外语言学家的首肯，也取得了巨大的成果。J. R. Martin 的系统评价理论是由系统功能语言学家在语篇分析的实践中发展和建立起来的，主要探讨的是语言资源所体现的态度，情感及意识形态。新闻语篇中的评价资源多种多样，但是近些年来的研究多集中于其显性评价方面，隐性评价关注不多。而新闻语篇文本所建构的态度和立场，只有通过对隐性评价的识别和解读才能全面地呈现在读者面前。

3.2 语篇中的隐性评价

“评价意义是所有语篇的核心，对语篇人际意义的分析都不可忽视它。”语篇中的评价可分为显性和隐性。显性评价态度易被读者识别，主要由那些像“happy”,“hate”和“misery”等态度意义的词汇来表达。而隐性评价是指通过使用那些貌似中性但却隐含评价意义的成分和句式而不是那些明晰的话语标记来表达评价意义。Martin & White 在《评估语言：英语的评价系统》一书中，分析了隐性评价的涵义及其建构。通常我们认为新闻语篇是对发生在人们身边的事件进行客观的语言描述而已，其实不然。媒体语篇善于运用看似客观、白描性质的语言来传递其隐含的态度，以建构与读者之间的人际关系，协调双方立场。因此新闻语篇的隐性评价分析研究有助于我们更好地理解媒体的态度和立场，建构媒体和读者之间和谐的人际互动关系。我们从以下三个方面来分析新闻语篇中的隐性评价。

3.2.1 词汇隐喻激发隐性评价

词汇隐喻激发（provoke）评价是指通过语篇中不同概念域之间的类比，来激发读者的认知态度。这种类比性质的隐喻言语，强化了对评价对象情感上的共鸣。在下面的描述中，词汇隐喻的运用起到了激发评价的作用：

(1)We were bought like a market. We was all lined up in white dresses, and they'd come round and pick you out like you was for sale……I remember all we children being herded up, like a mob of cattle, and feeling the humiliation of being graded by the color of our skins for the government records.

(2)This story's right, this story's true

I would not tell lies to you

Like the promises they did not keep

And how they fenced us in like sheep

Said to us come take our hand

Sent us off to mission land

Taught us to read, to write and pray

Then they took the children away...

上述两段落中，都出现了词汇隐喻的用法。在例 (1) 中，语篇的内在语言描述并没有表明政府机构非人性的行为举止，但是“对待原著居民就像对待商品一样”，尤其是三个比拟式的排比运用一“like a market，like you was for sale，like a mob of cattle”—明显激发出政府在读者心目中的那种无视和冷漠的态度。例 (2) 是一首歌曲，反映了澳大利亚“被偷走的一代”真实的生活写照。“被偷走的一代”是澳大利亚历史上充满悲剧色彩的群体，当时的澳大利亚政府，以改善土著儿童生活为由，将混血土著儿童强行从他们的家庭中带走，将其集中在保育所等处，接受白人文化教育。“And how they fenced us in like sheep”表达了“被偷走的一代”对政府这一野蛮政策的反对和声讨，因为政府对他们造成的心理创伤是无法弥合的。新闻报刊 China Daily 中同样存在着词汇隐喻的例子，例如：

(3) In contrast, the US turns a blind eye to Israel's possible ownership of nuclear weapons.

(4) Pro-Russia authorities and Moscow says the referendum is an example of self-determination like Kosovo's decision to leave Serbia, but Washington says it cannot be democratic because it is taking placing "under the barrel of a gun" .

例 (3) 中 turn a blind eye to 这一词汇隐喻，激发了读者对“美国无视以色列拥有核武器，却对别国拥核百般指责”的无赖态度的愤恨，同时也表达了在国际事务处理上美国采用双重标准政策的不满。例 (4) 中词汇隐喻“under the barrel of a gun”的使用表明：美国认为克里米亚的独立是俄罗斯军事恐吓的结果，是不民主的，暗示了美国对克里米亚公投不予承认的态度；而且此处是介入系统中多声资源的运用，拓展了作者与读者之间的对话空间，间接地隐含了作者的态度。

3.2.2 级差资源旗示隐性评价

级差是一种常见的语言学现象，将事物、品质、行为等进行量化，表达态度意义的强弱。级差语义部分在评价系统中处于核心地位，不仅可以表达概念意义，还具有强调、缓和、模糊等人际功能。概念意义的分级可旗示 (flag) 评价，旗示是指说话人以级差资源作为信号向读者暗示态度意义的存在。语势与聚焦为级差的两个子范畴，前者涉及质量、过程的强度与实体的数量，分别称为强化（intensification）和量化 (quantification)；后者是对事物范畴典型性或精确度的分级。聚焦关注评价对象是范畴的核心成员还是边缘成员。按语义值的强弱，聚焦可细化为锐化（sharpening）和柔化（softening）。请看下面的例子：

(5) Thousands of [语势：量化] Russian forces had arrived in Crimean in

the buildup to Sunday's referendum, in which Russian-majority Crimea voted overwhelmingly [语势：强化] to leave Ukraine and join Russia.

(6) Crimean voted overwhelmingly [强化：过程] on Sunday to secede from Ukraine and seek to join Russia. The hastily [强化：过程] called vote was held two weeks [量化：跨度] after Russian troops had moved into the Black Sea peninsula.

(7) Crimea's impending attachment to Russia has raised concerns that Ukraine may splinter further, dividing into a mostly [聚焦：锐化] ethnic-Ukrainian west and an ethnic-Russian east.

级差资源按照语义力度的大小可分为上升和下降两个方向，语义上升意味着作者的正面评价，语义下降预示作者的负面评价。在例 (5) 中上升力度的数量量化词语"Thousands of"和质量强化词语"overwhelmingly"，凸显了作者对俄罗斯占据克里米亚和克里米亚人民脱乌入俄的正面评价和支持。例 (6) 通过上升力度的过程强化词"overwhelmingly"和"hastily"以及时间分布跨度数量词"two weeks"来表达克里米亚人民脱离乌克兰加入俄罗斯的急迫愿望，暗含作者的正面评价。同样，例 (7) 中锐化聚焦词"mostly"的上升语义力度向读者传达出克里米亚的独立使乌克兰面临分裂的可能急剧增加。

3.2.3 概念意义的选择致使隐性评价

概念意义（功能）是系统功能语言学理论中三大语言元功能的子系统，是说话人对周围外部世界和人类内心世界经验的描述。概念意义致使 (afford) 隐性评价，是指语篇作者通过对概念意义成分的不同选择来表达其态度。White 指出唤起 (evocation) 和激发 (provocation) 是新闻篇章中最主要的隐性评价手段。唤起主要是通过语篇中纯粹的概念意义信息来唤起读者或听者积极或消极的情感反应，如下面的例子：

(8) Crimea, home to the Russian Black Sea Fleet and historically part of the

Russian Federation, was transferred in May 1954 to Ukraine, then a republic of the Soviet Union.

语篇作者在例 (8) 小句中，没有使用明确表明其态度意义或感情色彩的词语，只是在陈述一个事实：克里米亚作为俄罗斯黑海舰队的母港，历史上就是俄罗斯联邦的一部分；它在 1954 年被移交给乌克兰，当时的乌克兰是苏联的一个加盟共和国。但是此小句的信息却能唤起读者的正面情感反应，此情感反应的唤起主要源自于读者头脑中的价值取向和对社会文化定位的评判。

再看下面的例子：

(9) Preparations to become part of Russia-a process that could take months-are to begin this week if the referendum result is pro-Moscow.

例 (9) 中“preparations to become part of Russia” 是名物化 (nominalization) 的结构，转化为一致式为“Crimean people prepared to become part of Russia”。此例句由物质过程小句转化为名词短语，是命题（proposition）向实体（entity）的转化，且省略了动作者 (actor) 和情态（modality）成分。系统功能语言学认为在物质过程小句中动作者是对过程负责的参与者成分，对其后的目标（goal）施加一定的影响。因此，此例中动作者的缺失，意味着公投事件的发起者缺失，就在法理上找寻不到此事件的负责人，失去了支持或批评的对象，公投的有序安全进行也就获得了保障，含蓄地表达了媒体对此次公投的支持。

3.3 结论

评价是所有话语与语篇的核心，评价有显性和隐性之分。新闻媒介语篇通常会使用那些貌似中性但却隐含评价意义的成分和句式来表达媒体集团的声音和立场。本文从词汇隐喻、概念意义的选择和级差资源三个方面分析了隐性评价的体现形式，探究了其在语篇中的评价功能。新闻语篇中的隐性评价资源的识别与解读，需要借助于语境，借助于相关上下文语境和文化背景知识来激活。最后指出的是，语篇中的评价资源非常丰富，本文的研究角度和思路难免会顾此失彼；因此，新闻媒介语言的评价研究值得国内外学者们进一步探讨。

参考文献

[1] Fowler, R. Language in the News: Discourse and Ideology in the Press [M]. London: Routledge, 1991.

[2] Martin, J. R. & P. R. R. White. The Language of Evaluation: Appraisal in English [M]. London / New York: Palgrave Macmillan, in press, 2005.

[3] 王天华 . 新闻语篇隐性评价意义的语篇发生研究 [J]. 外语学刊 , 2012(1): 104-107

[4] 张蕾 , 苗兴伟 . 评价意义的语篇构建功能 [J]. 西安外国语大学学报 ,2010, (9):23-26.

[5] 冉志晗 . 英语新闻语篇的及物结构及其隐性评价功能研究 [J]. 安徽工业大学学报 (哲学社会版), 2013(3): 62-66.

[6]Thompson, G. & S. Hunston. Evaluation: An Introduction [A]. Hunston, S. & G. Thompson. Evaluation in Text: Authorial Stance and the Construction of Discourse [C]. Oxford: Oxford University Press, 2000, 1-27.

[7] 朱永生 . 概念意义中的隐性评价 [J]. 外语教学 , 2009 (4): 1-5.

[8] Martin Khor. Western Hypocrisy in Ukraine [N]. China Daily, 2014-3-18(9).

[9]Agencies. Ethnic Russians Confident in referendum [N]. China Daily, 2014-3-17(12).

[10]Li Xiaokun. Pro-Russians Storm Naval HQ [N]. China Daily, 2014-3-20(1).

[11]Agencies. Putin Defends Crimea Vote, Blasts West [N]. China Daily, 2014-3-19(11).

[12]Agencies. Russians in Eastern Ukraine Want Their Own Voice, Gorbachev Says [N]. China Daily, 2014-3-19(11).

[13]White, P. R. R. Subjectivity, evaluation and point of view in media discourse [A]. In C. Coffin (ed.). Applying English Grammar: Functional and Corpus Approaches [C]. London: Arnold, 2004.

[14]Agencies. Ukraine Crisis [N]. China Daily, 2014-3-21(9).

Chapter4
隐性评价在英语新闻语篇宏观层面上的体现

4.1 引言

任何语篇都是其作者思想情感、意识形态的反映。新闻语篇通过对新闻事件的解读，表达着报道者及其所代表的新闻媒体的态度。语言学家通过研究指出：新闻媒体通常运用一些读者不易识别的，隐藏在语篇背后的话语来暗示某种态度，以期联盟读者达到人际互动的目的。近几年来，运用马丁的评价系统理论来分析这些隐性的语言资源一直是语言学界的热门话题。新闻语篇中的隐性评价资源多种多样，但是近些年来的研究多集中于其微观层面，关注于词汇语法层面较多，关注语篇层面较少，因此是不全面的。新闻语篇中除了其微观层面的隐性评价之外，是否还存在着更多宏观层面的语言资源来体现隐性评价呢？这是本研究的出发点。

4.2 评价系统理论视角下的新闻语篇分析研究

评价系统理论是由系统功能语言学研究者创建和发展的，关注语篇中“所协商的各种态度，所涉及到的情感的强度，以及表明价值和联盟读者的各种方式”。语篇中的评价资源可归纳为三大系统：态度，介入和级差。三大系统又可分为多个子系统。评价又可分为显性评价和隐性评价，显性评价由那些明确表达作者态度的词汇来体现，如形容词“happy”、副词“angrily”和动词“hate”等。隐性评价是指通过那些没有明确态度意义的非核心词汇来表达。进入 21 世纪后将评价系统理论应用于语篇分析获得了快速发展，国内外学者从不同视角探讨了其在语篇分析方面的应用模式。马丁和怀特在《评估预言：英语评价系统》一书中详细阐释了评价理论及其在语篇中的应用。王振华是国内最早对英语硬新闻和社论进行评价理论运用研究的学者，单胜江从批评话语分析的角度研究了语篇中的评价；张蕾和苗兴伟认为新闻语篇中的评价资源具有语篇建构功能。从英语新闻语篇的隐性评价研究来看：魏在江认为语用预设具有隐性评价功能；王天华指出新闻语篇以隐性评价手段动态地建构新闻语篇和定位读者；冉志晗认为英语新闻语篇的及物性结构具有隐性评价功能。

综上所述，我们认为英语新闻语篇的隐性评价虽然获得了丰硕的成果，但是这些研究多集中于隐性评价资源的微观层面。英语新闻语篇中的隐性评价资源多种多样，不仅有微观层面的，更有宏观层面的。中国日报英文版 China Daily 是国内发行量最大的英文报刊，且具有较大社会影响力，因此本文拟以 China Daily 的新闻语料为分析对象。2014 年 3 月克里米亚公投加入了俄罗斯，世界各国对此反应不一。基于此事件的新闻报道，本文探讨隐性评价在语篇宏观层面上的体现形式。

4.3 宏观层面的隐性评价

梵迪克在其博士论文中，第一次提出“宏观结构 (macrostructure)”的概念。姜望琪认为：“话语和语篇中不仅仅在线性的展现中句子和句子之间存在着各种微观的连贯关系，从话语的整体和全局来看，存在着宏观结构，即管理话语篇章的整体形式或格局的摘要或图式结构。”在本文中宏观层面是指段落内部及段落之间或整个语篇上的语义结构或语境。我们从以下几个方面来识别和分析新闻语篇在宏观层面上的隐性评价资源。

4.3.1 篇章中的评价韵律

语篇中的人际意义的体现模式是呈现韵律性（prosodic）特征的，不仅体现在词汇和小句层面，同样弥漫于整个语篇中。马丁和怀特也认为“语篇中的韵律模式对于语篇中评价意义的分析具有十分重要的意义”，在此基础上，马丁针对人际意义提出了韵律结构的三种具体体现方式（图1）：渗透型、加强型和主导型。渗透型 (saturating) 结构指人际韵律的表达是随机的、任意的，可能出现在小句中的任何位置。加强型 (intensifying) 结构指人际韵律随着语篇的展开渐进增强；加强型韵律结构的词汇——语法体现方式包括重复、感叹句、修饰语和最高级等。主导型 (dominating) 结构指语篇的人际韵律受到其中心意义的支配；语篇在开端时设定了一定的基调，随后的人际韵律都围绕着该基调展开。

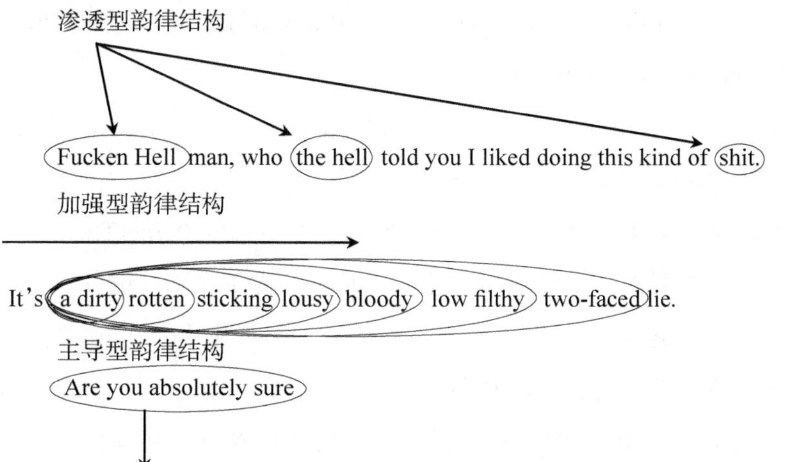

图 1　韵律结构类型

从上面的韵律分布图式来看，语篇的韵律模式是多样化的，不仅体现在某些个别词汇上，而且弥漫于整个语篇。因此语篇的韵律模式在宏观上弥补了单个词汇所体现的评价意义。我们认为这种无明显态度词汇表征的波浪型韵律特征也是隐性评价的体现形式。我们以例（1）为具体实例分析评价韵律模式。

（1）Oil, gas become issue

Meanwhile, many EU nations are heavily dependent on Russian oil and gas, and the EU is divided on how far it can go in cutting economic ties with one of its largest trading partners and a key energy supplier. EU efforts to diversify energy supplies after Russia cut delivery to Ukraine in 2006 and 2009 have so far failed to make much headway.

Russia fired another warning shot on this front on Friday. The Kommersant business daily said that when Moscow and Kiev revise their agreement on the Crimea base for the Black Sea fleet, Ukraine could lose the lower price it got in return for the 2010 accord.

If Kiev loses its ＄100 discount, it will end up paying up to ＄480 per 1,000 cubic meters for natural gas, the highest price of any of gas giant Gazprom's clients in Europe, the newspaper said.

A gas price hike of this order would be a huge blow for Ukraine and likely add to tensions. (China Daily 2014-3-22-23)

马丁和罗斯提出了宏观主位 (macroTheme) 和超主位 (hyperTheme) 的概念，超主位是语篇中各个段落的主题句，具有预测下文内容的作用。宏观主位位于超主位之上，是更高层次的主位结构（如整个篇章的题目），可以帮助读者预测段落的超主位和小句中的主位。因此，主位、超主位和宏观主位构成了整个语篇的结构框架，评价意义随着语篇结构的不断展开，起伏消长如同音乐中的韵律。上面的例证中“Oil, gas become issue”这一关系过程小句起到了宏观主题的作用，统辖了全文语篇发展的韵律方向，同时也奠定了整个新闻语篇的评价基调—对于乌克兰来说，石油和天然气成为一大难题。因此从宏观层面来看，评价韵律属于主导型。从段落间的评价韵律来看，语篇的宏观主题在第一、二、三段的论述中获到呼应和增强，评价意义呈现出加强型的韵律特征。尤其是语篇的最后一段，“a huge blow for Ukraine adds to tensions”与语篇的题目相呼应，整个语篇加强型韵律模式得以最终完成。

4.3.2 显性与隐性评价的互动模式

语篇中既有显性评价又有隐性评价，他们相互交织在一起，表达语篇作者的态度。胡德认为显性与隐性评价可共同存在于语篇中，显性评价辐射（radiate）即而产生隐性评价，隐性评价积聚则产生显性评价。例（2）如下：

（2）Russia's strategic and emotional ties to Crimea are especially deep. ① The Kremlin views Ukraine as essential to its attempts to establish a Eurasian Commission modeled after the European Commission, the governing arm of the EU. ② The majority of Crimea's population is ethnic Russian and the Kremlin has a long lease on a base there for its ultra-important Black Sea Fleet. ③ Tens of thousands of Russian military personnel were already stationed on the peninsula. ④ Russia also has deployed a big force opposite Ukraine's eastern border, the industrial heartland with a big Russian-speaking population. (China Daily 2014-3-21)

马丁和罗斯指出语篇中的超主位（段落主题句）和超新信息通常被用来表达作者的态度，具备显性评价的作用。上例中的首句为该段的主题句（超主位），体现了显性评价功能，同时超主位又具有预测其后语篇信息的作用。段首主题句的显性评价意义辐射到语篇的剩余部分，虽然语篇的剩余部分没有显性评价词汇，但是其表征的内容是主题句的语义辐射。①克里姆林宫视乌克兰为其建立类似于欧盟的欧亚联盟模式的重要一步；②克里米亚的大部分民众为俄罗斯族裔，并且俄罗斯长期租用克里米亚作为其黑海舰队的基地；③成千上万的俄罗斯军事力量已驻扎在克里米亚；④俄罗斯已在乌东部边境地区部署了大量武装力量。这些小句体现出的概念涵义隐含地表达了语篇中主题句（超主位）的评价意义——俄罗斯与克里米亚的战略和情感联系尤其至深。

再看下面的例（3）：

① It was after all the US that invaded Iraq in 2003, massively bombing its territory and killing hundreds of thousands, on the grounds that Iraqi leader Saddam Hussein had amassed weapons of mass destruction...

② The US has also waged war in Afghanistan that has caused thousands of deaths. In Libya, the US and its allies carried out massive bombing, which added opposition forces and led to the killing of Libya leader Muammar Gaddafi.

③ Even now there are sanctions on and the threat of military action against Iran because the West suspects Teheran wants to develop nuclear weapons. In contrast, the US turns a blind eye to Israel's possible ownership of nuclear weapons…

④ Just days ago the UN Human Rights Council published a Special Rapporteur's report detailing the deaths of civilians caused by US drone attacks…

⑤ All these actions were carried out in the 21st century, in addition to many other actions in the 20th century. It's thus remarkable that Obama and Kerry could, with a straight face, accuse Russia of not acting in a manner benefiting the 21st century and being on the wrong side of history.

⑥ There appears to be one law for still the most powerful country, and another for others. The former can invade and kill, while lecturing self-righteously to others. (China Daily 2014-3-18)

在此新闻报道中，我们开始虽然不能从①句中得出其评价基调，但是随着①至⑤小句信息的不断向前发展，作者的态度越来越明显，直到最后作者明确的主观态度才显现出来。末尾句⑥为语篇的超新信息，是整个篇章的显性评价所在。“There appears to be one law for still the most powerful country, and another for others”体现出作者对美国霸权主义两面派作风的指责。语篇中，评价韵律从语篇之首不断向前扩散，隐性评价信息不断推进和积累，至语篇终结显性评价得以最终显现。

4.3.3 历史文化背景引发隐性评价

语篇作者通过语言资源的运用，对新闻事件进行解读与剖析，来传达其显性抑或隐性的态度，联盟读者和人际交往的目的得以完成。语言是文化的载体，文化是语言的内容。任何语言都是一定社会阶层在文化和意识形态的体现。因此，文化的展现即昭示态度，语言背后所呈现的文化历史背景传递语言使用者的某种意识倾向。新闻语篇中出现的历史文化会触及阅读者的心理认知，因此作者的态度通过文化背景的激活便产生于读者的头脑中。例如：

(4) The Black Sea peninsula is inhabited mostly by ethnic Russians and has been seized by Russian forces over the past month after Ukraine's uprising, plunging US-Russia ties to their lowest point since the fall of the Berlin Wall in 1989 … Crimeans took to the polls on Sunday for a referendum on breaking away from Ukraine and joining Russia, part of a Cold War-style security crisis on Europe's eastern frontier that began with the toppling of Ukraine's central government at the end of February. (China Daily 2014-3-17)

段首句指出：乌克兰危机过后一个月，大部分由俄罗斯族裔居民居住的黑海半岛就被俄罗斯迅速占据；自柏林围墙倒塌以来，美俄关系降到了历史最低点。“柏林围墙的倒塌”被历史学家认为是东西方冷战终结和东西德统一的标志。冷战结束，世界进入了相对和平发展时期。“柏林围墙的倒塌”在段落中的引用，表达了作者对乌克兰危机不断升级的担忧。同样，将“克里米亚公投”看作是“冷战模式（a Cold War-style）”，易让读者联想到：乌克兰和俄罗斯的关系已进入敌对状态，战争冲突一触即发。

4.4 结论

评价是所有话语与语篇的核心，评价有显性和隐性之分。隐性评价的探究多聚焦于词汇语法等微观层面，宏观层面的隐性评价研究没有得到足够重视。本文从语篇的评价韵律、显性与隐性评价的互动和历史文化背景三个方面，分析和探究了隐性评价在新闻语篇中的体现。需要指出的是，新闻语篇中的隐性评价由态度标记不明显的成分来体现，在语言层面上不易被察觉。因此，新闻语篇中的隐性评价资源的识别与解读，需要借助于语境，借助于相关上下文语境来激活。本文从宏观层面的视角探讨了隐性评价在语篇中的体现形式，但也存在不足之处。语篇中的隐性评价资源非常丰富，仅从宏观层面来分析难免会顾此失彼。因此，新闻英语的评价研究值得语言研究者们进一步探讨。

参考文献

[1] Hodge, R. & G. Kress. Language as Ideology [M]. London: Routledge, 1979.

[2] Fowler, R. Language in the News: Discourse and Ideology in the Press [M]. London: Routledge, 1991.

[3] 张滟 . 态度评价 : 主体互联性劝说模式构建 [J]. 外语学刊 , 2008 (3): 71-75.

[4] Martin, J. R. & D, Rose. Working with Discourse: Meaning beyond the Clause [M]. London: Bookcraft Limited, 2003.

[5] 单胜江 . 新闻语篇的批评性话语分析 [J]. 外语学刊 , 2011(6): 78-81.

[6] 张蕾 , 苗兴伟 . 评价意义的语篇构建功能 [J]. 西安外国语大学学报 , 2010 (9):23-26.

[7] 魏在江 . 语用预设的语篇评价功能 [J]. 学术探索 , 2011 (2): 23-29.

[8] 王天华 . 新闻语篇隐性评价意义的语篇发生研究 [J]. 外语学刊, 2012 (1): 104-107

[9] 冉志晗 . 英语新闻语篇的及物结构及其隐性评价功能研究 [J]. 安徽

工业大学学报 (哲学社会版), 2013 (3): 62-66.

[10] Van Dijk, T. A. News Analysis: Case Studies of International and National News in the Press [M]. Hillsdale, New Jersey: Lawrence Erlbaum Associates Publishers, 1988.

[11] 姜望琪 . 语篇语言学研究 [M]. 北京 : 北京大学出版社 , 2011.

[12] Martin, J. R. & P. R. R. White. The Language of Evaluation: Appraisal in English [M]. London / New York: Palgrave Macmillan, in press, 2005.

[13] Hood, S. The persuasive power of prosodies: radiating values in academic writing [J]. Journal of English for Academic Purposes, 2006(5).

Chapter 5
隐性评价与大学“英文报刊选读”教学

5.1 引言

英文报刊选读课程是英语专业大学生的一门必修课，不少学校对非英语专业的学生也开设了这门选修课。通过阅读各种英文报纸杂志，可以使学生了解和学习世界各国的政治、经济和文化等方面的知识，同时对于开拓大学生的文化视野，培养英语语感，提高英语语言学习的效率也具有非常重要的作用。但是传统的课堂教学侧重于人文地理和风土人情的教学，多以分析语篇结构为主，忽视了对语篇作者以及媒体的态度和立场的探究。新闻报道看似具有客观性和真实性的特点，但是往往会以貌似中性但却隐含态度的语言资源，来表达其立场和观点。这些语言资源体现了语篇作者的某些隐性评价态度，因此在报刊教学中，发掘和探讨这些隐性评价资源，对于培养学生独立思考、批判性阅读的能力，具有十分重要的意义。

5.2 基于人际功能的隐性评价

系统功能语言学认为语言具有三大元功能：概念功能、人际功能和语篇功能。人际功能源于语言的社会符号性。语言作为一种符号，是其使用者运用语言策略来表达其身份地位和他对周围所发生事件的判断和评价的工具。马丁认为系统功能语言学的人际功能理论还不够完善，不能完全反映人类交际的特点，因此他又提出了评价系统 (Appraisal System) 理论。评价系统理论关注语篇中“所协商的各种态度，所涉及到的情感的强度，以及表明价值和联盟读者的各种方式。”评价可归纳为三大系统：态度，介入和级差。三大系统又可分为多个子系统。评价按照态度和情感意义的凸显程度又可分为显性评价和隐性评价，显性评价（explicit evaluation）是指通过那些明显表明作者态度的词汇来表达，如“happy、angrily”和“hate”等。隐性评价（implicit evaluation）是通过那些没有明显态度意义的非核心词汇及语义结构来表达。报刊语篇一般被认为通过客观、公正或白描式的语言来报道人类世界所发生的事情，但是报刊语篇又不同于其他语篇，通常会运用隐晦的或选择性的话语来体现报道者的意识形态和观点。我国的学者和英语教育者在运用评价理论进行英文报刊教学研究方面，进行了有益的探索和实践，也取得了一些成果。但是这些研究多以显性评价为主，对隐性评价的探讨不多。王天华指出新闻语篇往往以隐性的评价语言资源建构语篇、传递态度和定位读者。因此分析和探究这些隐性评价资源对于读者识别和解读媒体背后的态度具有十分重要的意义。

5.3 隐性评价在英文报刊中的体现

显性评价通常由具有明确态度意义的词汇来体现，因此报道者和媒体的态度及意识形态容易被读者所知晓，但是隐性评价是由那些态度意义不明显的非核心词汇和语义结构来体现的，所以不易被读者所察觉。[3](P67) Martin & White 指出语篇中的隐性评价主要由三种途径来体现：词汇隐喻激发（provoke）评价；概念意义致使 (afford) 评价；级差资源旗示 (flag) 评价。后来，Hood & Martin 又认为隐性评价主要由概念意义的选择和概念意义中语义程度的分级来体现。即时新闻报道往往以最新发生的事件和最鲜活的语言，吸引着英语学习者的兴趣。因此，在实际大学英语报刊选读课堂上，除了使用课程教材，我们通常会以中国日报英文版和华尔街日报为教学素材。之所以选用两类报刊是因为其社会影响力较大，其中中国日报是国内发行量最大的英文报纸，反映了国内媒体对世界发生事件的看法与态度；华尔街日报是美国国内发行量较大的政治经济类报刊，其世界影响力首屈一指。本文以这两类报刊为语料基础，识别和探讨英文报刊中的隐性评价资源，以期挖掘报刊媒体的态度和观点，培养学生批判性阅读的能力。

5.3.1 词汇隐喻激发评价

词汇隐喻是一种具有类比性质的语言学现象，词汇隐喻激发（provoke）评价是指通过语篇中不同概念域之间的对比，来激发读者的某种认知态度。这种类比性质的隐喻言语，强化了读者情感上的共鸣。在下面的语言描述中，词汇隐喻的运用起到了激发评价的作用：

（1）We were bought like a market. We was all lined up in white dresses, and they'd come round and pick you out like you was for sale……I remember all we children being herded up, like a mob of cattle, and feeling the humiliation of being graded by the color of our skins for the government records.

（2）This story's right, this story's true

I would not tell lies to you

Like the promises they did not keep

And how they fenced us in like sheep

Said to us come take our hand

Sent us off to mission land

Taught us to read, to write and pray

Then they took the children away...

上述两段落中，都出现了词汇隐喻的用法。在例（1）中，语篇的内在语言描述并没有表明政府机构非人性的行为举止，但是"对待原著居民就像对待商品一样"，尤其是三个比拟式的排比运用"like a market，like you was for sale，like a mob of cattle"明显激发出政府在读者心目中的那种无视和冷漠的态度。例（2）是一首歌曲，反映了澳大利亚"被偷走的一代"真实的生活写照。"被偷走的一代"是澳大利亚历史上充满悲剧色彩的群体，当时的澳大利亚政府，以改善土著儿童生活为由，将混血土著儿童强行从他们的家庭中带走，将其集中在保育所等处，接受白人文化教育。“And how they fenced us in like sheep”表达了“被偷走的一代”对政府这一野蛮政策的反对和声讨，因为政府对他们造成的心理创伤是无法弥合的。中国日报和华尔街日报中同样存在着词汇隐喻的例子，例如：

(3) In former US sectary of state Henry Kissinger’s words, it should try to play a bridge between the two sides instead of anyone’s chess piece.(China Daily, 2014-3-18).

(4) In this regard the banking system is Greece’s Achilles’ hell. Greek banks have lost more than 15% of their total deposits since November, with outflows of € 20.4 billion in the first two months of this year. (The Wall Street Journal, 2015-5-10).

在例 (3) 中，美国前国务卿基辛格将发展中美关系比作搭建“桥梁”，而不是各下各的“棋子”。此处是一种比喻的用法，虽然没有明确的态度词汇，但是“bridge”和“chess piece”词汇隐喻的使用，向读者暗示了中美关系的重要性。例 (4) 中的“Greece’s Achilles’ hell”同样是词汇隐喻的用法。作者将希腊的银行系统比作“阿卡琉斯之踵”，预示脆弱的银行体系是希腊经济的软肋，表达了对希腊国内经济情况的担忧。

5.3.2 概念意义致使评价

概念功能是系统功能语言学理论中三大语言元功能—概念功能、人际功能和语篇功能的子系统，是说话人对周围外部世界和人类内心世界经验的描述。概念意义致使隐性评价，是指语篇中概念意义成分的不同选择隐含了作者的态度和观点。White 指出唤起 (evocation) 和激发 (provocation) 是新闻篇章中最主要的隐性评价手段。唤起主要是通过语篇中纯粹的概念意义信息来唤起读者或听者积极或消极的情感反应，例如中国日报中关于克里米亚危机的报道：

(5) As well as the closer political ties, the European Commission has agreed to extend nearly 500 million euros in trade benefits to Ukraine, removing customs duties on a wide range of agricultural goods, textiles and other imports. (China Daily, 2014-3-22).

例 (5) 中没有明显态度意义的词汇，但是句子的概念意义却能唤起读者的负面情感反应。乌克兰因为此次危机导致国内经济和社会环境急剧恶化，欧盟不得不对乌克兰提供 5 亿欧元的优惠，以减除农产品、纺织品和其他进口商品的关税，来维护其摇摇欲坠的国内政权。此情感反应的唤起主要源自于读者头脑中的价值取向和对社会文化定位的评判。我们再看欧盟成员国法国和意大利在此次危机中的表现：

(6) France accounts for almost 22% of eurozone gross domestic product; Italy, more than 16%. Together, these two countries contribute more than 20 times Greece's portion of eurozone GDP.(The Wall Street Journal, 2015-5-10).

在上面的例子中，作者通过具体的数字对比来向读者传达了这样一个事实：法国和意大利的经济总量约占欧元区的 38%，对欧元区生产总值的贡献率远远高于希腊，是希腊的 20 多倍。因此读者头脑中不禁会产生这样一种意识：虽然希腊债务危机困扰着欧洲，但是法国和意大利的经济表现对欧盟的稳定也起着至关重要的作用。

5.3.3 级差资源旗示评价

级差是一种常见的语言学现象，将事物、品质、行为等进行量化，表达态度意义的强弱。级差语义部分在评价系统中处于核心地位，不仅可以表达概念意义，还具有强调、缓和、模糊等人际功能。级差资源旗示评价是指说话人以级差资源作为信号向读者暗示态度意义的存在。语势（force）与聚焦（focus）为级差的两个子范畴，前者涉及质量、过程的强度与实体的数量，分别称为强化（intensification）和量化 (quantification)；后者是对事物范畴典型性或精确度的分级。量化又可分为数量（number）、体积（mass）和跨度（extent）。聚焦关注评价对象是范畴的核心成员还是边缘成员。按语义值的强弱，聚焦可细化为锐化（sharpening）和柔化（softening）。语势和聚焦按语义值的高低可分为趋上和趋下两个轴。趋上（up-scale）语义力度凸显作者强调的内容，赋予正面评价；趋下（down-scale）语义力度弱化所讨论的内容，赋予负面评价。请看例(5)中华尔街日报关于亚洲基础设施投资银行的报道：

(7) According to the official Xinhua News Agency, by March 31st. [量化：跨度], 47st. countries [量化：数量] had applied to be founding members, of which 30 [量化：数量] had already been approved and others were still awaiting approval, including Australia.(The Wall Street Journal, 2015-5-10).

例 (7) 通过趋上语义力度的数量量化词 47 和 30 和时间跨度词 by March 31 凸显了世界各国争相参加亚投行，促进本国经济发展的决心，同时也隐含了对中国牵头成立亚投行行为的正面评判。

(8) The demand for cocoa product in Asia completely [强化：过程] stopped and the Asian market basically [强化：过程] shut down. The soft [聚焦：柔化] demand in Asia comes amid falling cocoa consumption in North America and Europe.(The Wall Street Journal, 2015-5-12).

例 (8) 中趋上语义力度的过程强化词“completely”和趋下语义力度过程强化词 basically 形成对比，分别修饰“stopped”和“shut down”，反映了亚洲可可产品市场的萎缩，从侧面凸显了对世界经济复苏乏力的担忧。上例中的“soft”是柔化聚焦词语，柔化聚焦在语篇中往往旗示一种负面态度，这种负面态度的旗示同样表达了对亚洲经济担忧的情感。

5.4 结论

通过对两类报刊的具体实例分析，我们认为隐性评价理论是探究和挖掘新闻报道者的主观态度和观点的强有力的工具。在英文报刊选读课程教学过程中，通过对隐性评价资源的探讨和分析，能够帮助学生理解新闻语篇的核心思想，识别和解读字里行间的隐含意义，辨别报刊媒体背后的立场和意识形态。这对于促进英文报刊选读课程教学目标的实现，良好教学效果的取得，以及探索一套务实和有效的教学方法具有积极的指导意义。

参考文献

[1] Martin, J. R. & D, Rose. Working with Discourse: Meaning beyond the Clause [M]. London: Bookcraft Limited, 2003.

[2] 王天华 . 新闻语篇隐性评价意义的语篇发生研究 [J]. 外语学刊, 2012 (1): 104-107

[3] Martin, J. R. & P. R. R. White. The Language of Evaluation: Appraisal in English [M]. London / New York: Palgrave Macmillan, in press, 2005.

[4] Hood, Susan and James R. Martin. 2007. Invoking attitude: the play of graduation in appraising discourse. In Ruqaiya Hasan, Christian M. I. M. Matthiessen and Jonathan Webster (eds.), Continuing Discourse on Language: A Functional Perspective. Volume 2. London: Equinox. 739-764.

[5] White, P. R. R. Subjectivity, evaluation and point of view in media discourse [A]. In C. Coffin (ed.). Applying English Grammar: Functional and Corpus Approaches [C]. London: Arnold, 2004.

Chapter 6
Comparison between Oriental Philosophy and Western Philosophy

6.1 Introduction

Research is our search-around in all directions imaginable. It inevitably turns to self-scrutinize to self-direct toward comprehensive interculture as interacting varied thinking-modes searching, methodologically on how research goes fittingly, a Socratic turn of research as philosophy, research of all researches. This essay unpacks the triune intimacy, from research via philosophy to interculture, in common sense. To cite a simple trivial example not simple trivial—nothing is simple trivial—we play peekaboo with a baby giggling at it; we giggle, too. We know how the baby is delighted with the surprise and we are not, yet we continue it. We may then ask why we giggle at what we are not surprised, and answer we enjoy being with an innocent baby; and then why being-with is delightful is now a delightful theme. Human sociality has long been prominently featured in Aristotle, Heidegger, Buber, Huizinga, Wach, Levinas, Wu, and countless others (Levinas & Lingis, 1969; Wu, 2008). We dig into why sociality ubiquitous— "peekaboo" enjoyed everywhere—is joy, why it is a joy to dig into social joy. "Hide and seek" more complex can be researched in the same way.Virginia Woolf (1882-1941), an experimental novelist, critic and essayist of the 20th century, has been classified as a major modernist writer, whose unique modernist views voice her concern about the modern world, precisely the world after the World War. Woolf is also one of the most important and influential feminist writers of the twentieth century and her works are dynamically engaged with the political, philosophical, historical and materialist issues of her time.

Philosophy is, generally speaking, divorced from real life, and therefore, monotonous and rigid. But the author maintains that philosophy must be poetic. He advocates philosophy with beautiful features. Western postmodern art is closely related to real life, so art becomes life-oriented and vitalized. Philosophy may be inspired by Western postmodern art as follows: It should philosophize about life; philosophers may use reason to argue for an art-oriented realm of life and achieve a philosophy featuring beauty. Traditional Western philosophy is typical of pursuit of abstract concepts and ideals and an estrangement from the sensible world and life. To make philosophy achieve artistic beauty, we must bring to an end traditional Western philosophy. With the end of old philosophy, a new philosophy came into being with the name of "post-philosophy" . One of the features of "post-philosophy" is the union of philosophy and poetry, which is no other than making philosophy achieve artistic beauty. The union of philosophy and poetry is also an important feature of most of traditional Chinese philosophy. Traditional Chinese philosophy, especially, that of Daoism is similar to Western post-modern art. Both of them stress the realm of life and uphold the beauty of life, mind and spirit. Since the middle of the last century, under the influence of traditional Western philosophy, Chinese philosophy lost its traditional beauty. To keep this beauty, we need to go further and understand philosophy as a discipline to upgrade the realm of life. The beauty of life realm comes before the beauty of philosophy.

Therefore, Chinese philosophy needs to become life-oriented like postmodern art. Inheriting and developing Daoism philosophy while absorbing the philosophy of life shown through postmodern art, seems to be a good way for us to enhance the realm of life and pursue the beauty of philosophy. Modern western thought stresses the importance of reason, which was originally a product of the counter-movement to theocracy in medieval times and has played a positive role in liberating humanity and mobilizing their free creativity. Unfortunately, supremacy of reason understands humanity one-sidedly as mere subject of reason, ignoring or denying such non-reason aspects as human feelings, sensations or instincts. Hegel didn't reject human feelings, in fact he highly praised Aristotle for his criticism of Socrates—Plato's definition of morality lacks illogical and irrational elements. He said clearly, however, that "morality should restrict passions" , and "something rational should prevail in morality" . (Hegel: Werke, 1981). His "pure concept" theory calls off all irrational elements in particular. As a matter of fact, humanity and their history and culture must be a unity of reason and non-reason. Rule of mere reason may turn life into a tough and rigid formula. Hegel claims that mind may enjoy freedom in "concept s" , but it is these rationalistic "concepts" that make humanity lose his integrity, creativity and freedom. Postmodernism claims that elements such as sensations, desires, instincts and the like are the source of our life and creativity. Postmodern art, especially some of the "art of actions" , is no other than free and full expression of our natural features, primitive desires and passions.

Facing the turbulence of the society, the social thinkers and writers, including Woolf, who were concerned about the predicament of man, began to criticize the society and reexamine the basis of human existence. In Woolf's works, she showed great concern about the plight of modern men, appealing for harmony between man and nature, men and women, man and civilization. Taoism's central principle is that, all life, all of the performance, is an integral part of the overall, an interrelated organic unification, it comes from a deep and mysterious, the source of nature cannot explain the word itself. Everything imaginable is contained within this principle. Laozi, as the ancestor of Taoism, is devoted to exploring the harmonious existence of mankind. After 2000 and 500, as a result of the rapid expansion of the imperialism, the outbreak of world war ii, and loss of faith, modern history entered the 20th century, has more and more influence on human social unrest.

Consequently, human beings come into a crucial period. More and more celebrated writers come to realize the all-pervading disharmonious elements in the world. Woolf is one of them. As far as her exploration of harmony is concerned, she happens to share similar views with the great Chinese sage Lao Tzu.

The speech acts theory was firstly proposed by the famous British philosopher John Langshaw Austin. In his book "Austin's Initial Distinction" in 1962, Austin was a speech about consistency and expressiveness. An expression is a kind of speech, which is roughly used to state the fact, to report something is the fact, or to describe what it is. On the other hand, there are three characteristics of discourse expression:

(a) they are saying something;

(b) it cannot be implemented unless the language is used;

(c) they and verb of sex, as a main verb, in the present tense, indicative, active voice, the first sentence made it clear that the speaker wants to do what in the sentence.Austin suggests that statements are merely one kind of speech act, that any statements, if only they are uttered in appropriate circumstances, may be regarded as implicit performatives. This leads to his new account: any speech act comprises at least two and typically three sub-acts: locutionary act, illocutionary act and perlocutionary act. According to Austin, the locutionary act “includes the utterance of certain noises, the utterance of certain words in a certain construction and the utterance of them with a certain 'meaning'" In other words, it is the act of conveying literal meaning by means of syntax, lexicon and extra-linguistic knowledge.

As Austin puts it, the illocutionary act can be regarded as the force with which the sentence was employed. "Saying something will often, or even normally, produce certain consequential effects upon the feelings, thoughts, or actions of the audience, or of the speaker, or of other persons…. we shall call the performance of an act of this kind the performance of a perlocutionary act or perlocution"

John searle in 1969, the famous American linguistic philosopher to improve the speech act theory by introducing the indirect speech act theory, he thought, in a particular part of the power of the significance, meaning the only determine the strength of a specific, these are not two different behaviors, but two different labels the same behavior, he came to the conclusion that only the illocutionary act. Searle thinks (1) the basic language unit is not a symbol, but a speech act; (2) speech ACTS are governed by two kinds of rules: the regularity rules (the dynamic rules of the non-verbal behavior) and the constitutive rules (the basic rules for the behavior of speech and prepositions).Duan Kaicheng and Gu Yueguo introduced Searle's speech acts theory, involving the classification of speech acts and formal questions. Gu Yueguo reviewed the sources and methods s of Austin's speech acts theory, highlighting the classification relating to illocutionary act and defects of analyzing perlocutionary acts.

One focus of the speech act study is the Pragmatic strategy of the implementation of indirect speech act and speech act. He Zhaoxiong discussed the indirect speech act, in particular the indirect requests in English. Zhang Shaojie and Wang Xiaotong comparatively studied of the implementation strategy of the "request" acts in English and Chinese. WANG Aihuacomparatively analyzed the expression patterns of refuse acts in English and Chinese.

In China, the study of Virginia Woolf began in the 1920s. After that, from 1930 to 1950, some of her literary theories were introduced and disseminated; Her novels have been translated very widely. Woolf's main novels and essays were fully translated from the 1980s to the 1990s. Since 2000, Woolf's literary works and literary theories have been systematically studied. Previous studies of Virginia Woolf focused on various interests: historical and cultural studies; Feminist and gender studies; Post-colonial studies; Language and style research; There are other studies, such as influence and intertextuality, global acceptance, modernism and postmodernism, and so on.

Our reflections on human life include, of course, the pursuit of universal laws, even the "most universal" laws. Science is the knowledge system; The science of the most common law is also a knowledge system. But will our rethinking of life stop when we reach the knowledge system? I don't think that just knowing certain laws, including "the most common law" , is not the culmination of our thinking about life or philosophy. Perhaps the pursuit of philosophy began when the laws of science were presented to us. The characteristic of philosophical thinking is that we keep asking questions until we reach the bottom of the question: what is the ultimate basis of these laws? What attitude should we adopt towards these laws? Why these attitudes? A problem like this suits philosophy, so no other science can replace it. Problems such as these can be simply called problems in the field of life. This is the ultimate question that philosophy should study. Philosophy is the science of life, designed to promote the realm of human life (not some claim that "the business of philosophy is the most universal law"). The area of life of one person or group of people determines their philosophy, so pessimism, optimism, egoism, anthropocentrism, non-anthropocentrism, and so on. People from all walks of life have different areas of life and therefore have different philosophies. Different countries have different areas of life, so different countries have different philosophies.

However, comparative study of Woolf's modernist ideas and Taoist philosophy is rarely touched upon, which can be regarded as a research blank. In some sense, Woolf is more of a philosopher than a writer. In all her life, she has never stopped her earnest pondering upon the meanings of life and human existence in the world. Harmony and unification is an important theme both in her literary theory and in her works, which can also be found in the doctrines of Lao Tzu's philosophy. Through a comparative study of the two eminent figures in literary history, we can have an opportunity to get in touch with some brilliant wisdom of them, which will guide us to create a harmonious society. Since research on the similarities between Woolf and Lao Tzu is relatively new, studies from other perspectives have given much inspiration to this topic. In the article of "On the New Revelation of the Essence of Western Civilization in To the Lighthouse", Shen Fuying has explicated Woolf's new insight into the Western civilization in To the Lighthouse by probing into Woolf's systematic idea of the relations between man and nature, man and society, man and man, man and himself. In "Harmony: seeking for unification in opposition", Wang Peng tries to explore Woolf's life-long ideas to reach harmony in the relations between man and nature, man and man, history and reality. In "Eco-feminist Interpretation of To the Lighthouse", Wang Ping advocates reexamining the relationships between human and nature, human and society in order to realize the reconciliation to nature and androgyny. Marilyn R. Farwell, in his article "Virginia Woolf and Androgyny", has explained Virginia Woolf's androgyny from the perspective of Taoist conceptions of Yin and Yang, "a pattern of balance and dialectic in which each quality in the set of opposites is equally valid and equally contributing to the whole." Furthermore, some books are contributed to the comparative study of the two, such as, Taoism and Androgynous Ideal by Roger T. Ames, who has explored the androgynous color in Taoist views about male and female; Helen Wussow's The Nightmare of History has discussed topics of war and history; Virginia Woolf and the Discourse of Science written by Holly Henry has explored Woolf's views on science and civilization.

The thesis makes a tentative endeavor to make a comparative study of Woolf's modernist ideas and Lao Tzu's Taoist philosophy, with the purpose of promoting the mutual understanding of the ancient Chinese philosophy and Western cultures and finding out solutions to restore us to a more balanced, harmonious, and satisfying mode of living.

6.2 Relationship between Man and Natural Environment

In the Caribbean, mankind has a very close relationship with the natural environment. Contact with the biological world has convinced us that since ancient times, man has been turning to nature to question it, especially the conditions that determine his own existence. For this reason, alien creatures in such an environment must observe all the elements that make up their essence, and can transmit the deepest secrets of fauna and flora, which are often merciless. Through these actions, we will understand that everything is connected to the plant world, regardless of the endogenous or exogenous, has quickly become the Allies of nature, in the so-called "human ecosystem" created a real contact.

This dynamic and empirical methods from anthropology and cultural groups are the first factors by many stories and legends, and Creole culture is bearing the weight of the various territorial conquest of relevant testimony. Isn't it true that many wonderful stories, Creole songs, literary works are a popular form, or a way of expressing our relationship with the real world? Nature seems to dominate these women and men's daily life, they draw the lessons of life, from observation of life and life in nature and biological behavior on some sort of philosophy, these creatures are plants and trees. That's why most stories take these natural elements out of reification, give them a soul and explain the world. Sustainable development is one of the most important problems in the world today. With the rapid growth of the global population and the increasing demand for natural resources, mankind is facing increasingly serious environmental problems.

After having experienced the calamities of the World Wars, Woolf was very much concerned about the existence of humankind in modern society. The increasingly serious problems of existential crisis urged her to think about solutions for human beings. At the same time, against the background of a worldwide ecological crisis, China's ancient culture and traditions which contain a high degree of ecological wisdom, have not only aroused the concern of Chinese scholars, but also stirred up great interests of many western ecologists. Especially, Lao Tzu's Taoist philosophy, with its own unique perspective and concern about the harmony between man and nature, has developed into unique ecological thinking. These conceptions, in some sense, have much in common with the ecological views of Virginia Woolf. This Chapter probes into the ecological ideas of Lao Tzu's Taoist philosophy and that of Virginia Woolf, so as to understand and analyze the similarities as well as dissimilarities of their ecological outlooks. Detecting deeply into the ecological thinking of Lao Tzu and Virginia Woolf will have great significance for the realization of a harmonious coexistence of humans and nature, and the sustained development of ecological environment.

Man understands that nature has a dual nature, because it gives life its wish. Here, it shows its dual divinity, which is both a wife and a mother. Human destiny is not only related to the change of time and weather. It also depends on the plant's formation, which may be beneficial, because it may be evil. This internal connection between man and nature is the result of plant diversity, which has witnessed a specific biological technology that enables human beings to learn the nature of their knowledge and their mastery of the world. The relationship between man and nature is mainly a sacred relationship. Taoist ecology is based on the idea of "harmony between man and nature" , which is highly appraised according to the relationship between man and nature according to modern ecological view. To some extent, Taoism is a philosophy based on nature, striving to achieve a harmonious state between man and nature. In the technocratic industrial society, nature is used as a tool for other purposes. Today, many people realize that our attitude toward nature is very wrong. Chinese Taoism is opposed to the idea that humans rule the earth and other inhabitants. The Taoist nature is a very valuable thing in itself. In the pursuit of sustainable development and environmental protection, mankind must abandon the traditional development model and overemphasize economic interests without considering the environmental supporting capacity. In this respect, our ancestors left a lot of legacy, among which the Taoist concept of "the unity of heaven and man" deserves our attention.

From the perspective of Lao Tzu, man cultivates himself as cultivating the nature. Man and nature are united in essence and they are merged in the Tao. Lao Tzu holds the view that:

Way; One produces two; Two produce three; Three produces everything. All things have left behind them the darkness (they have come out), and to embrace the brightness that they have revealed, and they are reconciled by the breath of emptiness. This article sums up Lao zi's world view and regards tao as the basic element. In Lao zi's view, tao is the essence of the universe, and it appears before the existence of heaven and earth. The path produces a swirling pattern of cloud energy called chi. This energy eventually develops into two complementary aspects: Yin, Yin, heavy, negative, Yang, bright, light, masculine. Yin can gather into the earth, Yang can rise to the sky, two kinds of energy harmony form people. Therefore, the human body has the energy of earth and heaven in it, making it a microcosm of the world.

Taoist ecology not only discusses the relationship between man and nature from the metaphysical point of view, but also puts forward many valuable viewpoints and thoughts on how to deal with the relationship between man and nature. On the basis of natural philosophy, Taoist ecology further puts forward three basic theories, namely "the unity of heaven and man" , "the father of heaven, the earth is the mother" and "according to the natural law of tao" . The unity of man, heaven, earth and nature emphasizes the harmony between man and nature. "Heaven is father, mother earth," as the heavens and the earth humanity's parents, to humans and they get along well with each other, and respect for nature, just as we respect filial piety we parents, this is a kind of attitude, the nature of things by Taoist ecological needs treatment. "According to viz. The natural principle" put forward the principle of protecting the natural environment, and ask our behavior is in line with the nature, protect nature, and nature coordination, it become a Taoist ecological principles according to deal with the relationship between human and nature, protect the natural environment, realize ecological balance. The whole theory of man and nature is the natural philosophy foundation of Taoism ecology, which is "the starting point of the relationship between man and nature" .

To define philosophy as a universal law will lead to a monotonous understanding of human life, but it is by no means a liberal philosophy, not to mention its beauty. With the development of science and socialization of the individual, human will see him and other things in the world, and others can be integrated into a unified, the pursuit of science cannot be separated from morality. With this knowledge, life is entering its third reality - moral state, to a certain extent, human liberated from the externality of the subject and object, have more freedom. (between science and moral activities, there are economic and political activities, including our natural desire (for example, the desire of the economic activity cannot be separated from natural self-protection) and unnatural. The former is close to scientific activity and the latter is moral activity.

Therefore, the freedom of economic and political activities is also between science and morality. The four areas of life I have discussed here are general, so I have not divided the economic and political spheres of life. However, morality is always constrained by the distance between ideal and reality. When the subject and object are not fully integrated, the moral "should" is an expression.

Laozi's aim is to "let nature take its course" , advocate the unity of man and the universe, and oppose the destruction of the natural environment. In other words, people should act according to the laws of nature, or they will be punished by nature. Taoists believe that man and nature are interrelated and bound by the relationship of reciprocity and retribution. The harmony between man and nature, the kindness of mankind, the world will be peaceful and harmonious, all will become prosperous — this is a good condition for mankind. If nature is harmed by human beings, it will retaliate against humanity, causing catastrophic suffering and extinction of species. If the pursuit of development runs counter to the harmony and balance of nature, even if it has great direct interests and interests, people should restrain themselves. Insatiable human desire will lead to overexploitation of natural resources. To succeed, we must set foot on the path of failure. In Chapter 23 of the tao te ching, Lao zi expounded his views:

To sum up, in the process of globalization, with the development of economy and the progress of the society, the relationship between human and nature as human is a very important problem, but for various reasons, the relationship is not harmonious, threaten the continued survival of mankind. In order to solve the ecological problems and save mankind from the crisis of survival, Woolf called on the public to change the central point of human beings and live in harmony with nature. Woolf spent her life exploring the harmony between man and nature. She believed that since man is the product of nature, only by obeying the laws of nature can we enjoy the infinite freedom and beauty of life. She believed that man should not conquer nature by overwhelming force. Only by harmonious coexistence between man and nature can we get rid of the damage caused by the over-exploitation of nature and live a happy life forever. Her view of the balance between man and nature is consistent with that of laozi, because Taoism is known for its unity of nature, which means the unity of man and nature. Both laozi and wulff both sought the harmonious relationship between man and nature and opposed the destruction of the natural environment.

Establish the relationship between human and nature, of course, is a new league, in this league, water, water and blood mixed together, into a woman's uterus, like the depths of the earth, the new and the disturbance of resurrection life. Trees and people find a balance between the universe and ontology. Of all the stories and all of the text, the open road as a woman's body, the evil tree was erased before new life, or in front of the hero, by the penetration of light lit up the darkness of the forest, and allow the bodily resurrection of the eaten. This image is associated with many of the legendary big consuming forest, especially in Larkin, Jose in particular the stasi, Rivera (Jose Eustacio Rivera) and Victor Hugo (Victor Hugo) found in the legend of the primeval forests for centuries to come. Let us remember the verses of the French poets who painted the forest images for us:

These trees are eating jaws.

Elements, scattered in the soft air.

The reading of the text is focused on the collective imagination of trees and plants, showing the ambivalence of this motivation among Caribbean writers. But let's take a closer look at the two totem trees mentioned in some of the texts, and they are a source of poetic imagination, Jacaranda and Kapok trees.

Philosophers disagree with what they study. Although the definition of philosophy is not the consensus of philosophers, there is a common view that can be derived from the different definitions they provide. This is the philosophical view of the sober quest for truth. Philosophy tries to understand reality and to find answers to basic questions about life, knowledge, morality and humanity. The early greeks defined it as the love of wisdom, the insatiable thirst for the world around us. Philosophy tries to answer questions such as "what is the meaning and purpose of life?" "What is happiness? "What is knowledge? "How do we know we know? In this way, philosophy promotes the exploration of wisdom, which helps us to free ourselves from ignorance, prejudice, self-deception, palo-chidism, and half-truth.

The influence of nature is everywhere in people's life. The first sentence of the novel, "of course, if it is fine tomorrow" (1) means that even a small thing (to the lighthouse) will be limited by the forces of nature. With the development of the novel, readers will feel the power of nature more strongly: nature affects the ultimate meaning of human life. The understanding and realization of this ultimate meaning epitomises the journey of the lighthouse, and the decisive factor of success is the weather condition; The accumulation of human cognition of the whole universe is the epitome of books, while the preservation of books depends on the humidity of air and the strength of wind. In addition, the living environment is the epitome of the island, and the survival of the island depends on the height of the waves.

In addition, we must note that no matter how human beings view nature, it exists objectively and measures the world in its own way. In the face of mankind, the firmness of nature reflects confrontation. Under the threat of all these uncontrollable factors, man's efforts to save his own civilization, like Mrs. McNab's, seem to be weak. Woolf published her most difficult novel, the waves. Both formally and content can be regarded as the peak of Woolf's literary career. In this novel, Woolf pursues the essence of human life and life.

In A sketch of the Past, Woolf recalls her past as a child. When she was watching a flower in the garden, she got the revelation that flower was not an isolated thing, and it was in fact connected and fused with the earth, human beings and the whole universe.

When talking about trees, Bernard discovered the firmness of nature. Recognizing that the universe is governed by immutable laws, everything in nature must follow these laws, and Woolf further argued that man should obey the laws of nature. People should respect the laws of nature and develop the mutually beneficial relationship between culture and nature, instead of using culture as a defense against nature. Only in this way can man truly understand and live in harmony with nature. At this point, Woolf follow the idea of natural law, and Lao tzu's "the way" thought is consistent, is essentially the principle of protecting the natural environment, the behavior of asked us to comply with nature, protect nature, the coordination of nature. The fusion of the natural scenes and the growth of human beings show the close relationship between the universe. In addition, Woolf conveys her the thought of "holistic" , namely everything on earth, whether living or dead, is said to have its own spirit, there should be a balance between man and nature, cannot be ignored, even can not be broken. In order to maintain this balance, Woolf does not allow a binary model, which is both positive and negative on one hand and dominant on the other. She believes that humans are equal to other species, such as plants, animals and the environment around them. "Of course we are animals," said Bernard. (Woolf, volume 245) this reminds us of the old man's philosophy of "unity of nature" . In fact, Woolf and Lao tzu both sought harmony between man and nature. According to Woolf ideas about "wholeness" , human should not alienate or isolate him, regard it as his enemies, conquered or occupation, because he is part of nature, he cannot live without it.

6.3 Traditional Thoughts of Ancient China's Philosophy

Historically, many survey method is in the spring and autumn period (770 BC - 476 BC), during the warring states period (475 BC - 221 BC), but most is interrupted, until after a long time never recovered, because the first emperor of qin dynasty and their burning books about unified China in 221 BC. This undoubtedly has a great impact not only on the development of research methods, but also on the entire Chinese civilization.

From the perspective of epistemology, the Chinese people are more holistic, intuitive, moralistic and immanent than westerners, under the profound influence of traditional Chinese Taoism and Confucianism. Lin yutang in his country and my people carefully analyzed China's development of natural science epistemological reasons. According to him, "the Chinese mind only likes moral platitudes." Experiments have never been considered and no scientific method has been developed. The Chinese believe in common sense and insight, and rely heavily on intuition to solve the mysteries of nature. One of the most important concepts of Taoism is wuwei. In the tao te jing, the principle of "nothing" is embodied in the full text. There are many explanations for this word; A form, usually accepted in a mild environmental thought, that works or ACTS in accord with nature. Although strictly translated as inaction or inaction, most writers do not regard wuwei as "no action" , but "no pretentious performance" . According to this view, wuwei refers to the cultivation of a state in which our actions are completely consistent with the ups and downs of the elements of the natural world. All of this makes it easy for us to respond to environmental needs, including ourselves.

The practice of wuwei is regarded as the highest form of virtue in Taoism. Lao tzu, with the supreme motto of wuwei, said, "Help everything to be natural and free from any interference." "(Legge, trans. The book of ethics 11. It can be seen from this chapter that Wuwei thought is the soul of Taoist philosophy. Laozi pays attention to wuwei, spontaneity, humanism, relativism and nihilism. If tao is the way, then Te or virtue is its active expression. Wuwei, or not to do practical things, is the central tenet of Taoism. This non-action can be compared to water:

The softest things in the world are the hardest. There is no such thing as a place where there is no crack. I know what it's good for. I don't do anything. There are few people in the world who can say nothing, not the benefits of action. (Legge trans. The tao te ching 17)

On the relationship between human and nature, the subject - object "dichotomy" is one of the traditional western culture analysis methodology, its performance is: in the process of acquiring knowledge, man's subjective world is objective world. Because nature itself is the object of cognition, it can be separated from others. In other words, man and nature are independent of each other. Consequently, advances in natural science followed. Greek culture is the origin of science. The greeks laid the foundation for natural science, because the Greek mind is essentially an analytical mind. Democritus' philosophy is basically natural philosophy, reflecting the external essence. Pythagorean philosophy approximates mathematics. Socrates, Plato and Aristotle further distinguish between man and nature. Wuwei in the human life, means to abandon the false morality, pursue the real life. Practice is to pursue the right attitude, morality and way of life. As a way of life, wuwei's way of life is to follow the tao. It aims to preserve individual freedom and spiritual freedom by escaping the bondage of the secular world. Wuwei does not mean to do nothing, but to be free from any interference. Instead, it means doing what needs to be done, not more. "Wu wei Tibet" is Lao zi's deep consciousness of social and political crisis at that time. In this sense, wuwei's theory actually expresses his unhappiness with the dark society. Therefore, wuwei can act as a form of resistance, not just passive obedience. It is the product of turbulent times, closely connected with the life experience of laozi. .

Western philosophers in modern times, including Descartes and Bacon, approached philosophical theories from the perspective of natural science. Kant engaged himself in a kind of philosophical study which was actually based on natural science, especially mathematics and physics.Living during the Spring and Autumn period (770-476 B.C.) and the period of Warring States (475-221 B.C.), Lao Tzu was relentless in criticizing the selfish and heartless ruling class. It was a time of turbulence, when wars, intrigues and usurpations were common occurrences.

In face with a society full of intrigues, hypocrisies and strife, he poignantly criticizes the inequitable social system and exposes the dark side of society with the stand of wu-wei. In Chapter 53 of Tao Te Ching, Lao Tzu relentlessly criticizes the luxury of rulers:

If I were suddenly to become known, and (put into a position to) conduct (a government) according to the Great Tao, what I should be most afraid of would be a boastful display. The great Tao (or way) is very level and easy; but people love the by-ways. Their court (yards and building) shall be well kept, but their fields shall be ill-cultivated, and their granaries very empty. They shall wear elegant and ornamented robes, carry a sharp sword at their girdle, pamper themselves in eating and drinking, and have a superabundance of property and wealth···-such (princes) may be called robbers and boasters. This is contrary to the Tao surely! (Legge, trans. Tao Te Ching 20)

Just because there is no analytical method, China lags behind in science. In the relationship between man and nature, China's cultural tradition USES the spirit of "man is an inseparable part of nature" , which is a holistic methodology combining man with nature. "Man is an inalienable part of nature" , which means that nature and human beings coexist. Therefore, in the process of acquiring knowledge, it is not an isolated cognitive object. Nature is closely bound up with human life. Naturally, people do not stress the so-called objective and natural research, but pay more attention to the state of communication between nature and people. Therefore, the focus of Chinese culture has always been on the discussion of people's spiritual activities and status, rather than natural or natural science.

The overall thinking is also clearly reflected in the summer calendar. According to the summer calendar, the combination of sky (universe), earth and man is the only way to explain any event. The belief that there are several important features: 1) human activities in the whole life system (people, animals, trees), operating in the life system in inanimate systems run (the material world, represented by the earth), the system is controlled by the (natural law represented by day). 2) emphasize the coordination of these elements in the universe. The harmony and stability of the universe depend on the unity of these elements. Maintaining the harmony of the universe is the only way for human activities to succeed. In this chapter, he explains how to manage a country by cooking small fish, which is not a simple task and requires more caution. Here, Lao tzu wanted to illustrate the significance of wuwei's reign in a country. Therefore, the essence of wuwei is the resistance to the corrupt and dark society.

6.4 Traditional Thoughts of Western Philosophy

As this article has revealed earlier, the goal of science is a coherent system. Therefore, in the field of science, logic is greatly enhanced — it plays an important role in epistemology, which provides a mechanism for the expansion of knowledge. As a by-product of reasoning, logic provides the recipe, that is, how people should reason. There are two modes of human reasoning: rationality and intuition. The west has devalued rational scientific knowledge and intuitive religious knowledge, whereas China has done the opposite.

As discussed in the first section, daoism believes that wuwei is not doing nothing, but is free of any interference. In this sense, wuwei can act as a form of resistance, not just passive obedience. In fact, the essence of wuwei is the rebellion against the dark society. Woolf lived in the age of imperialism and lived through world war. He was very concerned about human conditions. In her literary works, we can see a kind of wuwei complex which is consistent with the teachings of laozi. Virginia Woolf (1882-1941) lived in an age of despair.

Since Western culture sets seeking truth as the highest goal, it is bound to lay emphasis on logical reasoning, and analyzing is sure to be the cognitive method of knowing the object by the subject within the Western "subject- object dichotomy" framework. For one thing, the cognitive object is metaphysical matter, something beyond physical phenomenon. For another, seeking truth entails abstraction from phenomenon. So it is only through logical reasoning and analyzing that one can fulfill such process.

Aristotle's organic theory laid the foundation for deductive reasoning and formed formal logic. Inference is deductively valid, if and only if there is no possibility, all premises are true and the conclusion false. The concept of deductive validity can be strictly expressed as a system of formal logic, which is the semantic concept of understanding.

The 20th century witnessed the unprecedented prosperity of science and technology and brought a dazzling material civilization. But the progress of science and technology seems to have failed to bring a harmonious world to mankind. Contrast with the dazzling material achievement is the person's spiritual emptiness and anxiety. In Mrs. Dalloway's life, criticism of society was mainly reflected in the heroine, Clarissa Dalloway, who used wuwei as a manifestation of social resistance. Unlike the other characters in the novel, clarissa doesn't play an important role in life. She did not participate in religious, political, charitable or social reforms. She don't use religion as miss kilman, don't like lady bruton eager support social programs, not like Peter Walsh and seek personal passion, not to take part in social activities or the pursuit of power and Hugh William, and does not use science as an excuse for his own purpose of famous doctors - bradshaw. Clarissa refuses to conform to her social role, preferring to quit her private life. Her life was a kind of order and etiquette, and her posture was gentle. In the face of the alienated world destroyed by world war, she used her own way to prevent herself from being disturbed by the outside world. In this sense, her tendency to retire into private life is in line with the principles of lao-wei.

In contrast to her negative attitude towards those who are despotic, clarissa sympathises with siptimus and even agrees with himself, because he chooses death to rebel against authority. In the novel, siptimus Smith is portrayed as a young man going to war, and his thoughts are filled with idealism and passion. In the novel, he gets what he expects: friendship, promotion, survival, marriage, especially the dignity of men. When his friend Evans was killed, septimus "is far from showing any feelings, also don't realize that this is the end of a friendship, he was glad his feeling very little, and very reasonable." The war taught him. This is sublime. He went through the whole show, the friendship, the European war, the death, the promotion, less than 30 years old, doomed to live. But it won't last long. When he realized that he could not feel the death of Evans, he collapsed. His impotence frightened him, and he felt that it was an unforgivable sin, and that he was overwhelmed by guilt. He was unhinged by the experience of war. After a brutal war, he began to criticize the social system that led to war and refused to compromise with society. Dr Holmes and Mr Bradshaw heal the west partyms, hoping that they will overcome his resistance to social standards and eventually adapt him to social norms. In other words, he needs to be built by an existing ideology. Septimus has an ostracism to him. "once you're down," he said to himself, "human nature is on you. Sherlock Holmes and bradshaw are on you." They scoured the desert. They screamed and flew to the wild. The rack and thumb screws are applied. Human nature is cruel. By killing himself, he overcame those who made life unbearable. Although he had "abandoned life" , he did not lose the independence of his soul. Thus, the death of septimus was also a revolt against society, and clarissa meditated on his death: "death is resistance" . He found the meaning of death, and his death was seen as a revolt against the tyranny of personal liberty.

Clarissa most clearly asserts her rebellious thought when she identifies herself with Septimus. She understands his gesture of defiance against an authoritarian that would force his soul, for both of them are obsessed in different ways with a compulsive need for personal freedom and are at odds with the prescribed social codes. Through her sympathy with Septimus, Clarissa has also expressed her criticism on the war and military virtues, and even the social constitutes which initiates the war. And the traditional culture that denies the reality of war by covering it with images of glamour and heroism is also criticized.

Francis Bacon was the founder of inductive reasoning. The induction validity requires a reliable generalization of some observations. The task of providing this definition may be carried out in various ways, some less formal; Some of these definitions use mathematical models of probability. Induction is considered to be the method of scientific discovery.

The concept of positivism can be traced back to the inductive reasoning of Francis Bacon. Positivism believes that there is an external world outside. We can only understand the facts of the outside world through experiments and manipulation. Empirical observation is used to verify scientific hypotheses. As the observation increases, the likelihood of the hypothesis increases. Therefore, this is the only way to find out scientifically, that is to say, observation is the premise of theory. Woolf's criticism of the war did not contradict her wuwei complex. Because war and conflict are barriers to the arrival of humans in the country. In this sense, the criticism of military war reveals that Woolf is living a life of inaction. Wuwei's ultimate goal is to pursue the real life, which means a simple and harmonious spiritual free life, which is in harmony with nature. As long as you don't interfere in anything, you can achieve a lot and live a real life, because "the person standing on his toes is not firm. People who stretch their legs can't walk (easily). So people who show themselves don't shine; There is no difference between those who advocate their own views; He who boasts of himself does not find his good. Conceited people are not allowed to be superior. The tao te ching .

The real life was what clarissa was after. She always tries to penetrate the surface to see the true humanity. Of all the characters in the novel, clarissa is the only one who, through her inactivity, penetrates life, achieves unity without loss of personal integrity and spiritual freedom.

In her eyes, the moths were lovely, "how she likes the gray moths, on the cherry pie, on the primrose." when she felt lost themselves in the process of life, she felt a thrill of joy, just like the sun rises, as time went by, she found a sense of harmony and integrity. She was quiet in the midst of turmoil, creating order in a chaotic world. To attain spiritual freedom, we must first protect the privacy of the soul. Clarissa is a shrewd judge of character, he and septimus, instinctively despise Sir William bradshaw and all threats to privacy the angel of the transformation of the soul, "there is a kind of solemn things" . The old woman was only being herself, as if she were not old, an eternal ghost, under the shelter of distance and solitude. To experience life, one must be alone. Clarissa believes that a soul can neither govern nor obey. This is clarissa's "ultimate riddle" . Clarissa cherishes her spiritual life, and so cherishes the privacy of her soul. Her self-resignation is a way of protecting the privacy of the soul, to counter the forces that threaten it.

Only with the freedom of soul, can one immerge himself in the nature and become oneness with it. Clarissa has the exquisite feeling of the nature. In the flower shop, she is extremely excited at seeing the beautiful flowers, "And then, opening her eyes, how fresh…the roses looked; and dark and prim the red carnations, holding their heads up; and all the sweet peas spreading in their bowls, tinged violet, snow white, pale…as if it were the evening and girls in muslin frocks came out to pick sweet peas and roses after the superb summer's day" Intoxicated in the beauty of the flowers, she even feels "every flower seems to burn by itself, softly, purely in the misty beds"

On this basis, you can enter a world beyond and enjoy the beauty of life in spirit. Clarissa against interference in thoughts, take life as a simple, natural and harmonious, the rhythm of the waves, is constantly rising and falling, "the waves of the sea to collect, excessive balance, decrease; Collection and autumn; The whole world seemed to be saying that "all this" was getting heavier and heavier, until even the heart of the man lying on the beach said it was all. clarissa follows the natural rhythm and integrates into the movement of life. Clarissa's vision of life was a freedom. She freed herself from worldly bondage, lived in harmony with nature, and enjoyed absolute freedom in the stream of life.

Of all the ancient philosophers in the zhou dynasty, only Moses and humphreys developed a style similar to that of convincing reasoning. According to mohism, the three laws of true knowledge and reasoning are :1) must have foundation or foundation; 2) general investigation must be carried out; 3) there must be practical application. The second law is the beginning of the first empirical method in Chinese history. The first two laws have similar scientific method characteristics. There are five ways of reasoning: deduction, comparison, analogy, analogy and induction. The period between the first world war and the second world war was a period of transition, a period of division and stability. After two world wars, there is no doubt that social and cultural emotions are different. Due to the consequences of the great war, the post-industrial society has gone from high integration to division and conflict, and modern cultural and social structures have been destroyed. At that time, western civilization was experiencing a serious alienation crisis. Because traditional beliefs are shattered by threats from the outside world and from the inner world, feelings of loneliness, alienation, apathy, and emptiness pervades almost everyone's heart.

The alienation and dehumanization of modern humans have become one of the most distinctive themes of twentieth century literature. As Erich Fromm pointed out in his famous book, the society of reason:

6.5 Conclusion

Through comparing the epistemological differences between the West and China, it is safe for us to conclude that lack of science in ancient China can be attributed to distinct patterns of methodology, reasoning and truth-seeking, and dissimilar understanding of the relationship between man and nature.The thesis makes a tentative endeavor to make a comparative study on Western Philosophy and ancient China's philosophy, with the purpose of promoting the mutual understanding of the ancient Chinese philosophy and Western cultures and finding out solutions to restore us to a more balanced, harmonious, and satisfying mode of living.

Bibliography

[1]Ames, R. T. Taoism and the Androgynous Ideal. New York: Philo Press, 1981.

[2]Berman, Jessica. Modernist Fiction, Cosmopolitanism, and the Politics of Community. Cambridge: Cambridge University Press, 2001.

[3]Bloom, Harold, ed. Virginia Woolf's To the lighthouse. New York: Chelsea House Publishers, 1988

[4]Bond, Alma Halbert. Who killed Virginia Woolf? New York: Human Science Press, Inc, 1989.

[5]Collines, Robert G. Virginia Woolf's Black Arrows of Sensation: The

Waves. Devon: Arthur H. Stockwell Limited, 1962.

[6]De Beauvoir, Simore. The Second Sex. London: Jonathan Cape, 1972.

[7]Duyvendak, J. J. L. Tao Te Ching. London : John Murray, 1954.

[8]Farwell, Marilyn R. Contemporary Literature. Wisconsin: University of Wisconsin Press, 1975.

[9]Fleishman, Avrom. Virginia Woolf: a critical reading. Baltimore & London: the Johns Hopkins University Press, 1975.

[10]Fromm, E. The Sane Society. New York: Rinehart & Company, 1955.

[11]Glotfelty, Cheryll, and Herold Fromm. The Ecocriticism Reader: Landmarks in Literary Ecology. Georgia: The University of Georgia Press, 1996.

[12]Gordon, Lyndall. Virginia Woolf: A Writer's Life. London: Oxford University Press, 1984.

[13]Henry, Holly. Virginia Woolf and the Discourse of Science: The Aesthetics of Astronomy. Cambridge: Cambridge University Press, 2003.

[14]Heilbrun, Carolyn. "Woolf and Androgyny" in Morris Beja (ed.) Critical Essay on Virginia Woolf. Massachusettes: G. H. Hall & Co. Bost, 1985.

[15]Holtby, Winifred. Virginia Woolf. London: Wishart, 1932.

[16]Hussey, Mark, and Vara Neverow-Turk,ed. Virginia Woolf miscellanies. New York: Pace University Press, 1992.

[17]Meeker, Joseph W. The Comedy of Survival: Studies in Literary Ecology. New York: Charles Scribner's Sons, 1974.

[18]Schwartz, Benjamin I. The World of Thought in Ancient China. Cambridge：Harvard University Press, 1985.

[19]Sheehan, Paul. Modernism, Narrative and Humanism. Cambridge: Cambridge University Press, 2002.

[20]Smith, Mark J. Ecologism: Toward Ecological Citizenship. Barkingham: Open University Press, 1998.

[21]Taylor, Paul. Respect for Nature. Princeton: Princeton University Press, 1986.

[22]Tratner, Michael. Modernism and Mass Politics. California: Stanford University Press, 1995.

[23]Woolf, Virginia. Mrs. Dalloway. Hertfordshire: Wordsworth Editions Limited, 1996.

[24]Cabanne, P. (Trans.) (2003). Dialogues with duchamp. Beijing: China Renmin University, 46 .

[25]Wang, R. Y. (2004). Through duchamp. Beijing: China Renmin University. 221-223.

[26]Hegel, G. W. F. (1981). Theorie werkausgabe. Werke. Berlin: Suhrkamp Verlag. S134-S144,S2 23.

[27]Zhang, S.-Y. (2007). Realm and culture. Beijing: Renmin Press. 125-130, 160-162, 291.

[28]Zhang, S.-Y. (2007). Relations between heaven and man (2nd ed.). Beijing: Renmin Press. 157, 315- 329. The New Encyclopedia Britannica (1993). 25. 733.

[29] 高奋，鲁彦 . 近 20 年国内弗吉尼亚 · 伍尔夫研究述评 . 外国文学研究，2004(5).

[30] 葛荣晋 . 道家文化与现代文明 . 北京：中国人民大学出版社，1996.

[31] 李晓文 .《海浪》的生态视角解读 . 湖南农业大学学报，2006(4).

[32] 刘庆华 . 老子 · 庄子 . 广州：广州出版社，2001.

[33] 刘笑敢 . 论《老子》之雌性比喻的诠释问题 . 中央研究院中国文史哲研究集刊，2002(5).

[34] 林语堂 . 老子的智慧 . 长春：时代文艺出版社，1988.

[35] 老子 . 道德经 . 北京：蓝天出版社，2006.

[36] 裴广川 . 环境伦理学 . 北京：高等教育出版社，2002.

[37] 孙以楷 . 道家与中国哲学 · 先秦卷 . 北京：人民文学出版社，2004.

[38] 申富英 . 论《到灯塔去》对西方文明的再认识 . 山东大学学报，2003(1).

[39] 武跃速 . 宇宙人生的诉说—解读伍尔夫的诗小说 . 国外文学，2003(1).

[40] 庄子 . 庄子 . 北京：中华书局，2007.

Chapter 7
Textual Contrastive Studies

7.1 Introduction

The traditional concern of linguistics has been the abstract formal system (called "langue" , "competence" or "code") of language. In the last three decades, there has been a shift of focus in the study of language. An increasing interest arose in analyzing the way sentences work in sequence to produce coherent stretches of language. In fact the search for larger linguistic units and structures has been pursued by scholars from many disciplines. Linguists: investigate the features of language that binds sentences when they are used in sequence;Ethnographers (ethnography: scientific study of different races of people) and sociologists: study the structure of social interaction, esp. as manifested in the way people enter into dialogue;Anthropologists: analyze the structure of myths and folk-tales;Psychologists: carry out experiments on the mental processes underlying comprehension;And further contributions have come from those concerned with artificial intelligence, rhetoric, philosophy, and style.The common concern of the approaches: they stress the need to see language as a dynamic, social, interactive phenomenon——whether between speaker and listener, or writer and reader.

It is against this intellectual background that macro-linguistics emerged and developed. Macrolinguistics can be characterized by three points:

A concern for communicative competence rather than for "linguistic" competence in Chomsky's senses;

An attempt to describe linguistic events within their extralinguistic settings;

The search for units of linguistic organization larger than the single sentence.

(James, 1980:100-2)

when searching for some relevant information to Context on the net, I came across an impressive statement: An utterance in isolation can mean a thousand things: a more determinate meaning exists only by virtue of the rich background against which the utterance was produced.

e.g. Flying planes can be dangerous.

This is undoubtedly an ambiguous sentence. Then what if this sentence is expanded to include more words or sentences which can provide a richer language environment?

e.g. Don't fly kite on the runway of the airport. Flying planes can be dangerous.

His father is a pilot. He definitely knows that flying planes can be dangerous.

From the above example, we can see the importance of studying the interrelationship between sentences, rather than sentences in isolation. In fact, textual analysis or discourse analysis is one of the most important current trends in linguistic research.

7.2 Text and Discourse

Text is a piece of spoken or written language. One important feature of a text is that a full understanding of it is often impossible without reference to the context in which in occurs.

It may be of considerably length, e.g. a fairy tale, a novel, or a sermon;

It may consist of only one word, e.g. DANGER on the warning sign of a power substation

Discourse is a general term for examples of language use, i.e. language that has been

produced as the result of an act of communication. According to van Dijk (1980:29), the difference between text and discourse lies in that the former is a theoretical conception related to a language users' Competence while the latter is a notion realistically perceived which is related to the user's Performance.

Text Analysis and Discourse Analysis

In this study, we see the two terms as complementary, believing that text analysis starts with linguistic forms and works outwards to investigate in which contexts they are appropriate, whereas discourse analysis starts with the communicative situations and works inwards to find the formal linguistic correlates to the situational variables. TA is concerned with the formal devices used for establishing inter-sentential connections, and units "above" the sentence; DA handles considerations of language use.

Essential characteristics of text

De Beaugrande and Dressler (1981) (Introduction of Text Linguisitcs) proposed seven defining characteristics of a text or, in their terms, seven standards of textuality. (All seven can be regarded as CT.)

intentionality (the fulfillment of the author's intentions)

acceptability (relevance to the text receiver)

informativity (right amount of information with regard to the reader)

situationality (location in a discrete socio-cultural context in a real time and place)

intertextuality (relationship with other texts which share characteristics with it) cohesion, and coherence.

Failure to comply with any of these seven characteristics makes a text non-communicative. Of these seven characteristics the most important two are cohesion and coherence.

Cohesion and coherence are related to the appropriateness of what one writes or speaks in verbal communication. A well-formed sentence can be appropriate to its context in two ways:

Formally appropriate: not violating the rules of textual organization;(cohesion-related)

Functionally appropriate: communicating what the speaker intends. (coherence-related)

Formal inappropriacy to linguistic context results in incohesion of the text, while functional inappropriacy will lead to a breakdown in communication, that is incoherence.

Cohesion refers to the structural and/or semantic relationships holding between the different elements o a text. (between different sentences; between different parts of a sentence)

A: Will Tom do it?

B: Yes, he will.

Link between Tom and he and between will and will.Coherence refers to the relationships which link the meanings of sentences in a text or the utterances in a discourse. The links may be based on the shared knowledge of the participants in a communicative event, e.g.

A: Could you give me a lift home?

B: Sorry, I'm visiting my sister.

There is no grammatical or lexical link (cohesive ties) between A's question and B's reply but the exchange has coherence because both A and B knows that

B's sister lives in the opposite direction to A's home. (presupposition)

The structure of text mainly concerns two aspects: cohesion (form) & coherence (meaning).(Cohesion in English, by Halliday and Hasan, 1976) (Coherence in Spontaneous Text, edited by Gernsbacher & T. Givon, 1995)

Cohesive devices (according to Halliday and Hasan,

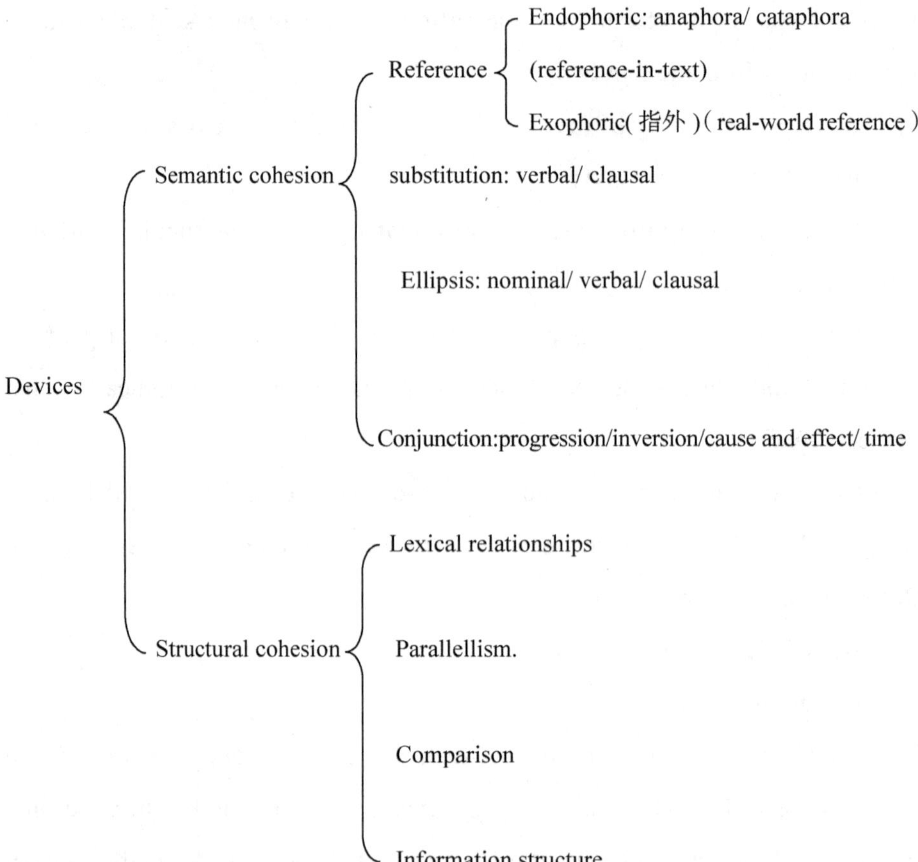

According to Xu Yulong, there are 'semantic cohesive devices', and 'structural cohesive devices', which are: information structure (given/new-tone-tone group), thematic structure (theme/rheme-starting point/contents, when theme happens to be a given information, it is called 'topic', and the rest 'comment'), parallel structure, etc.

Substitution

Substitution refers to the replacement of a previous expression with a pro-form.

1) We invited Mary and John to dinner because we liked them.

2) I've got a pencil. Do you have one?

3)A: Will we get there on time?

B: I think so.（Sometimes auxiliaries may even encode the whole of the predicates in the preceding sentence.)

4) 甲：我们能买这本书吗？

乙：我想能（买这本书）。

英汉替代手段对比

Category	English	Chinese
Nominal substitution	One, ones, the same, so	的，者，同样（的），一样（的）
Verbal substitution	Do, do so	干，来，弄，搞
Clausal substitution	So, not	（不）这样，（不）这么，（不）是，不然，要不

差异：

英语有词的屈折变化形式，所以名词性替代词有单复数形式的区分，动词替代词有时态上的形式变化，而汉语则无。inflection 非一一对应，如英语中的替代关系在相应的汉语表达中可能体现为照应关系。

汉语中替代现象出现的频率要低于英语，主要原因在于汉语往往使用原词复现的方式来达到语篇的衔接。（朱永生等 P59）re-occurrence of the original words

Ellipsis: nominal, verbal, clausal ellipsis

Ellipsis is to create cohesion by leaving out what can be taken over from preceding discourse. (Halliday and Hasan, 1976:196) . In other words, it leaves something unsaid that is understood or inferable from the context.

Ellipsis is usually anaphoric in English, but may also be cataphoric.

A: Have you been to Moscow?

B: (I have) never (been to Moscow). anaphoric

Because Alice won't (dust the furniture), Mary has to dust the furniture. cataphoric

Zero-anaphora: a form of personal reference; a special kind of ellipsis that characterizes the textual organization of Chinese.

贾母一面说，一面来看宝玉，只见今日这顿打，不比往日，有是心疼，有是生气，也抱着哭个不了。——《红楼梦》

From the sight that met her eyes she could tell that this had been no ordinary beating. It filled her with anguish for the sufferer and fresh anger for the man who had inflicted it, and for a long time she clung to the inert form and wept…… (D. Hawkes, Trans. The Story of the Stone)

In the above passage, all the personal pronouns referring anaphorically to "贾母" (the Old Ancestress), which appears only initially in the text, are ellipted.

Zero-anaphora occurs more frequently in Chinese than in English.

Zero-anaphora can only occur with languages in which the subject and predicate of a clause are not bound by formal grammatical ties. Since English is a language in which the Subject and the predicate verb must be in agreement to each other in terms of person and number, zero-anaphora usually does not apply with its texts.

Conjunction:

This method has been widely adopted. However, it is not yet clear that it is the best method.

Lastly, could I ask all of you to keep this information a secret?

1) additives: and, besides

2) adversatives: however, instead

3) temporals: then, lastly

4) continuatives: now, anyway

Winter (1971) (Connection in science material. Science and Technology in a Second Language. CILT, London) identifies the five most frequent categories of connectives in scientific texts:

1) logical sequence: thus, therefore, then, thence, consequently, so..

2) contrast: however, in fact, conversely···

3) doubt and certainty: probably, possibly, indubitably

4) non-contrast: moreover, likewise, similarly..

5) expansion: for example, in particular···

These account for 89% of all the connectives in the texts analyzed.

(A discourse marker is a word or phrase used in conversation to signal the speaker's intention to mark a boundary.Anyway, I have to be going now.)

Discourse marker

Some words and phrases help to develop ideas and relate them to one another. These kinds of words and phrases are often called discourse markers. Note that most of these discourse markers are formal and used when speaking in a formal context or when presenting complicated information in writing. with regard to; regarding; as regards; as far as ··· is concerned, as for These expressions focus attention on what follows in the sentence. This is done by announcing the subject in advance. As regards and as far as…is concerned usually indicate a change of subject

Examples:

His grades in science subjects are excellent. As regards humanities … With regard to the latest market figures we can see that ... Regarding our efforts to improve the local economy, we have made ... As far as I am concerned, we should continue to develop our resources. As for John's thoughts, let's take a look at this report he sent me.

on the other hand; while; whereas

These expressions give expression to two ideas which contrast but do not contradict each other. For Examples:

Football is popular in England, while in Australia they prefer cricket. We've been steadily improving our customer service center. On the other hand our shipping department needs to be redesigned. Jack thinks we're ready to begin whereas Tom things we still need to wait.

however, nonetheless, nevertheless

All these words are used to present two contrasting ideas. Examples:

Smoking is proved to be dangerous to the health. Nonetheless, 40% of the population smokes.

Our teacher promised to take us on a field trip. However, he changed his mind last week.

Peter was warned not to invest all of his savings in the stock market. Nevertheless, he invested and lost everything.

moreover, furthermore, in addition

We use these expressions to add information to what has been said. The usage of these words is much more elegant than just making a list or using the conjunction ‘and’. Examples:

His problems with his parents are extremely frustrating. Moreover, there seems to be no easy solution to them.

I assured him that I would come to his presentation. Furthermore, I also invited a number of important representatives from the local chamber of commerce.

Our energy bills have been increasing steadily. In addition to these costs, our telephone costs have doubled over the past six months.

therefore, as a result, consequently

These expressions show that the second statement follows logically from the first statement. Examples:

He reduced the amount of time studying for his final exams. As a result, his marks were rather low.

We’ve lost over 3,000 customers over the past six months. Consequently, we have been forced to cut back our advertising budget.

The government has drastically reduced its spending. Therefore, a number of programs have been canceled.

Lexical Relationships (Lexical Cohesion)

Semantic cohesion may also be achieved by having one lexical item entering into a structural relationship with another.

The flowers were lovely. He liked the tulips best.

Foremost among the lexical relationships are synonymy and hyponymy.

Parallelism

Have you ever seen a pig fly? Have you ever seen a fish walk? (rhetoric questions)

My paintings the visitors admired. My sculptures they disliked. (Object-Subject-Verb sequences)

Comparison

Geographically, Canada is greater than the United States.

Art is long; life is short.

Information Structure: refers to the use of word order, intonation, stress and other devices to indicate how the message expressed by a sentence is to be understood.

Theme: the known information (the information which is not new to the reader or listener).

Rheme: the unknown information (the information that is new to the reader or listener).

Topic is the part of a sentence which names the person, thing, or idea about which something is said (Comment). Like the concept of Theme and Rheme, the concept of topic and Comment is different from the Subject and Predicate in that the former is related to the information structure of a sentence while the latter to the grammatical structure of a sentence (Syntax).

As for your suggestion, we will discuss it at tomorrow's meeting.

(Subject) (Predicate)

(Topic) (comment)

Not frequently, though, Topic-Comment and Subject-Predicate may coincide with each other in a sentence, for example:

We went downtown with Peter.

Most languages fall into two groups in terms of their information structure: Subject-prominent languages and topic-prominent languages. A Subject-Prominent language is a language in which the grammatical units of Subject and Predicate are basic to the structure of sentences and in which sentences usually have Subject-Predicate structure. English is a SP language, since sentences such as the following are a usual sentence type:

He has already been to the new airport. (Subject+Predicate)

A TP language is one in which the informational units of topic and comment are basic to the structure of sentences. Chinese is a typical Topic-Prominent language, since sentences with Topic-Comment structure are a usual sentence type in it. The information carries in the above English, the Subject of a sentence is often, but not always, its Theme.

Different languages preferring different cohesive devices. One thing we are sure about is that while every language has at its disposal a set of devices for maintaining textual cohesion, different languages have preferences for certain of these devices and neglect the other. Coherence: Coherence seems to have been given more emphasis or attention than cohesion in the past twenty years:

Halliday & Hasan: On the basis of studying cohesive devices, they explore the semantic relations between different components inside text.

Fries (1983), Danes (1974): Thematic progression(主位推进) (see 朱永生等 P103-104) (A sentence is normally composed of a theme and a rheme) (see the major types of patterns of thematic progression, P103)

Brown, Yule, Widdowson, etc.: They study coherence from the extra-linguistic angle, i.e. shared knowledge.

Givon, etc.: They believe that coherence is a mental phenomenon, so their analysis is basically psychological or cognitive.

One of the most influential articles of this school of thought is: Coherence in text vs. coherence in mind. By T. Givon (1995)

Classic remarks: (p1, by T. Givon)

"The coherence we are really after is not the coherence of the external text but rather the coherence of the mind that produce, store and retrieve the mental text…we study the coherence of external text as a useful heuristic in order to get insights about the coherence of mental text, and about the mind that produces it."

(tool —— target)

e.g. Accessibility Theory proposed by Ariel

high accessibility markers —— zero, pronoun

medium accessibility markers —— this/that + NP

low accessibility markers —— proper noun, the +NP

(The antecedent of each type can be found in linguistic context, physical context and encyclopedic context respectively.)

Based on his study of the papers written in English by international students, Kaplan (1966) (Cultural thought patterns in intercultural education. *Language Learning*, 16:1&2, 1-20) concludes that people with different linguistic and cultural backgrounds tend to think in different modes or patterns, and he illustrates the major thinking patterns graphically in different diagrams.

7.3 Conclusion

English texts are characterized by linear organization and development. Typically, English articles, essays, feature stories, or even book length works tend to start with an introductory paragraph or part, which usually states in an explicit way what the writer is going to be concerned with in the work and, esp. in the case of argumentative writings, the basic views of the author as well. The rest part of the work is normally organized around the subject or argument the writer proposed at the very start. The same holds true with the paragraph as well: the use of the topic sentence.

Reference

[1]Bloor, T. & M. Bloor. The Functional Analysis of English: A Hallidayan Approach. 北京：外语教学与研究出版社，1995/2001.

[2]Brown, G. & Yule, G. Discourse Analysis. Cambridge: Cambridge University Press，1983.

[3]Eggins, S. An Introduction to Systemic Functional Linguistics. London: Pinter,1994.

[4]Halliday, M A.K. and R Hasan. Cohesion in English. London: Longman, 1976.

[5]Halliday, M A.K. and R Hasan Language, context, and text: aspects of language in a social-semiotic perspective. Oxford: OUP, 1989.

[6]Huang, G. & M. Ghadessy Functional Discourse Analysis. Shanghai: Shanghai Foreign Language Education Press,2006.

[7]Martin, J. English Text: System and Structure. Amsterdam: Benjamins, 1992.

[8]Martin, J. & D. Rose. 2007. Working with Discourse: Meaning beyond the Clause. 2nd edition. London: Continuum.

[9]Schiffrin, D. 1994. Approaches to Discourse. Oxford: Blackwell.

[10]Van Dijk, T. Discourse Studies: A Multidisciplinary Introduction. 2 Vols

(ed.). London, Thousand Oaks, New Delhi: Sage. ,1997.

[11] 胡壮麟 . 语篇的衔接与连贯 . 上海：上海外语教育出版，1994.

[12] 黄国文 . 语篇分析的理论与实践 . 上海：上海外语教育出版社，2001.

Chapter 8
政治语篇中的评价意义研究

8.1 引言

政治语篇是人们在社会生活中经常见到的一种文体，它可以用来宣传政治主张、发表个人见解、交流彼此思想，具有强烈的宣传、教育和鼓动作用。演说者又试图通过演说来调节人际关系，赢得听众支持，因此，人际意义在演说词中具有关键地位。本文试以奥巴马（Obama）在芝加哥竞选获胜时的演说词及北京申奥语篇为例，运用系统功能语言学的评价理论来分析语篇的评价意义。

8.2 评价理论渊源

评价理论 (appraisal theory) 是在 Halliday 的系统功能语言学的基础上发展起来的理论。Halliday（1994：36）认为，语言具有三个元功能，即概念 (ideational) 功能、人际 (interpersonal) 功能和语篇 (textual) 功能。人际功能是指语言可用来建立和维持人际关系，也可用来表达说话者的观点态度及影响他人的态度或行为。在系统功能语法中，人际功能可以通过语气 (mood)、情态 (modality) 等语法系统来体现。然而，语气和情态可以揭示人际关系的亲疏，却无法阐明说话者对事物的评价。鉴于此，功能语言学家 J.R. Martin 和他的学生 White 及其他一些学者对系统功能语言学的人际功能理论进行了发展，从而形成了目前的评价理论系统。评价理论是系统功能语言学在人际意义的研究中发展起来的语义资源系统，是探讨、描述和解释说话者 / 作者如何使用语言进行评价、表明立场、构建语篇人物角色以及协调人际立场和人际关系的一种方法。该理论框架包含三大次系统：介入 (Engagement) 、态度 (Attitude) 和级差 (Graduation) ，它们又分别次系统化。介入次系统化为自言 (monogloss) 和借言 (heterogloss) ，态度次系统化为情感 (affect) 、判断 (judgment) 和鉴赏 (appreciation) ，级差次系统化为语势 (force) 和聚焦 (focus) 。其中态度系统是整个评价系统的核心。态度系统指人们参照情感反应或文化制约下的价值体系对参与者和过程进行主体间性 (intersubjective) 评价的意义资源，即 Martin 所说的“说话者 / 作者对人、人类行为、事物和人类情感的价值资源”。态度的三个次系统情感、判断和鉴赏分别属于心理、伦理和美学范畴。情感是整个态度系统的中心，用以表达语言使用者对事件或现象的情感反应；判断指根据一系列制度化的规范对人们的行为做出评价；鉴赏是对事物的价值，如对文本、产品、现象和过程等的评价。这三个次系统又分别有各自的子系统。态度的表达方式有肯定和否定、隐性和显性之分，并可根据强度分级来调节评价的值，表示感情的强弱程度。

8.3 政治语篇中的评价资源分析

情感是构建感情反应的资源，是对评价对象的态度最明显、最主观化的表达方式。该语篇情感资源的使用特点是构建情感的类别多样化，而且绝大部分是积极的快乐情感，用以表达演讲者对所评述事件的积极情感反应，并以此来感染听众。此外，该语篇还成功运用了情感诱发判断模式 (affect-invoking judgment pattern) ，即表达情感的方式往往不是把人作为经历感情的主体，而是与文章主题相关的活动或事件，如：

(1) And I guarantee，their gratitude will pour out in open expressions of affection for you and the great movement that you guide.

话语，作者将更多的态度编码作为奖励的指南，即“情感系统成为一个命题 (事物)”而不是对人们的行为或性格进行情感反应或评论，以避免个人倾向，使评价更加客观。在上面的例子中，情感被包装成名词结构，如感恩，使情感的感觉主体模糊和背景，并给予经验本身，使评价更加制度化和客观化。评价系统主要通过评价词汇表来表达语言使用者对实体、事件或过程的态度。由于表达表达资源的态度通常是形容词，名词和副词，翻译英语和汉语的话语，这两种语言的对应的源语言和目标语言，形容词，名词和副词通常可以直译翻译可能提供，如刚性支架(坚定的支持)，党派之争(政治)，等等，这种情况下的文本语音和两个翻译，在不同的例子。然而，根据语言是选择一个系统和语言元素的概念，任何部分的话语同时呈现经验，建立关系和身份。韩礼德把它看作是一种将“行为潜力”编码为“意义潜能”的手段，它是一个由语义、词汇语法和语言组成的系统。意义是一种强大的力量，不是因为我们拥有如此多的武器和财富。民主、自由、机会和不屈的希望是这个国家持久的力量。这部分的划线部分是承认或否定，这取决于读者的阅读位置。不同的读者对此会有不同的评论。但是译者有责任准确地解释发言人的态度。判断是对人类行为的评价。在资源的选择上，作者着重于对能力和合法性的肯定评价，以使观众相信北京完全有能力举办奥运会。就判断的表达而言，除了一些主导能力的判断和合理的词语，比如你可能会理解为什么：“我们的女子足球队今天表现如此出色；这是一个千百万友好的城市；作者是中国最伟大的艺术家，也是世界上最伟大的艺术家。”更像是一个信息内容和过程描述的“隐含标记”。

欣赏是对评价对象特征的评价，是事件或客体命题的情感本质。话语倾向于选择更多的鉴赏，这是将个人的情感转化为事件的内在本质，从而避免直接的情感反应或对人类行为的判断。欣赏为个人情感提供了客观的外衣。在鉴赏资源的选择中，笔者对北京申奥的重要性、价值和社会意义有着强烈的偏好。作者运用大量的显性价值评价来评价北京的申奥和它的优势，从而引导观众与演讲者产生共鸣，并做出最终一致的立场。升值：估值代表了社会的参考价值，从鉴赏者的感官反应(鉴赏力：反应)和从某种内在质量现象(欣赏：构成)的角度来看。在语言资源的欣赏方面，有很多的属性和态度名词，如：中国的体育传奇，一片神奇的土地，等等，除了许多积极的修饰词之外。这些高水平的明确的升值，足以给北京的历史、文化和申办权留下深刻印象。

Thompson & Hunston(2000) 指出，用评估来操纵读者是非常有效的。子句中的位置越不明显，它就越能操纵读者。根据评价理论，我们应该分析显性编码的态度，分析隐性的态度变化。层次系统是一种层次的资源，用于态度的参与程度，包括力量和焦点。语言的潜力可以调节一种分类态度的强度，比如强 (涨) 或弱 (低)。重点是不能分类的态度分类。重点 (锐化) 和模糊 (软化)。这是一种含蓄的表达主观态度的方式，通过调整语言的强度和焦点清晰度来表达主观态度。语言或焦点的增加可以使论点更有力，降低了价值，降低了论点的攻击性。

原　文：To those who would tear the world down: We will defeat you. To those who seek peace and security: We support you. And to all those who have wondered if America’s beacon still burns as bright: Tonight we proved once more that the true strength of our nation comes not from the might of our arms or the scale of our wealth, but from the enduring power of our ideals: democracy, liberty, opportunity and unyielding hope.

译文：对于那些想要毁灭这个世界的人，我们将打败你们。对于那些寻求和平与安全的人，我们将支持你们。我们今天晚上再次证明：美国真正的权力来源不是军事力量或财富，而是我们理想的永恒力量：民主、自由、机会和不屈的希望。

A 将隐喻直译为“go on the arc of history”，加上“forward”一词可以反映出说话者的积极评价，在“调整”的背后，“朝向更美好的未来继续形成一个连贯的体系”。虽然观察说话人给出的是积极的态度，但也许是出于对表达的尊重，完全取代了隐喻系列，尤其是在短语“stand up”中，让人感到困惑。当然，译者在面对语言和文化不可逾越的障碍时，可以改变隐喻。然而，历史的比喻是指“前面的路是曲折的”。弯曲……希望有

更好的一天意味着“再次控制它……”朝着更好的方向发展。隐喻汉语的认知系统也可以接受。为了保持对原文的积极评价，

除了大量的明确的评论之外，作者还成功地运用了各种关联和隐含的机制来激励观众去评价北京申奥的积极态度。首先，纯信息的内容或话语的体验性质具有明显的触发态度评价的潜力。如：

(8) In China，the torch will pass through Tibet，cross Yangtze and Yellow Rivers，travel the Great Wall and visit Hong Kong，Macau，Taiwan，and the 56 ethnic communities who make up our society.

例 (8) 这不是为某些词汇本身有一定的价值，但是，信息内容——北京奥运会计划在时间和空间跨度——特定的话语中隐含的计划的影响和意义的传播奥林匹克精神的积极的价值判断。这些“事实”的信息内容与话语中明确的态度相互作用，共同建构对整个话语的积极态度。隐藏的态度资源不容易掌握，或者经常被翻译人员忽略。从以上的描述和分析来看，翻译的主体是直译，译文的翻译主要是翻译的态度和语气。但这并不意味着直译是翻译评价的唯一策略。由于评价性词汇的存在，该短语没有预先设定，因此需要使用上下文来识别一些边缘的评价表达式。此外，评价意义不仅是作者的表达个人的观点和态度，以及与读者沟通，协商人际意义，译者还需要考虑表达方法和读者接受等因素，目标语言规范，对于“忠实”原文的评价意义，根据需要采用的方法、解释和调整。此外，由于阶级差异造成的隐性态度资源往往被忽视，这也是译者的特别注意。

8.4 结论

同样重要的是要注意，在语言中有许多评价方法，这些方法都显示在各个级别。在声音系统层中可以体现在标签的重音和模式中，层次可以体现在词汇表项的评价倾向中，在语法层可以体现在一些特殊的句子模式中，文本层可以体现在叙事性的视角和语义的连贯性上。由于分析工具的局限性，本文只关注词汇层的讨论。这篇文章是指原语已成为一篇书面文

本，但在演讲的领域中，说话者将在音响系统中甚至是超语言水平来表达评价的意思，也需要现场录音、视频资料进行分析。

参考文献

[1]Halliday, M. A. K.Language as social semiotic: The social interpretation of language and meaning[M]. London:Edward Arnold,1978.

[2]Halliday, M. A. K.Introduction to Functional Grammar.2nd edition[M]. London: Edward Arnold,1994.

[3]Martin, J.R. & Rose, David.Working with Discourse[M] London & New York:Continuum,2003.

[4]Thompson, G. & Hunston, S.Evaluation in text-Au-thorialStance and the Construction of Discourse[C]. Oxford:Oxford UP,2000.

[5] 巴拉克 奥巴马 . 无畏的希望 [M]. 北京 : 法律出版社 ,2008.

[6] 陈明瑶 . 新闻语篇态度资源的评价性分析及其翻译 [J]. 上海翻译 ,2007(1).

Chapter 9
新闻语篇中概念意义的隐性评价

9.1 引言

语篇都体现评价意义，通过评价意义的表达反映着语篇组织者的态度，情感及其意识形态。新闻语篇也不例外，同样表达着新闻媒体对某一事件的解读，传递着各种各样的间接或直接、支持或反对的态度。媒体对新闻事件的报道通常会使用一些隐性的，不易被读者识别的，隐藏在语篇字里行间中能传递一定态度的语言资源（Hodge & Kress, 1979; Fowler, 1991；Van Dijk, 1988）。通过这些隐性表达方式，新闻语篇可引导读者接受其价值定位，达到联盟读者建构双方主体间性，达到人际互动的目的。

近些年来，运用 Martin 的评价系统理论研究英语新闻语篇中的隐性评价资源是语言学界的热门话题。Martin & White（2005）指出语篇中的隐性评价主要由三种途径来引发（invoke）：词汇隐喻的激发（provocation），级差资源的旗示 (flagging) 和概念意义的致使 (affording)。后来 Hood & Martin (2007) 又认为隐性评价主要由概念意义的选择和概念意义中语义程度的分级来体现。迄今为止，语篇的评价意义研究大多从人际意义的角度展开，这似乎给我们一种假象：即语篇的评价意义仅仅与人际意义相关，与概念意义没有丝毫的联系。其实不然，评价意义的生成与识别和概念意义是息息相关的。蕴含态度意义的词汇语义结构激发评价，而这些词汇语义结构与句中特定的言语行为过程、动作的发出者和承受者以及句中环境等成分是密切相关的。因此，语篇中的评价意义研究不能与概念意义相分离。概念意义是说话人对周围外部世界和人类内心世界经验的描述。概念意义中的隐性评价主要由及物性系统来体现。及物性是一个语义系统，由现实世界中的若干种“过程”（process），与各种过程相关的“参与者”（participant）和“环境成分”（circumstantial element）组成。语篇组织者对及物性语义系统的不同选择体现了其某种意图和态度，具有明显的评价意义。现阶段对语篇评价的研究探讨显性评价的居多，对隐性评价的探讨，尤其是从概念意义方面来分析探究不多。

9.2 评价理论视角下的英语新闻语篇分析现状

评价理论“关注语篇中所协商的各种态度，所涉及到的情感的强度，以及表明价值和联盟读者的各种方式（Martin & Rose, 2003:22）。”评价又可分为显性评价和隐性评价，显性评价是指通过那些明显表明作者态度的词汇来表达，如形容词、副词和动词等。隐性评价则是是由那些隐含作者态度及情感的中性词语或语义结构来引发的。进入21世纪后运用评价理论进行语篇分析获得了快速发展，国外学者从不同方面探讨了其在语篇分析方面的应用模式（Hunston & Thompson, 2000; Martin & Rose, 2003; Martin & White, 2005; Hood & Martin, 2007）。Martin的评价理论由张德禄（1998）和王振华（2001）引入中国，之后获得了快速发展，不少学者在评价理论的发展和运用方面取得了丰硕的成果（李战子, 2004; 杨信彰, 2003; 刘世铸, 2007, 2010; 苗兴伟, 2007; 朱永生, 2009; 胡壮麟, 2009; 刘世生, 2012等）。

国内学者在英语新闻语篇的评价意义研究方面也取得了不少成果。对英语硬新闻和社论进行理论运用研究的有王振华（2004a）、刘世铸，韩金龙（2004）、陈明瑶（2007）、陈晓燕（2007）和陈令君（2011）等。从评价的研究方法上可分为：评价的批评性阅读策略研究（刘承宇, 2002），社会认知模式及互文性分析研究（张蕾, 2007），批评话语分析研究（单胜江，2011）和语篇建构功能分析研究（张蕾，苗兴伟，2010）。从英语新闻语篇的隐性评价研究来看主要有如下成果：魏在江（2011）认为语用预设具有隐性评价功能；王天华（2012）指出新闻语篇以隐性评价手段动态地建构新闻语篇和定位读者；冉志晗（2013）认为英语新闻语篇中物质、言语、关系三种及物性过程具有隐性评价功能。

综上所述，我们认为英语新闻语篇的隐性评价研究虽然获得了丰硕的成果，但是这些研究多集中于隐性评价资源的某一方面，尤其是对概念意义的隐性评价研究还不够深入。评价系统由态度、介入和级差三大成分构成，他们是相互联系不可分割的一个整体。因此，本文拟从介入和级差视角来分析新闻语篇中的隐性态度资源，探究隐性态度资源定位读者和联盟读者，达成主体间一致性的功能。本文以2014年乌克兰危机这一事件为例，以新闻报刊China Daily（2014年3月17日～23日）与此事件相关的23篇新闻报道为语料基础，采用定性分析的方法来探讨新闻语篇中概念意义的隐性评价。

9.3 概念意义中的隐性评价与介入

朱永生（2009）认为概念意义的隐性评价是指说话人通过运用及物性系统中看似客观描写性质的词汇语义结构，来含蓄地表达自己的态度。语篇通过对及物性过程以及与各种过程相关的参与者和环境成分的不同选择和句中位置安排，来凸显作者的某种态度。评价系统理论由J. R. Martin在韩礼德系统功能语言学理论人际意义功能的基础上发展而来的，分为三个子系统：态度（attitude）、介入（engagement）和级差（graduation）。在精密度上，态度又可分为情感（affect）、判断（judgment）和鉴赏（appreciation）；介入分为单声（monogloss）和多声（heterogloss）；级差分为语势（force）和聚焦（focus）。介入子系统基于Bakhtin（1981）的“多声”和“互文性”语言学理论，关注语篇中态度和声音的来源和出处。介入和态度相互关联，密不可分：只要作者介入事态，就会昭示态度；介入的方式可调节态度的强弱程度。从本质上来说，介入系统是发话人参与交际的方式，是其建构人际关系的策略。介入可协调自己和受话人的声音，调节双方之间立场并期盼读者共享彼此价值观和信念。单声又称为单纯性断言（bare assertion），是指语篇中仅存在一种声音（即语篇作者的声音），排除对话性。多声意味着对话性，语篇中存在多种声音，作者邀请和操控其他声音来达到协调立场，传递态度的目的。

9.3.1 隐性评价与单声系统

单声系统意味着排除对话性，只存在一种声音；在语篇中仅仅作者的声音在描述发生的事情，因此单声亦称为主观性介入。Lyons(1977: 794) 将单声理解为客观化的单纯性断言，认为其是事实性的。但是在看似客观的概念意义描述中，虽没有明显态度意义词汇，作者也可通过及物性结构各种成分的选择，传达着作者的态度，比如：

（1）Earlier this week, the EU and the United States imposed sanctions on certain individuals that were involved in the referendum in Crimea over joining the Russian Federation.

（2）Eastern and southern regions of Ukraine that are home to huge members of ethnic Russians will, supported by Russia, continue to demand more autonomy from Kiev.

例（1）中第一个小句为物质过程小句，过程动词 imposed 解释为 forced somebody or something to have to deal with something that is difficult or unpleasant，带有明显的强制态度意义，其贬义色彩意味浓重；同时此小句的“动作者”（actor）为欧盟和美国两个世界超级大国集团，而“领受者”（recipient）为某些个人，这就形成了大国对个人的制裁，明显具有两大势力集团以大欺小的姿态，暗示作者对欧盟和美国行为的负面判断评价。例（2）中第一个小句为关系过程小句，“属性”（attribute）成分为“home”，此句指出乌克兰的东南部地区是大批俄罗斯族裔群体的“家园”，凸显此地区的人们渴望脱离乌克兰加入俄罗斯的决心。再看下面的例子：

（3）The last straw was a move by the European Union to draw Ukraine closer to the West through a political association agreement.

（4）Preparations to become part of Russia-a process that could take months –are to begin this week if the referendum result is pro-Moscow.

（5）Two sets of the documents were passed around the table for the EU' s leaders and Yatseniuk.

（6）The fact is that the Cold War ended by negotiation to the advantage of both sides.

例（3）中 the last straw 是词汇隐喻，是关系过程小句中的载体（carrier）。Martin & White（2005）认为词汇隐喻可以激发隐性评价。在国际形势急转直下的情况下，欧盟为了拉拢乌克兰，保住其在乌克兰的利益，想方设法达成某些政治协定便成为其最后的救命稻草。例（4）中划线部分是名物化 (nominalization) 结构，作为整个存在过程小句中“存在物”（existent）。朱永生 (2006:85) 指出名物化具有使句子意义客观化的作用。此名物化结构由物质过程小句转化为名词短语，是过程向事物的转变；施事成分的缺失，使句子体现的命题意义——“持续数月的克里米亚加入俄罗斯的准备活动”——变得客观与理所当然。例（6）中同样存在名物化的结构，在句中作为方式环境成分（manner）的次范畴—手段 (means) 的构成部分；言语过程转化为环境成分、协商参与者的故意缺失使“冷战结束是因为利益攸关方协商的结果”这一命题看起来显得有理有据。例（5）的句子是典型的被动语态，此物质过程中没有出现施事，作者的交际意图非常明显，信息提供者所承担的责任得以避免。

9.3.2 隐性评价与多声系统

多声系统表征对话性，存在着作者声音和外部不同声音和观点的互动和碰撞。多声又分为话语收缩（dialogic contraction）和话语扩展（dialogic expansion），话语收缩是指语篇作者通过言语策略的运用来挑战或排斥与之相左的立场和声音，关闭对话多样性的空间。与之相反，话语扩展则运用言语策略来接纳或承认其他声音与立场，开启对话多样性的空间。在语义精密度上，话语收缩又可分为否认（disclaim）和公告（proclaim），话语扩展分为接纳（entertain）和归属（attribute）。收缩和扩展实质上是把话语、语篇或交际环境建构为一个多种声音和观点相互交织在一起的语义场，反映作者与其他声音作者之间的主体间性。

请看下面的例子：

（7）We now have grounds to state the measures being taken today are enough to prevent a repeat of the Crimean scenario in Ukraine's southeastern regions.

（8）The post-Cold War era seems to be over as we enter what could be renamed the inter-Cold War era.

（9）It is also probable that Russia will seek to stall Ukraine's integration with the EU by pressing for a federalization process in Ukraine, which would entitle the eastern and southern parts a veto over major foreign policy decisions.

例（7）是话语收缩中公告的子范畴——宣告。说话人通过宣告明确地介入或干预语篇，强势表达自己的观点，对其他观点提出挑战，从而压缩了与不同意见之间的对话空间。“We now have grounds to state……”强烈表达了这一观点：对于防止克里米亚自治在乌东南部地区再次发生，我们所采取的措施是足够的和正确的。例（8）和例（9）属于话语扩展中的接纳。与宣告不同，接纳允许不同声音的出现，创造多声的空间。作者将反对的意见投射于一部分读者，与这些读者形成了联盟。接纳通常由情态和言据性的语言资源来体现。例（8）中“后冷战时代看起来结束了”这一命题预示另一命题的存在：后冷战时代其实没有结束。例（9）中关系过程小句“It is also probable…”表明后面命题的可能性，也含蓄地表达了与之相反命题的存在。

(10) In former US sectary of state Henry Kissinger's words, it should try to play a "bridge" between the two sides.

(11) Andriy Parubiy, secretary of Ukraine Security and Defense Council, said Kiev was drawing up plans to evacuate its outnumbered troops from Crimean and will seek UN support to turn the peninsula into a demilitarized zone.

例（10）和例（11）是话语扩展中归属子范畴—承认的例证。承认是指所表达的命题来自于外部声音或立场，作者没有为自己的立场提供明显的线索，而是转述他人的观点。承认主要通过转述动词或是与此类动词相对应的名物化结构来体现。Hood (2004) 认为转述的信息来源若是权威人士，该信息的可信度会提升；相反，信息的可信度会降低。例 (10) 中"In former US sectary of state Henry Kissinger's words"是小句中的"角度"（angle）环境成分，作者引用原美国国务卿基辛格的话语来佐证观点，凸显所表达命题的可信度很高。作者在例 (11) 中以乌克兰安全与国防部长 Andriy Parubiy 的言语作为信息来源，从国家的高度表明信息的高度可信性。此外，转述动词所投射的话语中概念意义成分的不同选择也表征了作者的态度。在例 (11) 中物质过程动词"evacuate"和目标（goal）"its outnumbered troops"等成分凸显了乌克兰在此危机中的被动性。

9.4 概念意义中的隐性评价与级差

级差是一种常见的语言学现象，将事物、品质、行为等进行量化，表达态度意义的强弱。级差语义部分在评价系统中处于核心地位（Martin & White, 2005:136），不仅可以表达概念意义，还具有强调、缓和、模糊等人际功能。Hood & Martin (2007) 指出概念意义的分级可旗示评价，旗示是指说话人以级差资源作为信号向读者暗示态度意义的存在。语势与聚焦为级差的两个子范畴，前者涉及质量、过程的强度与实体的数量，分别称为强化（intensification）和量化 (quantification)；后者是对事物范畴典型性或精确度的分级。聚焦关注的是评价对象是范畴的核心成员还是边缘成员。按语义值的强弱，聚焦可细化为锐化（sharpening）和柔化（softening）。级差系统网络图示如下：

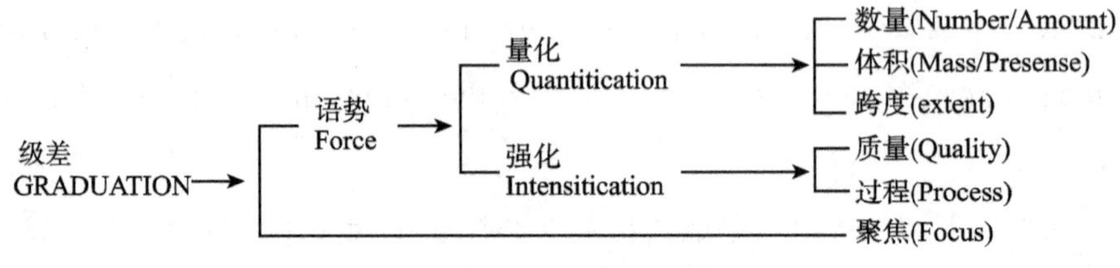

图 1　级差系统（**Martin & White 2005：154**）

9.4.1 隐性评价与语势

按照所适用的对象，语势可细化为量化和强化，两者为析取关系。强化是评价质量和过程，通常由副词来体现，这些副词可以修饰形容词、副词和过程动词等，例如，"slightly different，increase greatly"。量化则是对实体的数量、体积和跨度等特征的评价。跨度在精密度上又分为时间上的和空间上的临近和分布。从体现方式（mode）来看，Martin & White (2005:141-144) 认为语势可区分为孤立型（isolation）和注入型（infusion）。前者指级差意义通过词汇意义单独表达，例如"a bloody awful day"；后者指词汇不仅具有级差意义，还包含经验意义，例如"prices skyrocketed"。语势和聚焦按语义值的高低可分为上升和下降两个方向。语义力度上升凸显作者强调的内容，赋予正面评价；语义力度下降弱化所讨论的内容，赋予负面评价。那么级差如何在新闻语篇中旗示态度呢，请看下面的例子：

(12) UN Secretary-Ban Ki-moon is visiting Moscow on Thursday[量化：跨度] and is to come to Ukraine[量化：跨度] on Friday[量化：跨度]. His visit will follow hot on the heels of tense scenes at the UN Security Council in New York[量化：跨度]. It was the council's eighth meeting [量化：数量] in less than three weeks [量化：跨度] on Ukraine.

(13) Crimean voted overwhelmingly[强化：过程] on Sunday to secede

from Ukraine and seek to join Russia. The hastily [强化：过程]called vote was held two weeks[量化：跨度] after Russian troops had moved into the Black Sea peninsula.

例 (12) 中数量词 “eighth” 和下降力度的分布性时间跨度成分 “in less than three weeks”，表明联合国在乌克兰问题决议上进展缓慢，凸显美欧和俄罗斯利益裂痕之深，赋予一定程度上的负面判断评价。此例中的时间跨度量化词 “on Thursday” 和 “on Friday” 以及空间跨度量化词 “to Ukraine” 和 “at the UN Security Council in New York”，凸显联合国秘书长为乌克兰危机来回穿梭于俄罗斯和乌克兰，俄乌领土争端问题的复杂性跃然纸上。例 (13) 通过上升力度的过程强化词 “overwhelmingly” 和 “hastily” 以及时间分布跨度数量词 “two weeks” 来表达克里米亚人民脱离乌克兰加入俄罗斯的急迫愿望，暗含作者的正面评价。从级差体现方式来看，以上两例都是孤立型的，级差意义通过单独的词汇来表达。再看下面的例子：

(14) That set off a chain of [量化：数量]events that led to the outer of the Ukrainian president and, ultimately, to Crimean residents voting to join the Russian Federation.

(15) Tensions have escalated[强化：过程] in mostly[强化：质量] Russian-speaking parts of eastern Ukraine ahead of the referendum[量化：跨度].

例 (14) 和例 (15) 都属于词汇注入型的例证。例 (15) 中的 “escalated” 相当于 “rose quickly”，和例 (14) 中的 “a chain of”，同样既具有经验意义又具有级差意义。例 (15) 中上升力度的质量强化词 “mostly” 和临近性时间跨度词 “ahead of the referendum”，同注入型词汇 “escalated” 一起表达出大多数讲俄语的乌克兰东部民众与政府冲突的加剧，隐含了作者对乌东部民众加入俄罗斯意愿的正面评价。

9.4.2 隐性评价与聚焦

聚焦把本来不具有经验意义的事物进行分级，按照事物的典型范畴进行划分，区别中心成员抑或边缘成员。因此事物的典型性程度就被赋予了态度意义，锐化性聚焦常常旗示一种正面态度（如“a real/true husband”），相反柔化性聚焦则旗示一种负面态度（如“jazz of sorts”）(姜望琪 2005：XVII)。具体分析事例如下：

(16) From the very start[聚焦：锐化], the West has dismissed possibilities of armed intervention in the Crimean issue….. However, Wu from Tsinghua University warned of possible[聚焦：柔化]conflicts between Russia and Ukraine.

(17) Moscow will not seek to restore the Soviet Union, but it will try to consolidate the Eastern Slav/Orthodox countries, as well as areas inhabited by some Muslim Turkic peoples, into a new Eurasian-compact[聚焦：柔化]……

例 (16) 中“very”表示锐化聚焦，其上升的语义力度明确表明“从一开始，西方势力就没有武力干涉克里米亚的意图”，凸显作者对这一命题的确信无疑，蕴涵正面评价的意思。相反，柔化聚焦词“possible”的运用表明：命题—“俄罗斯与乌克兰发生冲突”的真实性存在不确定性，旗示了作者对这一命题的怀疑态度。与“possible”相同，例 (17) 中的“Eurasian”，表示柔化聚焦，属于下降语义力度词语。此例句表示俄罗斯试图把东正教国家和穆斯林突厥民族地区发展成为一个新的“亚欧”协约集团。柔化聚焦词“Eurasian”表明这一新的集团既有亚洲特点又有欧洲特点，突出了它似是而非的特点。

9.5 结论

本文从介入和级差视角探讨了英语新闻语篇中概念意义中的隐性评价。任何语篇的生成都体现着作者的态度，或是显性或是隐性。隐性态度通常由那些没有明显态度意义的词汇语法结构来引发。态度、介入和级差是评价系统理论的三大子系统，他们是相互联系的整体。

介入系统表明态度来源，在概念意义的表述中介入系统建构主体间对话空间，限制或包容不同观点；在此人际互动中作者与读者结成结盟，其意图和态度也得到了传递和承认。级差通过旗示策略引发态度，即通过概念意义的语义值特征引导读者的阅读立场，而间接表达态度。

参考文献

[1] Bakhtin, M. M. The Dialogic Imagination[M]. Austin: University of Texas Press, 1981.

[2] Fowler, R. Language in the News: Discourse and Ideology in the Press [M]. London: Routledge, 1991.

[3] Hodge, R. & G. Kress. Language as Ideology [M]. London: Routledge, 1979.

[4] Hood, Susan. Appraising Research: Taking a Stance in Academic Writing. Ph.D. Dissertation. Sydney: Sydney University of Technology, 2004.

[5] Hood, Susan and James R. Martin. Invoking attitude: the play of graduation in appraising discourse. In Ruqaiya Hasan, Christian M. I. M. Matthiessen and Jonathan Webster (eds.), Continuing Discourse on Language: A Functional Perspective. Volume 2. London: Equinox, 2007 :739-764.

[6] Lyons, J. Semantics. Cambridge: Cambridge University Press, 1977.

[7] Martin, J. R. & D, Rose. Working with Discourse: Meaning beyond the Clause [M]. London: Bookcraft Limited, 2003.

[8] Martin, J. R. & P. R. R. White. The Language of Evaluation: Appraisal in English [M]. London / New York: Palgrave Macmillan, in press, 2005.

[9] Thompson, G. & S. Hunston. Evaluation: An Introduction [A].Hunston, S. & G. Thompson. Evaluation in Text: Authorial Stance and the Construction of Discourse [C]. Oxford: Oxford University Press, 2000, 1-27.

[10] van Dijk, T. A. News Analysis: Case Studies of International and

National News in the Press [M]. Hillsdale, New Jersey: Lawrence Erlbaum Associates Publishers, 1988.

[11] 陈明瑶 . 新闻语篇态度资源的评价性分析及其翻译 [J]. 上海翻译，2007（1）：23-27.

[12] 陈晓燕 . 英汉社论语篇态度资源对比分析 [J]. 外国语，2007（3）：39-46.

[13] 胡壮麟 . 语篇的评价研究 [J]. 外语教学，2009（1）：1-6.

[14] 姜望琪 . 评估语言：英语的评价系统 [M]. 北京：外语教学与研究出版社，2005.

[15] 李战子 . 评价理论：在话语分析中的应用和问题 [J]. 外语研究，2004a（5）：1-6+80.

[16] 李战子 . 评价与文化模式 [J]. 山东外语教学，2004b（2）：3-8.

[17] 刘承宇 . 英语报刊语篇评价系统与批评性阅读 [J]. 山东师大外国语学院学报，2002（4）：25-29.

[18] 刘世铸，韩金龙 . 新闻话语的评价系统 [J]. 外语电化教学，2004（5）：17-21.

[19] 刘世铸 . 态度的结构潜势 / 话语评价的语法视角 [M]. 北京：中国社会科学出版社，2007.

[20] 刘世铸 . 评价理论在中国的发展 [J]. 外语与外语教学，2010（5）：33-37.

[21] 苗兴伟 . 英语的评价型强势主位结构 [J]. 山东外语教学，2007（2）：54-57.

[22] 冉志晗 . 英语新闻语篇的及物结构及其隐性评价功能研究 [J]. 安徽工业大学学报（哲学社会版），2013（3）：62-66.

[23] 单胜江 . 新闻语篇的批评性话语分析 [J]. 外语学刊，2011（6）：78-81.

[24] 王天华 . 新闻语篇隐性评价意义的语篇发生研究 [J]. 外语学刊，

2012（1）：104-107

[25] 王振华．评价系统及其运作 [J]. 外国语，2001（6）：13-20.

[26] 王振华．“硬新闻”的态度研究—“评价系统”应用研究之二 [J]. 外语教学，2004a（5）：31-36.

[27] 魏在江．语用预设的语篇评价功能 [J]. 学术探索，2011（2）:23-29.

[28] 杨信彰．语篇中的评价性手段 [J]. 外语与外语教学，2003（1）：11-14.

[29] 张德禄．论话语基调的范围与体现 [J]. 外语教学与研究，1998（1）：10-16+80.

[30] 张蕾．新闻报道语篇中评价意义研究 [J]. 天津外国语学院学报，2007（5）：19-23.

[31] 张蕾，苗兴伟．评价意义的语篇构建功能 [J]. 西安外国语大学学报，2010（9）：23-26.

[32] 张滟．态度评价：主体互联性劝说模式构建 [J]. 外语学刊，2008（3）：71-75.

[33] 朱永生．名词化、动词化与语法隐喻 [J]. 外语教学与研究，2006（2）：83-90.

[34] 朱永生．概念意义中的隐性评价 [J]. 外语教学，2009（4）：1-5.

Chapter 10
泰山茶文化内涵翻译研究

10.1 引言

在任何语际翻译的实践中，寻找源语文本和译语文本之间的等值成分和实现二者的对等都是翻译理论研究的中心问题之一。在过去 50 年里，等值论一直是人们争论的热点。在翻译领域，许多理论家运用不同方法来研究翻译过程中的等值现象，有的采用语言学方法 (linguistic approach) 进行研究，有的则主张用语用法 (pragmatic approach) 或语义法 (semantic approach) 进行移译。语言是一门最能体现文化内涵的艺术。翻译不仅是不同语言之间的互译，同时也包含着不同的文化习惯和文化背景。互文视阈下的茶文化内涵翻译有利于中西文化交流和融合，实现中国茶文化的传播。

习近平总书记提出了“一带一路”的战略思想，同时山东又被确定为重要海上战略支点。因此，这一伟大战略构想的实施必将为泰山茶文化的国际传播提供新的历史发展机遇。泰山茶文化要融入“一带一路”建设中去，需要加强人文交流，加快国内优秀茶文化作品的翻译研究工作，为茶文化的国际传播的长期发展铺平道路。

以泰山茶文化作品为语料，探讨茶文化的外宣策略研究，以期深入挖掘、提炼升华泰山茶文化中的精神内涵，进一步增强我市文化建设的感染力、影响力和渗透力，有助于提升泰山文化的国外影响力，促进泰安经济的大发展和大繁荣。茶文化是一种历史悠久的文化，它体现的是中华民族所固有的文化传统和思想特征。笔者通过对泰山茶文化内涵翻译进行探讨和分析，提出一些意见和建议。

10.2 茶文化渊源

文化是二十一世纪推动经济社会发展的重要战略性资源，加快文化产业发展、加强中国文化输出和提高文化软实力成为国家的重大发展战略。文化内涵是指某一民族或社会团体所固有的传统和思想特征。中西茶文化渊源不仅仅是把茶文化用另一种语言形式翻译出来，更重要的是，翻译过程中应该保持茶文化特色和独特的民族文化色彩。中国的茶距今已有数千年的历史，它指的并不仅仅是茶叶，还包括茶树、茶饮料等。茶文化作为中国传统文化的重要组成部分，是茶与文化的有机融合。“茶之为饮，发乎神农氏，闻于鲁周公”，据历史记载，神农氏是中国发现茶的饮用功能的始祖，而西周鲁国周公则使茶得以闻名于世，由此可见山东茶文化发展源远流长。“一带一路”战略呼吁文化先行，注重从人文领域做起，重视民间交往、舆论宣传等人文交流的先导作用。因此，泰山茶文化的国际推广，必须加强中西人文交流，进一步深化泰山茶文化的译介研究。加强齐鲁茶文化的对外宣传和推介，有助于山东经济文化的发展，早日实现经济文化强省战略。

10.3 泰山茶文化研究现状

茶文化是中国经典文化要素之一，随着中西方文化交流的不断加强，中国茶文化在世界范围内的影响越来越大，中西茶文化交流带动了互文视阈下的茶文化内涵翻译研究。由于传统习俗和文化的制约，互文视阈下的茶文化研究仍然不够成熟，相关从业人员应该加大对茶文化传播的重视力度，把茶文化的内涵和精粹在互文视阈下表现出来。首先，对互文视阈下茶文化内涵翻译研究来说，目前从事这方面研究的专业人员比较少，并且对茶文化内涵的翻译仍处于起步开发阶段。在国家“一带一路”战略背景下，为弘扬泰山茶文化，加强中西文化交流，本研究对泰山茶文化作品的内涵翻译进行探讨和分析，以期为茶文化的外宣翻译策略研究提出一些意见和建议。本研究将筛选一批中国传统茶文化和优秀泰山茶文化作品进行多语种的翻译和推介，加强茶文化的对外宣传，加快文化强市战略的实施。

首先，本研究将优先推介在国外已经有一定知名度的古今中国诗人、文人的茶文学、茶书画作品。另外，民间流传甚广的茶歌、戏剧、影视话剧作品等都可进行外译和推介，比如冯玉祥将军曾写了一首《大碗茶》诗，描写的是山东泰安地区民间饮茶的习俗。

其次，我们将翻译和推介独具泰山特色的茶文化。“南茶北引”以来，泰山茶产业获得了快速发展，形成了鲁中南茶叶主产区，出现了不同地域的泰山茶文化，形成了享誉国内外的“泰山女儿茶”等茶叶品牌。

最后，我们将探究泰山茶文化的历史与文化渊源。我们将着重介绍泰山茶文化与宗教祭祀、泰山茶文化与文学艺术和泰山饮茶习俗与佛教等内容。

唐代茶诗中所体现的和谐美。茶诗作为茶文化的一部分，体现了茶文化的精髓，即“和谐”。摘要唐代是儒家思想的中心，儒家思想在意识形态领域占有主导地位，因此受儒家思想影响很深，儒家思想也非常丰富。“天人合一”、“天人合一”、“和谐”的儒家价值观，在茶诗中表现出的“和谐”精神也是显而易见的。陆羽的《茶书》洋溢着和谐与和谐，正是他对茶的意境和意境的精确表现。对于唐代文人来说，茶是和平与积极的象征，饮茶是他们追求生活理想和精神境界的表现。当时，文人士大夫，有很多有才华的人，然后他们在心里涌动，他们想通过喝茶来保护国家的情绪，作为一首诗来表达。伟大的诗人白居易的一生坎坷曲折，官场生涯，所以他潜行于山中，在悠闲的下午茶中静静地，享受着生命，而可能，内在的“无乐，长任天涯”的优雅韵文。

10.4 结论

本研究主要选取泰山茶文化作品为研究对象，基于语言与文化内在关系，探讨文化作品对外宣传翻译过程中的策略研究。茶文化翻译，不是简单地将一种语言形式转化为另一种语言形式，而是在翻译过程中涵盖了文化背景及其作者的思想等因素。

茶文化的对外译介对凸显中国文化的普世性和齐鲁儒家文化的独特魅力，提升泰山文化的世界影响力具有非常重要的意义。在国家“一带一路”战略背景下，茶文化的国际传播不仅能够让更多的西方人士了解到泰山茶文化的丰富内涵，更能让西方世界体会到中国文化的博大精深。

本研究可以为本科高校的英语教学提供新的教学思路，促进大学英语教师把语言教学与文化教学有机结合起来，避免忽视了文化教学，有利于培养学生的跨文化交际能力，有利于新课标下大学英语教学目标的实现。

参考文献

[1] 刘明东 . 文化图式的可译性及其实现手段 [J]，中国翻译，2003（2）: 87.

[2] 阚文文．泰山地区茶文化旅游开发路径与策略 [J]，泰山学院学报，2012（5）: 47.

[3] 阚文文 . 泰山茶文化 [M]. 北京 : 中国农业出版社，2015 : 103.

[4] 张美芳 . 翻译研究的功能途径 [M]. 上海 : 上海外语教育出版社 ,2005:71.

[5] 周郢．女儿茶小考 [J]. 红楼梦研究，1987（3）:77.

[6]Yang Xianyi,Cladys Yang.A Dream of Red Mansions[M].Beijing:Foreign Language Press, 1994:624.

[7]Hawkes, David, John Minford.The Story of the Stone[M]. London: Penguin Books L d., 1973: 828.